ART

A Community Connection

Cover, and above: Malcah Zeldis, *Baseball*, 1990. Oil on board, 24" x 36"
(61 x 91 cm). Courtesy the artist and Art Resource, New York.

Art and the Human Experience

ART

A Community Connection

Eldon Katter
Marilyn G. Stewart

Davis Publications, Inc.
Worcester, Massachusetts

Foundations **What Is Art?**

Page 13

Page 27

Page 41

Page 53

Themes Art Is a Community Connection

Page 73

Page 104

Page 129

Printed in U.S.A.
ISBN: 0-87192-491-9
LC No.: 00-130408
10 9 8 7 6 5 4 3 2
WPC 05 04 03

Page 158

Page 180

Page 208

Page 231

Page 259

Page 293

Make the most of your time and your text. Artists across time and space have celebrated the events and values that unite a community. *Art: A Community Connection* dedicates a chapter to each of these universal, community-building themes.

Icons, symbols, logos and signs shape the message and the art of
Telling

Page 70

Page 131

Page 105

Memorials, monuments, festivals, and plazas express a community's ideals and sense of
Belonging

Through landscape paintings, gardens, and parks, artists foster community by
Connecting to Place

Still life paintings, portraits, and murals chronicle life and celebrate
Living

Refining its forms, patterns, and shapes, artists find inspiration
Responding to Nature

Page 151

Page 184

A Community Connection

Page 232

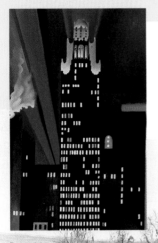

Page 207

Historical photographs, paintings, and sculptures record the **Changing** of landscapes and attitudes

Whether it's carousels, costumes, parades, or posters, the arts build for the future by **Celebrating** the past

Page 256

Through new materials, techniques, subjects, and styles, artists begin **Looking Beyond**

Through installations, murals, wood-cuts, and quilts, artists explore ways of **Making a Difference**

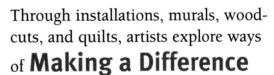

Page 292

Foundations in Art

This text opens with an exploration of the fundamental **hows and whys of art.**

- Why do people make art?
- Does art serve a function?
- How do artists choose their subjects?
- Are there different styles of art?
- What is a 2-D art form?
- Why are the elements of design important?
- How are art historians and critics different?

In answering these questions, these introductory lessons provide a sound foundation on which to build your understanding of art.

Make the most of each chapter!

A unique **CORE PLUS 4** chapter organization provides a structured exploration of art with the flexibility to zoom in on topics that interest you.

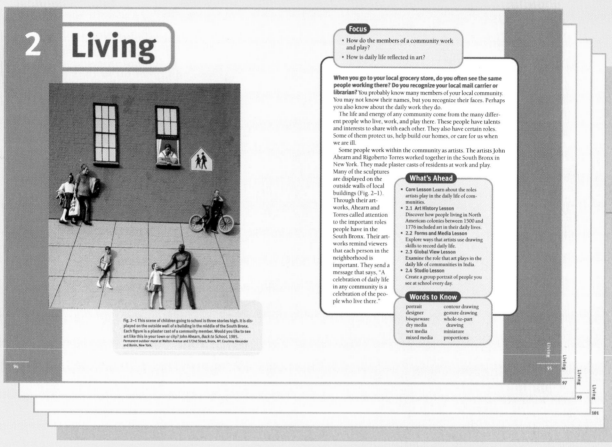

Sample pages from Chapter 2

Each theme opens with a CORE Lesson that provides a comprehensive overview of the topic.

In this theme you will examine how artists record and shape a community's daily life.

Each theme concludes with a studio activity that challenges you to apply what you have learned in a hands-on art project.

In this studio exercise you design and decorate a clay pot to be used in your daily life.

PLUS 4

4 regular follow-up lessons reinforce and extend the CORE Lesson.

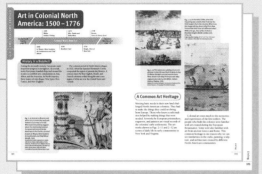

1 The first lesson examines the theme from the perspective of **art history**. *This lesson studies how the American colonists included art in their daily lives.*

2 The second lesson explores the theme through different **forms and media**. *This lesson examines how artists use drawing skills to record and document daily life.*

3 The third lesson looks at the theme from a **global or multicultural viewpoint**. *This lesson considers how artists from India have used a range of art forms to chronicle daily life in their communities.*

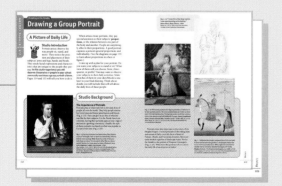

4 The fourth lesson studies the theme through a **studio activity**. *In this project you will make a portrait of people you see at school every day.*

At the end of each chapter the themes **Connect to...**

- **Careers**
- **Technology**
- **Other Subjects**
- **Other Arts**
- **Your World**

Make the most of each lesson!

There are a number of carefully-crafted features that will help you read, understand, and apply the information in each lesson.

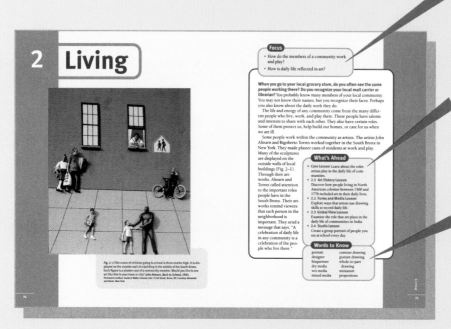

Read with purpose and direction.

Thinking about these Focus questions will help you read with greater understanding.

Prepare for What's Ahead!

See how all the lessons are related? Like a map, this will help you plan where you want to go.

Build your vocabulary.

The first time these key terms are used they are highlighted in bold type and defined. *These terms are also defined in the Glossary.*

Organize your thoughts.

By dividing the lesson into manageable sections, these headings will help you organize the key concepts in each lesson.

"Read" the visuals with the text.

Note how the visuals are referenced in the text. Following these connections will help you understand the topic.

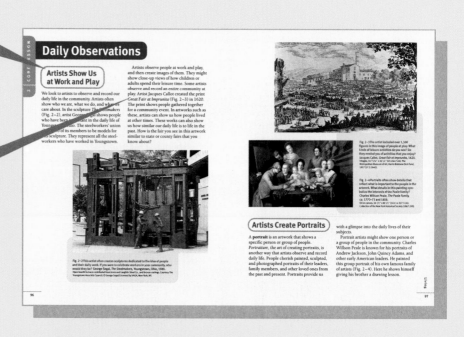

Images and Ideas

Use the captions to "see" the art.
These statements and questions direct you to key aspects of the artwork. Responding to the captions will help you see how the image relates to the text.

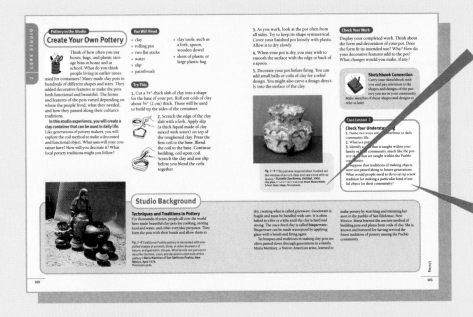

Who made this?
When was it made?
What is it made of?
These and other important questions are answered by the credits that accompany each visual. This information will help you appreciate the art more fully.

Check Your Understanding!
In addition to helping you monitor your reading comprehension, these questions highlight the significant ideas in each lesson.

Don't Miss

Timelines
Each **Art History** lesson is supported by a timeline that locates the lesson in history. As you read this timeline consider how the art reflects the historic events that surround it.

Locator Maps
Each **Global View** lesson is supported by a map that highlights the lesson's location in the world. As you read this map, consider how the art reflects the geography and culture of the place.

Work with Your Mind

Make the most of each studio opportunity!

Core Studio

An expansive studio assignment concludes and summarizes each CORE Lesson.

Studio Lesson

A comprehensive studio lesson caps off each chapter by tying the theme's key concepts together.

Sketchbook Connections
Quick process-oriented activities help you hone your technical and observation skills.

Studio Connections

Practical real-world studio projects explore concepts through hands-on activities.

Computer Options

An alternative to traditional art materials, the computer can be used to do all or part of the lesson.

2.4 STUDIO LESSON

Drawing in the Studio
Drawing a Group Portrait

A Picture of Daily Life

Studio Introduction
Portrait artists observe the way people sit, stand, and move. They notice the position and placement of their subjects' arms and legs, hands and heads. They study facial expressions and characteristics that are unique to the people they portray. **In this studio experience you will observe classmates or people in your school community and draw a group portrait of them.** Pages 114 and 115 will tell you how to do it.

When artists create portraits, they pay special attention to their subjects' **proportions**, or the relation between one part of the body and another. People are surprisingly alike in their proportions. A good portrait captures a person's general proportions and individuality. (See the diagrams on page 114 to learn about proportions in a face or figure.)

Come up with a plan for your portrait. Do you want your subjects to stand or sit? What view of them will you choose: front, three-quarter, or profile? You may want to observe your subjects in their daily activities. Make sketches of them in your sketchbook to use later in your final drawing. Think about details you will include that will tell about the daily lives of these people.

Studio Background

The Importance of Portraits
Portraits play an important role in the daily lives of people all over the world. They help people remember loved ones and honor great leaders and heroes (Fig. 2–23). They can give us an idea of what life was like for their subjects. For the North American colonists, having their portraits painted was a sign of success in a growing community. Usually, the style of these portraits was based on what was popular in Europe at the time (Fig. 2–25).

Fig. 2–23 During the American Revolution, Paul Revere made a "midnight ride" to warn his community that the British were coming. What does the artist of this portrait show us about Paul Revere's daily life as a silversmith? Notice the three-quarter view of Revere's face. John Singleton Copley, *Paul Revere,* 1768. Oil on canvas, 35 1/8" x 28 1/2" (89.2 x 72.4 cm). Gift of Joseph W. Revere, William B. Revere and Edward H. R. Revere. Courtesy Museum of Fine Arts, Boston. Reproduced with permission. ©1999 Museum of Fine Arts, Boston. All Rights Reserved.

Fig. 2–24 "I drew... I was experimenting... James Mast, Ma... Pencil, 16" x 10 1/2"... Christian School, Sea...

Fig. 2–25 This artist painted fo... formal garden scenes. Paren... their children's pleasures... nities that parents had... Kuhn, *Eleanor Darnall*... Oil on canvas, 54" x 44 1/2"... Society, Baltimore, Mar...

Portrait... re also import... Mughal... ure. Formal portrai... and s... of daily court life sho... Persi... Hindu, and European e... t... clude a garden or landsc... ails in the portrait of Emp... g. 2–26). What does this por... daily life of an emperor in Ir...

112

Build background knowledge

Artists regularly draw from the lessons of history. This background information chronicles how artists from the past approached similar artistic endeavors.

Learn from your peers.

An example of student artwork allows you to see how others responded to these hands-on exercises.

Think with Your Hands

Try This!

These directions and illustrations guide you step-by-step through the studio experience.

Check Your Work

One way to evaluate your art is through constructive group critiques. These strategies help you organize peer reviews.

Drawing in the Studio

Drawing Your Portrait

You Will Need
- drawing paper
- charcoal, pencil, or pastels

Try This

1. Observe the people you want to draw. Notice the shape and features of their faces. Notice whether your subjects are tall, thin, short, or plump. Then set up guidelines for proportion in your portrait.

2. Decide which view of each person you want to show. Will you show any profile or three-quarter views?

3. Draw your portrait. Work on the character or special qualities of your subjects. For example, you might use thin, wiry lines for a thin, nervous person. Capture important details. These might include the shape of the eyebrows, a dimple in the chin, a sparkle in the eyes, or a unique hair style.

4. Remember to include backgrounds and props that tell about the daily lives of the people in your portrait. Think about the mood or feeling you want to show. Are the lives of the people in your portrait serious or joyful? How can you show this detail?

5. Try shading your drawing. Imagine shining a strong light on your subjects. Where would you see the highlights and shadows?

Check Your Work

What guidelines for proportions did you use to start your drawing? Did they help you? Were you able to capture the mood and unique characteristics of your subjects? What details from their daily lives did you show?

Sketchbook Connection

The sketches you make of things you observe are one of the best sources of ideas for artworks. Sketch the most important or interesting elements of your community. Draw the people you know and see regularly. Sketch scenes of daily life in your neighborhood. Try filling a page with *thumbnail sketches*, or small drawings. Sketch your subject from different views or with different amounts of detail.

Computer Option

Look at some artists' self-portraits on the Internet. Then use paint or draw software to create your self-portrait. Add symbols that represent your interests, community, and/or culture.

Fig. 2–27 "The picture that I have drawn is of a girl on the school basketball team. Drawing her hair, the basketball, and her uniform was easy. The difficult parts were drawing her face (mostly her eyes) and shading." Mackenzie Granger, *Warrior in Waiting*, 2000.
Pastel, 12" x 9" (30.5 x 29 cm). Thomas Prince School, Princeton, Massachusetts.

114

115

This book shows you how artists across time have celebrated the events and values that unite a community. Through this study you'll understand your own communities better. You'll also learn how making and perceiving art helps build community connections.

Student Gallery

As you become fluent in the universal language of art, a wealth of studio opportunities will help you find your own voice. The artworks on these four pages show how students just like you express their own unique insights and concerns.

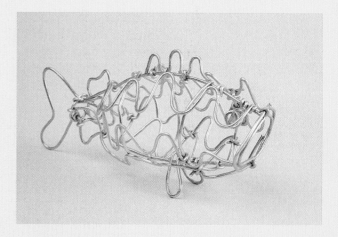

Page 30 William C. Tate, *Large-mouth Bass*, 1998. Aluminum wire, 8 ¼" x 3 ¼" x 3 ¼" (21 x 8 x 8 cm). Daniel Boone Area Middle School, Birdsboro, Pennsylvania.

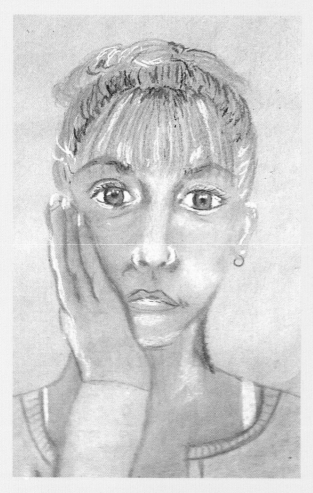

Page 16 Megan Verhelst, *Self-Portrait*, 1999. Conté crayon, 14" x 20" (35.5 x 51 cm). Verona Area Middle School, Verona, Wisconsin.

Page 64 Veronica Martinez, *Fly Away*, 1999. Clay and acrylic, 4" x 5" x 3" (10 x 13 x 7.5 cm). Sweetwater Middle School, Sweetwater, Texas.

Page 92 **Students from Los Cerros Middle School,** *Collaborative Sculpture,* **1999.**
Markers, 3 ¾" (9.5 cm) cubes. Danville, California.

Page 118 **Stacey Fong,** *Contemplation,* **1999.**
Papier mâché, wire, tape, tempera, 8" x 6" x 6" (20 x 15 x 15 cm). Los Cerros Middle School, Danville, California.

Page 127 **Nicolette Schlichting,** *Its Fleece Was White as Snow,* **2000.**
Colored pencil, 12" x 18" (30.5 x 46 cm). Chocksett Middle School, Sterling, Massachusetts.

Student Gallery

Page 248 **Stephen Torosian,** *Caught in the Act,* **1997.**
Clay. Remington Middle School, Franklin, Massachusetts.

Page 170 **Keith Bush,** *Deep Blue Sea,* **2000.**
Markers, 16" diam. (40.5 cm). Sarasota Middle School, Sarasota, Florida.

Page 222 **Meg Weeks,**
Twilight Trek to Freedom,
1999.
Construction paper collage, 18" x
24" (46 x 61 cm). Winsor School,
Boston, Massachusetts.

Page 196 **Heidi McEvoy,** *Animal,* **1999.**
Acrylic paint, 8 1/2" x 23 1/2" (21.5 x 59.5 cm). Fairhaven Middle School, Bellingham, Washington.

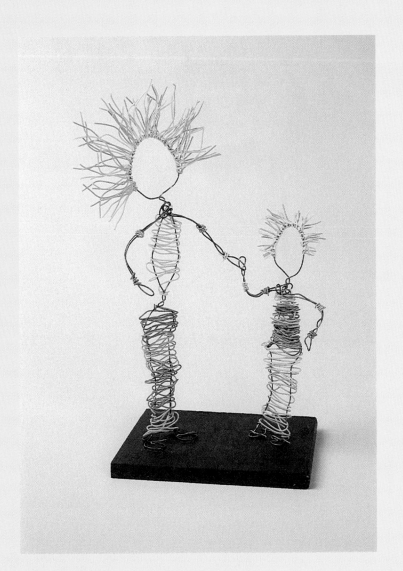

Page 295 **Deborah Mduruwa, Curtis Breer, Orion Stand-Grai, Noah Abrahams,** *Low Rider,* **1999.**
Videotape, Samford Middle School, Auburn, Alabama.

Page 274 **Micale Mitchell,** *Mother and Child,* **1999.**
Wire, wood base, 11 1/2" (29 cm) high. Desert Sands School, Phoenix, Arizona.

Foundations

What Is Art?

If you ask three friends what art is, they probably won't give the same answer. Throughout history, art has meant different things to different people. And that remains true today.

Many art museums display beautiful objects from different cultures. Even though we call these objects works of art, the people who made them may not have thought of them as art. In fact, some cultures have no word for art. Yet they take great care in making beautiful pottery, jewelry, and masks.

Whether or not it is intended as art, an object made by a person shows that individual's creativity and skill. The artist, designer, or craftsperson must have thought about why he or she was making the object. Something he or she saw or imagined must have provided inspiration. Once the object is made, other people may see it as a work of art, or they may not. How they see and appreciate the object depends on their sensitivity and their own ideas about what art is.

Look carefully at some of the objects pictured in this book. Write down the names of the ones that interest you, including their page numbers. Which objects do you consider works of art? Why? Why do you feel that other objects are not art? Write down your answers. When you are finished with Part 1 of this book, look at the objects again. How have your opinions changed?

The Whys and Hows of Art

Focus

- Why do people all over the world create works of art?
- How do artists make their work unique?

Do you remember the first time you painted a picture? You might have painted an animal or a scene from nature. Or perhaps you just painted swirling lines and shapes because you liked the way the colors looked together. No matter what the subject of the painting, there are many questions we can ask about how your first painting came to be. For example, what made you want to create it? How did you use paint to express your ideas? Why did you decide to paint the picture instead of draw it with crayons or a pencil? How was your painting similar to others you had seen?

These are questions we can ask about any work of art, whether it be your creation or someone else's. When artists work, they might not always think about these questions, but the answers are there. And while the answers might differ from one artist to the next, the whys and hows of art can lead us to a world of wonder.

What's Ahead

- **F1.1 The Functions of Art**
  Learn about the many roles that art plays in peoples' lives.
- **F1.2 Subjects and Themes for Artworks**
  Recognize that objects, ideas, and feelings inspire people to create art.
- **F1.3 Styles of Art**
  Understand why there can be similarities among certain artworks, even though every work of art is different.

Words to Know

subject
theme
style

Fig. F1–1 Sheila Hicks piled up separate fiber bundles for this sculpture. How do you think her title relates to the artwork? Sheila Hicks, *The Evolving Tapestry: Blue,* 1967–68.
Linen, silk, 27 pieces, average, each piece: 2" x 23" x 15" (5 x 59 x 38 cm) installed size will vary. Gift of Vivian and Edward Marrin, 80: 1992.1-.25, The St. Louis Art Museum (Decorative Arts and Design) [ISN 26181].

Fig. F1–2 The Tairona of Colombia were known as great warriors. Can you find the bird and animal heads in the headdress of the fierce human figure? Colombia, Sierra Nevada area, Tairona Style, *Pendant Figure with Headdress,* 14–16th century.
Gold, 5 1/4" x 6 1/2" (13.4 x 16.5 cm). The Metropolitan Museum of Art, Gift of H. L. Bache Foundation, 1969. (69.7.10) Photograph © 1982 The Metropolitan Museum of Art.

Fig. F1–3 In traditional African cultures, artists create works for royal rulers that often relate these people to their ancestors or the gods. How would you design a chair to communicate a ruler's power? Africa, Cameroon grasslands, *Chair,* late 19th century.
Wood, 31 3/4" x 21" x 17 1/2" (80.7 x 53.3 x 44.5 cm). © The Cleveland Museum of Art. Gift in memory of his parents, Wheeler B. and Dorothy Preston, by Mary and John Preston. 1983.33.

Fig. F1–4 Are human figures or the environment the main subject of Vincent van Gogh's painting? How do his brushstrokes and color communicate the passionate spirit of nature? Vincent van Gogh, *Entrance to the Public Gardens in Arles,* 1888.
Oil on canvas, 28 1/2" x 35 3/4" (72.3 x 90.8 cm). Acquired 1930, The Phillips Collection, Washington, DC.

The Functions of Art

Although people create art for many reasons, most artworks belong to one of three broad categories: practical, cultural, or personal. These categories describe the function, or role, of an artwork.

Practical Functions

Much of the world's art has been created to help people meet their daily needs. For example, architecture came from the need for shelter. People also needed clothing, furniture, tools, and containers for food. For thousands of years, artists and craftspeople carefully made these practical objects by hand. Today, almost all everyday objects that are designed by artists are mass-produced by machines.

Think about the clothes you wear and the items in your home and school. How do they compare to similar objects from earlier times or from other cultures? Which do you think are beautiful or interesting to look at? Why?

Fig. F1–5 Practical. It takes many years for Kuna women to master the challenging method of reverse appliqué. First they carefully cut through the top layers of cloth. Then they tuck and stitch them under to reveal brilliant, jewel-like fabrics below. Why might reverse appliqué be considered an art technique? Panama, Kuna Yala, *Mola* (woman's blouse), early 20th century.
Length 23 3/8" (59.5 cm). Courtesy the National Museum of the American Indian, Smithsonian Institution (16.6425). Photo by David Heald.

Fig. F1–6 Cultural. Can you locate Buddha in the sculpture? If you were to create a stele such as this, where would you place the most important figure? China, Honan, Wei Dynasty (535–557 AD), *Votive Stela,* 551 AD.
Limestone, 39" x 20" x 11" (99 x 50.8 x 27.9 cm). Courtesy the University of Pennsylvania Museum.

Cultural Functions

We can learn a lot about different cultures by studying their art and architecture. Some buildings and artworks were made to honor leaders and heroes. Other works help teach religious and cultural beliefs. Sometimes art commemorates important historical events or identifies an important person or group.

Many artists continue to create artworks for cultural reasons. What examples can you think of in your community or state that serve a social, political, religious, or historical purpose? How are they different from artworks that have a practical function?

Personal Functions

An artist often creates a work of art to express his or her thoughts and feelings. The materials an artist chooses and the way he or she makes the artwork reflect the artist's personal style. The work might communicate an idea or an opinion that the artist has about the subject matter. Or it might simply record something that the artist finds particularly beautiful. Such personal works are created in many forms, including drawing, painting, sculpture,

Fig. F1–7 Personal. Archibald Motley was one of the leading artists of the Harlem Renaissance (1919–29), a period when art, music, literature, and poetry flourished. What part of the African-American heritage does Motley seem to care about? Archibald Motley, *Barbeque*, 1934.
Oil on canvas. 39 1/2" x 44" (100 x 111.8 cm). The Howard University Gallery of Art, Washington, DC.

cartooning, and photography. What artworks do you know about that were created for personal expression or sheer beauty?

Fig. F1–8 What does this artwork express about the student who made it? Why might she have chosen to create a sculpture instead of a painting? Adrienne Lastoskie, *Untitled*, 1998.
Plaster, 13 1/2" x 5 1/2" x 6" (34 x 14 x 15 cm). Daniel Boone Area Middle School, Birdsboro, Pennsylvania.

Try This

Create a three-dimensional artwork out of objects, such as hardware, plastics, and other materials found in the modern industrial world. Your artwork should reflect both a practical and cultural function. Write a label for the work that asks viewers to think about how your piece fulfills a practical and cultural purpose.

Foundation Lesson 1.1

Check Your Understanding

1. What are three broad categories of reasons that art is created? Select an artwork from another lesson in this book to illustrate each of these functions.
2. Name and describe a piece of art in your community that serves a cultural purpose.

Subjects and Themes for Artworks

Artists are observers. They find subjects and themes for their work in almost everything they see and do. The **subject** of an artwork is what you see in the work. For example, the subject of a group portrait is the people shown in the portrait. Other familiar subjects for artworks include living and nonliving things, elements of a fantasy, historical events, places, and everyday activities.

You can usually recognize the subject of an artwork. Sometimes, however, an artist creates a work that shows only line, shape, color, or form. The artwork might suggest a mood or feeling, but there is no recognizable subject. This kind of artwork is called *nonobjective*.

Fig. F1–9 **Look carefully at this group portrait. The artist has arranged the figures according to rank. What details did the artist use to help express the ranking of the different people?** Africa, Nigeria, Edo, Court of Benin, *Warrior Chief, Warriors, and Attendants,* late 17th century.
Brass, 18 7/8" (47.9 cm). The Metropolitan Museum of Art, Gift of Mr. and Mrs. Klaus G. Perls, 1990. (1990.332) Photograph © 1991 The Metropolitan Museum of Art.

Fig. F1–10 **Do you see a restaurant in this painting? Why can this artwork be considered nonobjective?** Grace Hartigan, *Broadway Restaurant*, 1957. Oil on canvas, 79" x 62 ³/₄" (200.7 x 159.4 cm). The Nelson-Atkins Museum of Art, Kansas City, Missouri. (Purchase: Nelson Trust) (F57-56)

Fig. F1–11 **Do you think Marsden Hartley was more interested in realistically showing a *still life* — an arrangement of objects — or exploring shape, line, and color? Why do you think so?** Marsden Hartley, *Still Life,* ca. 1929–30. Oil on cardboard, 25 ³/₄" x 18 ³/₄" (65.4 x 47.6 cm). Santa Barbara Museum of Art, Gift of Wright S. Ludington. (1950.3)

Fig. F1–12 **In 1932, artist William H. Johnson said, "My aim is to express in a natural way what I feel, what is in me, both rhythmically and spiritually." What other theme besides his feelings does Johnson express in this artwork?** William H. Johnson, *Soap Box Racing,* ca. 1939–40. Tempera, pen and ink on paper mounted on paperboard, 14 1/8" x 17 7/8" (35.9 x 45.4 cm). National Museum of American Art, Smithsonian Institution, Washington, DC / Art Resource, NY.

The **theme** of an artwork is the topic or idea that the artist expresses through his or her subject. For example, the theme of the group portrait might be family togetherness or community support. Themes in art can be related to work, play, religion, nature, or just life in general. They can also be based on feelings, such as sadness, love, anger, and peace.

Artworks all over the world can reflect the same theme, but will still look entirely different. Why? Because the subjects used to express the theme probably won't be the same. For example, imagine that an artist in Australia and an artist in Canada each create a painting about natural beauty. Would the Canadian artist show a kangaroo? Probably not.

Look at the artworks in this lesson. What subjects do you see? What themes are suggested?

Try This

Create a self-portrait by drawing objects you carry around. Empty your school bag and pockets on the desk. Arrange the items you select in a composition that says something important about yourself. Remember: You are the subject of your work. Can you choose objects that suggest a theme?

Computer Option

Arrange objects from your school bag, knapsack, or pockets on a flatbed scanner. Scan them into an image-editing or paint program. Use the application's tools to add new elements that represent you. Move and alter all of the elements to create an effective composition.

Fig. F1–13 **Why might some people say that work is the theme of this painting? Why might others say that community is the theme?** Joseph Jean-Gilles, *Haitian Landscape*, 1971. Oil on canvas, 30" x 48" (76 x 122 cm). Purchase Fund, 1974, Art Museum of the Americas.

Fig. F1–14 **Nature is a popular theme in art. Why might this artist want us to see a close-up view of nature?** Tim Barwise, *Untitled*, 1999. Tempera paint, 24" x 18" (61 x 46 cm). Chocksett Middle School, Sterling, Massachusetts.

Foundation Lesson 1.2

Check Your Understanding

1. What is the theme and subject of Fig. F1-7, *Barbeque* by Archibald Motley? How is this similar to Fig. F1-12, *Soap Box Racing* by William Johnson?

2. Identify a nonobjective artwork in another section of this book. Explain why it is nonobjective.

Styles of Art

A **style** is a similarity you can see in a group of artworks. The artworks might represent the style of one artist or an entire culture. Or they may reflect a style that was popular during a particular period in history.

You can recognize an artist's *individual* style in the way he or she uses art materials, such as paint or clay. An artist can adopt certain elements of design and expression that create a similar look in a group of his or her works. Sometimes an artist uses the same kind of subject matter again and again.

Artworks that reflect *cultural* and *historical* styles have features that come from a certain place or time. For example, Japanese painters often depict scenes from nature with simple brushstrokes. From an historical perspective, the columns used in ancient Greek architecture have characteristics that are immediately recognizable.

As explained in the following sections, there are also four *general* style categories that art experts use to describe artworks from very different times and cultures.

Expressionism

In an expressionist artwork, the mood or feeling the artist evokes in the viewer is more important than creating an accurate picture of a subject. The artist might use unexpected colors, bold lines, and unusual shapes to create the image. Expressionist artists sometimes leave out important details or exaggerate them. When you look at an expressionist work of art, you get a definite feeling about its subject or theme.

Fig. F1–15 **How did the German Expressionist Ernst Ludwig Kirchner use diagonal shapes and lines to create a feeling of tension? Would the painting have the same feeling if his shapes were rounded and scattered throughout the canvas?** Ernst Ludwig Kirchner, *The Red Tower in Halle,* 1915. Oil on canvas, 47 1/4" x 35 5/8" (120 x 90.5 cm). Museum Folkwang Goethestr. 41, D-4300 Essen 1

Fig. F1–16 **Why might Richard Estes' artwork fall into a style dubbed Photo or Super Realism? How is his work different from a photograph?** Richard Estes, *Prescriptions Filled* (Municipal Building), 1983.
Oil on canvas, 36" x 72" (91.4 x 182.9 cm). Private Collection, photo courtesy Allan Stone Gallery, NY. © Richard Estes / Licensed by VAGA, New York, NY/ Marlborough Gallery, NY.

Realism

Some artists want to show real life in fresh and memorable ways. They choose their subjects from everyday objects, people, places, and events. Then they choose details and colors that make the subjects look real.

Sometimes a particular mood is suggested in the artwork. Artists who work in this style often make ordinary things appear extraordinary. Some of their paintings and drawings look like photographs.

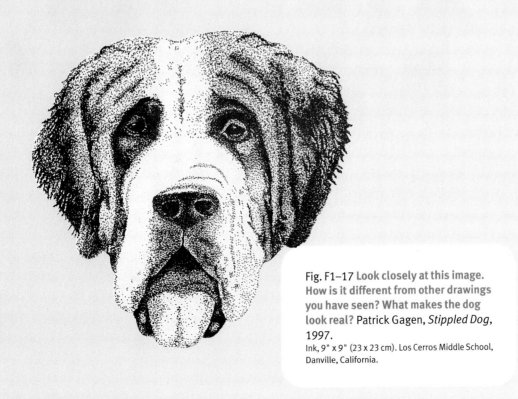

Fig. F1–17 **Look closely at this image. How is it different from other drawings you have seen? What makes the dog look real?** Patrick Gagen, *Stippled Dog*, 1997.
Ink, 9" x 9" (23 x 23 cm). Los Cerros Middle School, Danville, California.

Abstraction

Artists who work in an abstract style arrange colors, lines, and shapes in fascinating ways. They find new ways to show common objects or ideas. Their artworks appeal to the mind and senses. For example, most people see and feel flowing curved lines as graceful. Jagged lines remind people of sharp objects or sudden, unexpected events, such as lightning. Nonobjective artworks usually fall into this style category.

Fig. F1–18 **Can you see features of a city in this painting? How does it make you feel? Why?** Robert Delaunay, *Window on the City No. 3* (La Fenetre sur la ville no. 3), 1911–12. Oil on canvas, 44 3/4" x 51 1/2" (113.7 x 130.8 cm). Solomon R. Guggenheim Museum, New York. Photography by David Heald © The Solomon R. Guggenheim Foundation, New York.

Fig. F1–19 **What features of this scene look like they come from a dream?** Marc Chagall, *Paris Through the Window,* 1913. Oil on canvas, 53 1/2" x 55 3/4" (135.8 x 141.4 cm). Solomon R. Guggenheim Museum, New York, Gift, Solomon R. Guggenheim, 1937. Photograph by David Heald © The Solomon R. Guggenheim Foundation, New York (FN 37.438) © 2000 Artist Rights Society (ARS), New York / ADAGP, Paris.

Fantasy

The images you see in fantasy art often look like they came from a dream. When fantasy artists put subjects and scenes together, they create images that appear unreal. While the subject might be familiar, the details in the artwork might not seem to make sense.

Try This

Write two short sentences about something you see in the room. Place each word on a separate note card. Mix the cards up and then randomly pick five to eight cards. Place the words in any order to create a title for a drawing. Create the drawing, using one of the styles discussed in this lesson. When you are finished, gather together with the students who worked in the same style as you. As a group, discuss how you captured elements of that style in your drawings.

Sketchbook Connection

Find a simple object and create several sketches of it. Look at the object from different angles. Experiment with your drawing media and technique. Sketch the object alone or arranged with one or two other objects. When you are finished sketching, write about your experience. What did you learn about your individual style?

Foundation Lesson 1.3

Check Your Understanding

1. Compare and contrast the styles, themes, and subjects of two of the artworks in this lesson.

2. From another section of this book select an example of each of these styles: expressionism, realism, abstraction, and fantasy. Explain why each is a good example of its style of art.

The Hows and Whys of Art

Connect to...

Careers

Who is most likely to influence your beliefs about and responses to art? For most students, that person is an elementary- or secondary-school **art teacher**. Teachers of art provide meaningful opportunities and experiences for students to respond to art creatively, think about art, interpret art, and take part in artistic expression. Along with a solid foundation in art criticism, aesthetics, and art history, art teachers must be familiar with a wide variety of forms of visual expression and have a working knowledge of a broad range of media. Art teachers select themes, subjects, styles, media, and techniques to help students explore many ways to communicate. Art teachers also plan, lead

discussions, demonstrate, evaluate, and display the work of students while also remaining life-long learners in the visual arts. The program of study for an art teacher includes both education and art; most state colleges and universities offer an art-education degree through their education department.

F1–20 **Many art teachers are also practicing artists. Not only do they help you look at art and interpret what you see, they also help you create art that is meaningful to you.**
Photo courtesy *SchoolArts*.

Daily Life

F1–21 **Imagine walking past this sculpture. What might be your first impression? How could you learn more about why the artist created it for this site? What function does it serve?** Louise Nevelson, *Dawn Shadows,* 1983.
Painted steel, height: 30' (9.15 m). Madison Plaza Building, Chicago. ©2000 Estate of Louise Nelvelson/Artists Rights Society (ARS), New York.

Just as taking math is unlikely to make you a mathematician, there is no guarantee that taking art will turn you into an artist. But taking art classes can make you more aware of your visual environment and help you develop an appreciation of the artistic expression of others. If you approach the **study of art** with an open mind, the experience may heighten your perceptions and broaden your **personal concepts of art**. Think about the following questions as you begin your experiences in art, and return to them at the end of your course to see if your thoughts about art have changed: Is there a certain artist or artistic style you prefer? Does art play any part in your daily life? Do you ever visit museums on your own or with your family?

Mathematics

Can you think of any parallels between mathematics and art? **Mathematical concepts that connect to art** include measurement, symmetry, scale and proportion, congruent shapes and tessellations, and technical drawing. Geometry connects to art through two-dimensional shapes and three-dimensional forms, perspective, and geometric patterns. Look around you. What examples of these concepts can you identify?

Social Studies

Have you noticed that your social-studies text is illustrated with artworks? How can works of art teach us about a culture? If we are to explore artworks fully, we must consider **ideas common to both art history and social studies**. Concepts of history, stories of people and places, cultural practices, traditions, and beliefs all contribute to an understanding of both social studies and art. Choose a work of art from your social-studies book. Do you think its choice for use in the book was appropriate?

F1–22 This painting's subject is an historical event: the forced march of the Cherokee tribe from Georgia to Oklahoma in 1838. The route became known as the Trail of Tears. Why might it be important to include this work in a social-studies or history book? Robert Lindneux, *The Trail of Tears*, 1942.
Oil on canvas, 42" x 64" (106.6 x 162 cm). From the collection of the Woolaroc Museum, Bartlesville, Oklahoma.

Language Arts

Art and language arts share—or have parallel—concepts and terms. How are theme, subject, style, composition, mood, sequence, balance, and unity similarly expressed in both subjects? What are the parallels between meaning and main idea? Artist and author? Portrait and biography? Drawing and writing? How can these ideas extend your thinking about art?

Music

If someone asks you to define *art*, you might have to stop and think. Are you able to give a definition after studying this chapter? Take music. We all know what music is…don't we?

Is your **definition of music** "sounds that I like"? Is there a difference between noise and music? Between speech and music?

Listen to a CD of environmental sounds, such as the ocean or bird songs. Is this music? If so, what makes it music? If not, what would it take to turn these sounds into music? What about whales' "songs"? These have been recorded and made into CDs. Are these sounds music? Is music something made only by people?

Internet Connection
For more activities related to this chapter, go to the Davis website at **www.davis-art.com.**

Portfolio

"Our work of art was intended to be a dragon, but as we worked it seemed to transform right in front of our eyes into something that looked like a warrior."
Frederick Ceratt and Jason Lewis

F1–24 Frederick Ceratt and Jason Lewis, *Dark Knight,* 1999.
Wood, tempera, 24" tall (61 cm). Jordan-Elbridge Middle School, Jordan, New York.

F1–23 Megan Verhelst, *Self-portrait,* 1999.
Conté crayon, 14" x 20" (35.5 x 51 cm). Verona Area Middle School, Verona, Wisconsin.

"I enjoyed using the medium of colored pencil for this piece. You work with the colors much like you would in a painting. It helped me expand from using just ebony pencil, which I had been mainly using up to that point."
Heather Waldeck

F1–25 Heather Waldeck, *Invented Insect,* 1996.
Colored pencil, 12" x 18" (30.5 x 46 cm). Verona Area Middle School, Verona, Wisconsin.

CD-ROM Connection
To see more student art, check out the Community Connection Student Gallery.

Foundation 1 Review

Recall

Define expressionism and realism.

Understand

Explain the difference between subjects and themes.

Apply

Design a functional piece of clothing that also relates something about the culture from which your family originates (*see example below*). How can the piece's material, colors, purpose, and design reflect ideas about your heritage?

Page 4

Analyze

Classify the works on page 3 and pages 6–13 according to their function, as discussed in Foundation 1.1. Then compare and contrast selected examples within each group. What similarities and differences can you find among the items?

Synthesize

Find and read poetry that reflects something about the land or nature. Use the examples as the basis for your own artwork that reflects a landscape theme, with the specifics of the subject matter inspired by the poem itself.

Evaluate

Select the reproduction from this chapter that best illustrates expressionism, supporting your answers with what you see in the art itself.

Keeping a Sketchbook

Most artists fill many sketchbooks over the course of their careers. You can fill your own sketchbook pages with ideas for your artworks, notes about artworks you have seen, and pasted images from magazines and other sources. You can practice drawing and write your thoughts about art. When you fill the pages of one sketchbook, date it, and begin filling the pages of another!

Keeping a Portfolio

Many artists create portfolios to showcase their best works. Think of your portfolio as evidence of your learning in art. Provide evidence that you are learning to make art and that you are learning about the history and meaning of art. Keep your completed and dated artworks, essays, reports, and statements about art. On occasion, take a look at what you have placed in your portfolio and reflect on what you have accomplished.

For Your Portfolio

After completing each chapter of your book, insert a page into your portfolio, telling about what you have learned. Get into the habit of comparing your new artworks and ideas to those of the past.

Forms and Media

Focus

- What are the differences between two-dimensional art forms and three-dimensional art forms?
- What materials do artists use to create two-dimensional and three-dimensional artworks?

When you tell someone that you just created a painting or a sculpture, you are naming the art form you used to express yourself. **Art forms** can be two-dimensional, as in painting, drawing, printmaking, and collage. Or they can be three-dimensional, as in sculpture, architecture, and even furniture.

When artists plan a work of art, they decide which art form will best express their idea. Then they work in that art form. For example, an artist who wants to express an opinion about nature might create a painting or a drawing. An artist who wants to honor an important person might create a sculpture.

The differences you see between artworks of any one form are vast. This is because artists use a wide variety of materials, or **art media,** to create their artworks. For example, a painter might choose to use oil paints or watercolor. He or she might paint on paper, canvas, or even glass. Similarly, a sculptor might work with clay, stone, or any object that best expresses his or her idea. Imagine seeing a sculpture made from a beach umbrella or a car!

The lessons in this chapter explore art forms and the media most commonly used by artists.

What's Ahead

- **F2.1 Two-dimensional Artworks**
  Explore a variety of two-dimensional art forms and the media artists use to create them.
- **F2.2 Three-dimensional Artworks**
  Explore a variety of three-dimensional art forms and the media artists use to create them.

Words to Know

art form	mobile
art media	relief sculpture
fresco	ceramics
montage	mosaic

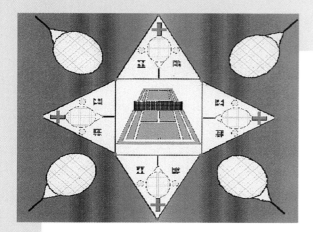

Fig. F2–1 **What ideas are expressed in this computer-generated artwork? How might the work look different if it was created as a painting? Do you think it would have the same kind of feeling? Why or why not?** Adam Hahn, *The Things I Thank*, 1999. Computer art, 6 ½" x 9" (16.5 x 23 cm). Plymouth Middle School, Plymouth, Minnesota.

Fig. F2–2 **Artist Romare Bearden focused on daily and seasonal rituals, including family meals, planting, and listening to jazz or blues music. What ideas might he be expressing in this collage? Do you see any photographs that represent daily life?** Romare Bearden, *Mysteries*, 1964.
Collage, 11 ¼" x 14 ¼" (28.6 x 36.2 cm). Ellen Kelleran Gardner Fund. Courtesy Museum of Fine Arts, Boston. Reproduced with permission. ©1999 Museum of Fine Arts, Boston. All Rights Reserved. © Romare Bearden Foundation / Licensed by VAGA, New York, NY.

Fig. F2–3 **British artist Henry Moore used bronze to create this sculpture of the family group. How has he simplified the features of each person in the sculpture?** Henry Moore, *Family Group*, 1944.
Bronze, 5 ⅞" x 5" x 2 ¾" (14.9 x 12.7 x 7 cm). The Metropolitan Museum of Art, Anonymous Gift, in honor of Alfred H. Barr, Jr., 1981 (1981.488.4) Photograph © 1997 The Metropolitan Museum of Art.

Two-dimensional Artworks

Drawing, painting, and other two-dimensional (2-D) art forms have height and width but no depth. To create 2-D artworks, such as those you see in this lesson, artists work with different types of art media.

Drawing and Painting

The most common media for drawing are pencil, pen and ink, crayon, charcoal, chalk, pastel, and computer software programs. Artists who draw choose from a wide range of papers on which to create their images.

Although many artists use drawing media to plan other artworks, drawings can also be finished works of art.

Oils, tempera, watercolor, and acrylics are common media used to create paintings. An artist might apply paint to a variety of surfaces, including paper, cardboard, wood, canvas, tile, and plaster. A **fresco**, for example, is a tempera painting created on a wet plaster surface.

Fig. F2–4 Artist Diego Rivera was involved in the Mexican mural movement, which revived the art of fresco painting. What does this fresco tell you about the city of Detroit? Diego M. Rivera, *Mural: Detroit Industry,* South Wall (detail), 1932–33. Fresco. Gift of Edsel B. Ford, Photograph © The Detroit Institute of Arts.

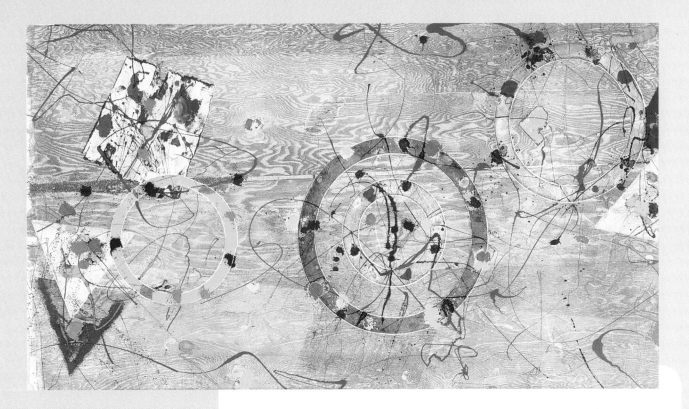

Fig. F2–5 **Notice the strong geometric elements in this print. How did artist Sam Francis keep this artwork from looking strictly geometric? What material did he use to create the work? How can you tell?** Sam Francis, *Untitled,* 1982.
Woodcut monotype, oil and dry pigment on paper, 43" x 78 1/2" (109.2 x 199.4 cm). Santa Barbara Museum of Art, Museum purchase, Vote for Art Fund. © 2000 Estate of Sam Francis / Artists Rights Society (ARS), New York.

Collage

To create a collage, an artist pastes flat materials, such as pieces of fabric and paper, onto a background. Some artists combine collage with drawing and painting. Others use unexpected materials, such as cellophane, foil, or bread wrappers. Look back at Fig. F2–2, the collage created by Romare Bearden, on page 19. A collage made from photographs is called a **montage.** How does Bearden's montage compare with the montage in Fig. F2–7?

Printmaking

This form of art can be broken down into several different kinds of processes. The main idea is the same for all: transferring an inked design from one surface to another. The design itself might be carved into wood or cut out of paper before it is inked. Then it is pressed by hand onto paper, fabric, or some other surface.

The most common printmaking processes are gadget, stencil, relief, and monoprint. Other more complex processes include lithography, etching, and silkscreen. An artist can print a single image many times using any printmaking process, except monoprinting; as the "mono" in its name suggests, an image can only be printed once.

Graphic Design

Graphic designers create original designs. Some of them print their designs by hand. They combine type and pictures to create posters, signs, corporate logos or symbols, advertisements, magazines, and books.

Most graphic designs are mass-produced on high-speed printing presses. Look around you. What examples of graphic design can you find in your classroom?

Fig. F2–6 Sometimes a graphic designer will hand-print a small edition and from one of those prints, a commercial printer will produce hundreds or thousands of copies using a high-speed press. What effect do you think such a process might bring to the finished, printed piece? How do you think a literary magazine such as *The Lark* might have benefitted from such an effect? Florence Lundborg, *Cover illustration for* The Lark, *November 1895.*
Woodcut, green and blue on Japanese paper, 16 3/8 x 9 7/8" (41.5 x 25.1 cm). Metropolitan Museum of Art, Gift of David Silve 1936. (36.23.14) Photograph by Bobby Hansson. Photograph © 1986 The Metropolitan Museum of Art.

Fig. F2–7 **Did David Hockney take only one photograph of each element in his composition? Why might he include multiple views of the same subject? How does this affect your sense of time and perception?** David Hockney, *Christopher Isherwood Talking to Bob Holman, (Santa Monica, March 14, 1983) #3*, 1983.
Photographic collage, 43 1/2" x 64 1/2" (110.5 x 163.8 cm). © David Hockney.

Photography, Film, and Computer Art

These 2-D art forms are fairly new in the history of art. The camera was invented in the 1830s, followed by moving pictures about sixty years later. Since their invention, photography and film have become two of the most popular media. Today, video cameras and computers offer even more media for artists working in the film or TV industry. Although individuals may use a single camera or computer to create art, feature films and television shows are usually created by a team of artists.

Try This

Artists face a certain set of challenges when creating work in two dimensions and different ones when working in three dimensions. Choose a three-dimensional artwork that is shown in this book. Recreate it as a two-dimensional artwork. When you are finished, ask yourself what surprised you most about the process. Compare your experience with classmates.

Computer Option
Choose an artwork that you have completed, and try to reproduce it on the computer. Compare the processes. How was one easier to create or change than the other?

Foundation Lesson 2.1

Check Your Understanding
1. Give an example of an art form. Then list the media that are often used in this art form.
2. Explain the difference between a fresco and an oil painting.

Three-dimensional Artworks

Architecture, sculpture, and other three-dimensional (3-D) art forms have height, width, and depth. To create 3-D artworks, such as those you see in this lesson, artists work with different types of art media.

Architecture and Environmental Design

Architects design the buildings in which we live, work, and play. They think about what a building will be used for, how it will look, and the way it will relate to its surroundings.

Architects combine materials such as wood, steel, stone, glass, brick, and concrete to create the buildings they design. Then interior designers plan how spaces inside the buildings will look. They choose paint colors or wallpaper, carpeting, and upholstery fabrics. They also suggest how the furniture should be arranged.

Environmental and landscape designers plan parks, landscape streets, and design other outdoor spaces. They use trees, shrubs, flowers, grasses, lighting fixtures, and benches. They also use materials such as stone, brick, and concrete to create paths, sidewalks, and patios.

Fig. F2–8 Whereas painters might use sketches, architects use models to work out their plans. How does Richard Meier make use of a mountain in his 110-acre building complex? Richard Meier & Partners, model of *The Getty Center,* 1991.
© J. Paul Getty Trust and Richard Meier & Partners. Photo by Tom Bonner.

Fig. F2–9 **Alexander Calder specialized in making sculptures that move. Why might you react differently to a sculpture that moves than you would to one that doesn't move?** Alexander Sterling Calder, *Tricolor on Pyramid,* 1965. Painted sheet metal and steel wire, 48" x 78" (121.9 x 198 cm). North Carolina Museum of Art, Raleigh, Purchased with funds from the National Endowment for the Arts and the North Carolina Art Society (Robert F. Phifer Bequest) © 2000 Estate of Alexander Calder / Artists Rights Society (ARS), New York.

Sculpture

Sculptures come in many forms. Most are designed to be viewed from all sides. You are probably most familiar with statues. A statue is a sculpture that stands alone, sometimes on a base. It can be life-size, as are the monuments you see in some parks. Or it can be small enough to place on a table or mantelpiece. A **mobile** is a hanging sculpture that has moving parts. The design on a **relief sculpture** is raised from a background surface and is intended to be viewed from only one side.

In addition to having many forms of sculpture to choose from, a sculptor can select from a great variety of media. Traditional materials include wood, clay, various metals, and stone such as marble. Sculptors also work with glass, plastic, wire, and even found objects.

Crafts

The term *crafts* applies to artworks made by hand that are both practical and beautiful. Among the many crafts are ceramics, fiber arts, mosaics, and jewelry making. **Ceramics** are objects that have been made from clay and then fired in a kiln. Fiber arts include objects that have been woven, stitched, or knotted from materials such as wool, silk, cotton, and nylon. A **mosaic** is a design made of tiny pieces of colored glass, stone, or other materials. Artists who make crafts such as jewelry and other personal adornments might use gold, silver, wood, fabric, leather, and beads. Look at the clothing and jewelry your classmates are wearing. What materials are they made of?

Fig. F2–10 **This example of fiber art is intended to hang from a hook. Why might the artist have named this *The Hat?*** Danielle McConaghy, *The Hat*, 1999.
Wire, yarn, 10" x 10" x 22" (25.5 x 25.5 x 56 cm). Penn View Christian School, Souderton, Pennsylvania.

Fig. F2–11 **This mosaic shows the hunting of dangerous animals. Why might artists choose to create a mosaic instead of a painting? Would you? Why or why not?** Roman, Antioch, *Hunting Scene*, 6th century AD.
Mosaic, 96 1/2" x 110 2/3" (245.5 x 281 cm). Worcester Art Museum, Worcester, Massachusetts, Museum Purchase.

Industrial Design

Artists who design three-dimensional products for mass production are called industrial or product designers. They design everything from spoons and chairs to bicycles and cruise ships. Industrial designers pay great attention to a product's function and appearance. They use materials such as metal, plastic, rubber, fabric, glass, wood, and ceramics. The next time you're in a grocery or department store, note the many examples of industrial design all around you.

Try This

Although we often study architecture from the outside, real people live and work inside these structures. Find an image in this book of a building façade (exterior) you like. Imagine walking through the building itself. What do you think its light, space, colors, and so forth are like? Make sketches of what you think the building's interior looks like.

Computer Option

Create an electronic representation of a three-dimensional space. Place a figure in the space, and imagine what the figure would "see." Draw the scene from the perspective of the figure.

Sketchbook Connection

Sketch a design for a ceramic object, fiber work, or piece of jewelry. Then write a brief paragraph about how your creation would look as a finished work of art. What materials would you use to create the piece? What function would your piece serve? How would you make it beautiful?

Foundation Lesson 2.2

Check Your Understanding

1. Why is a "bullet" train featured in an art book?

2. What two types of artwork form Calder's *Tricolor on Pyramid*, Fig. F2-9?

Fig. F2–12 Can you tell why this locomotive is called a "bullet" train? If you had to design a moving vehicle, how would you convey a sense of speed? *Bullet Train Between Paris and Lyon.*
© Chuck O'Rear, Courtesy Woodfin Camp.

Connect to...

Careers

What news stories can you recall about the deliberate damage of an artwork? In recent times, a few artworks in museums have been splattered with paint, struck with hammers, or scratched or torn. After an incident like any of these, museums rely on conservators to repair the damage. Though such an effort draws the attention of the press, most restoration work by conservators goes on quietly behind the scenes. Every major museum employs or works with a conservator who is responsible for the protection, authentication, cleaning, restoration, and repair of the museum's artworks on a regular basis. As a result of study and training in art history and in specialized areas, such as painting, conservators fully understand art forms and media, techniques, and styles. Only a few universities offer pro-

F2–13 Conservators carefully repair damage caused by weather, vandalism, or the effects of time. How could an understanding of the orginal artist's style and techniques help the conservator pictured here do a good job? Conservator working on Fra Angelico's San Marco fresco, ca. 1974.
Photo © David Lees/CORBIS.

grams in conservation, but extensive training is a prerequisite for success in this demanding career.

Other Arts

Music

Some people feel that all music may be classified as either song or dance. Do you agree? Your opinion probably depends on your definition of song and dance. Some people refer to any music they hear as a "song," but, technically, a song is music performed by the voice. The main feature of a song is its melody or tune. We listen to the words to understand what the song is about. A dance is music performed by instruments. The main feature is the rhythm, the way the music moves in time. We don't think about words; we may just want to get up and move!

Music, like art, is created in many forms. Each type of music is related to a purpose: to tell a story, for religious ceremonies, for public events, for entertainment. The media of music are instruments and voices. The specific instruments and types of voices fulfill the purpose of the music, and also provide important clues about its cultural background.

Internet Connection
For more activities related to this chapter, go to the Davis website at **www.davis-art.com.**

F2–14 **How are personal collections different from collections found in museums? How are they similar?** Photo courtesy H. Ronan.

Daily Life

Do you collect something? Baseball or other trading cards? Stuffed toys? CDs? What are some other collectibles? Although adults are more likely than you to collect artworks, stamps, coins, or antiques, the desire to acquire objects seems to appeal to people of all ages. Why, do you think, do people have a desire to collect and display things? What does a collection tell us about the collector's life?

Other Subjects

Language Arts

Do you prefer a certain type or form of art? Just as art has various forms, so does literature. The literary form, or genre, called narrative is sometimes accompanied by illustrations. Do you think literary and art forms are more

meaningful alone, or together? How else could a literary genre be improved by visual art?

Social Studies

Have you ever constructed and used a time line in your social-studies class? In your art class? A time line is a graphic form for studying dates and events in chronological sequence. It might span centuries, or just a few years. You can use textbooks and other reference materials to identify and order events and then place them on a time line. How does the time line on page 76 help you to understand art in early North America?

Science

Are you familiar with the chemical elements? Use a table of the elements as a guide to names of colors, by determining what elements are associated with a color. Why would this information be of interest to artists today? Why might such knowledge have been of interest to artists of the past?

F2–15 **This book was printed in Italy in 1478. Could this page be considered an early example of graphic design? Why or why not?** Girolamo da Cremona, frontispiece for the *Vitae illustrium virorum* (Lives) by Plutarch. Text printed in Venice by Nicolas Jenson, 2 January 1478. (Vol. II, frontispiece. PML 77565) The Pierpont Morgan Library/Art Resource, NY.

Portfolio

"For eighth grade art class we were required to create a wire sculpture of an animal. I really like fishing, so I chose my favorite fish, the large-mouth bass. I drew several sketches that showed how the bass would be constructed. I used my sketches to recreate the fish using wire."
William C. Tate

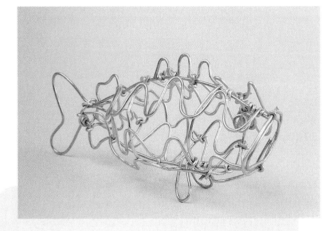

F2–17 William C. Tate, *Large-mouth Bass,* 1998.
Aluminum wire, 8 1/4" x 3 1/4" x 3 1/4" (21 x 8 x 8 cm). Daniel Boone Area Middle School, Birdsboro, Pennsylvania.

F2–16 Alicia A. Bartholemew, *Still Life with Mosaic Vase,* 1999.
Construction paper, painted paper, marker, 18" x 10" (46 x 25.5 cm). Roosevelt School, Worcester, Massachusetts.

 **CD-ROM Connection**
To see more student art, check out the Community Connection Student Gallery.

F2–18 Emma Berkey, *William H. Johnson,* 1999.
Colored pencil, 11" x 8 1/2" (28 x 21.5 cm). Asheville Middle School, Asheville, North Carolina.

Foundation 2 Review

Recall

Define two-dimensional and three-dimensional artworks.

Understand

Explain why architecture is a three-dimensional art form whereas a photograph of a building is not.

Apply

Search through magazines for what you think is a successful advertisement for sneakers. Describe what makes the advertisement appealing. How did the graphic designer catch your attention and get you to want the product? How could you alter the advertisement to make it even better?

Analyze

Write a label as a curator of an exhibition of three-dimensional artwork that explains why the bullet train (Fig. F2–12) is an example of industrial design while the mosaic and fiber artworks (Figs. F2–10 and F2–11) are examples of craft.

Synthesize

Transform either Fig. F2–4 or Fig. F2–5 into a three-dimensional artwork. What materials will you use to translate the flat image to one with actual depth?

Evaluate

Describe the problem with identifying the ancient Roman mosaic (Fig. F2–11, below) as a two-dimensional rather than a three-dimensional artwork.

Page 26

For Your Sketchbook
Review the art forms you have studied in this chapter. Write a statement about each art form in your sketchbook, using this form: "If I could make a _____ (sculpture, painting, etc.), I would make it out of _____ (wood, watercolor, etc.) and it would be about _____ (animals, people, swimming, etc.)." For each statement, make a quick sketch of how the artwork might look. This will help you think of ideas for future artworks.

For Your Portfolio
Whenever you add an artwork to your portfolio, make sure to sign and date it. Attach a page to the artwork, explaining the assignment, what you learned, and why you have selected this artwork for your portfolio. This information will be useful when you return to consider how you have developed as an artist.

Elements and Principles of Design

Focus

- What are the elements and principles of design?
- How do artists use the elements and principles of design in their artworks?

Artists use their imagination when they work. They experiment with ideas and art media, and invent new ways to create artworks. But before they actually get down to making a work of art, they must have a plan, or design, in mind.

In art, the process of design is similar to putting a puzzle together. The basic pieces or components that an artist has to choose from are called the *elements of design*. Line, shape, form, color, value, space, and texture are the elements of design. The different ways that an artist can arrange the pieces to express his or her idea are called the *principles of design*. Balance, unity, variety, movement and rhythm, proportion, emphasis, and pattern are the principles of design. When an artist is happy with the arrangement, the design is complete.

As you learn about the elements and principles of design, think about how they can help you plan and create your own art. Soon you will see that they can also help you understand and appreciate the artworks of others.

What's Ahead

- **F3.1 Elements of Design**
  Learn how artists can use the elements of design to create certain effects in their artworks.
- **F3.2 Principles of Design**
  Learn ways that the principles of design can make an artwork exciting to look at.

Words to Know

Elements of Design		Principles of Design	
line	value	balance	pattern
shape	space	unity	proportion
form	texture	variety	movement
color		emphasis	rhythm

Fig. F3–1 Duane Hanson's sculptures look so real that at exhibitions viewers sometimes nearly bump into them, mistaking the figures for actual people. What elements and principles of design do you think add to the realistic look of this sculpture? Duane Hanson, *Tourists,* 1990. Bondo and mixed-media, life-size. Courtesy Mrs. Duane Hanson.

Fig. F3–2 How does this mural, painted in 1974 by Latino artist Oscar Martinez, compare to the fresco that Diego Rivera painted in 1933 (Fig. F2–4)? Consider both the style and subject matter. Chicago Mural Group, *Latino and Asian-American History,* 1974, Left: *Hispanic Immigration* by Oscar Martinez. (912 West Sheridan, Chicago) Courtesy the Chicago Public Art Group.

Fig. F3–3 What elements and principles of design do you think you see in this artwork? Write down your answers. When you are finished with this chapter, see if you want to change your list. Kelly Bass, *Exploration of Art Elements,* 1999. Pencil, colored pencil, computer art, markers, 18" x 25" (46 x 63.5 cm). Verona Area Middle School, Verona, Wisconsin.

The Elements of Design

Line

Many people think of a **line** as the shortest distance between two points. To artists, a line is a mark that has length and direction. Lines can have many different qualities that help artists express their ideas. They can be thick or thin, wavy, straight, curly, or jagged. Artists use lines to outline shapes and forms or to suggest different kinds of movement. Sometimes artists use *implied* line. An implied line is not actually drawn, but is suggested by parts of an image or sculpture, such as a row of trees or a path of footprints.

If you look closely, you can find examples of line in every work of art you see. Notice how they affect the mood of an artwork. For example, how might a drawing with thick, zigzag lines be different from one with light, curved lines?

Fig. F3–4 Isabel Bishop's varied lines create a sense of solid three-dimensional form. How did she also use line to suggest motion? Isabel Bishop (1902–88), *Waiting*, 1935.
Ink on paper, 7 ½" x 6" (18 x 15 cm). © 1997: Whitney Museum of American Art, New York. Purchase.

Fig. F3–5 Notice how this student has used lines to create this portrait. How many different line qualities do you see? Do any suggest movement? Therese Ruhde, *Face with Line Patterns*, 1999.
Marker on brown paper, 14" x 20" (35.5 x 51 cm). Verona Area Middle School, Verona, Wisconsin.

Fig. F3–6 **Think about the sound of a clock ticking. Why might this artist's use of shape make you think of a ticking clock?** Niles Spencer, *The Watch Factory,* 1950.
Oil on canvas, 28" x 42" (71.1 x 106.7 cm). Courtesy The Butler Institute of American Art, Youngstown, Ohio.

Shape and Form

A line that surrounds a space or color creates a **shape.** Shapes are flat, or two-dimensional. A circle and a square are both shapes. A **form** is three-dimensional: It has height, width, and depth. A sphere and a cube are examples of forms.

Shapes and forms may be organic or geometric. *Organic* shapes and forms—such as leaves, clouds, people, ponds, and other natural objects—are often curved or irregular. *Geometric* shapes and forms—such as circles, spheres, triangles, pyramids, and cylinders—are usually precise and regular.

Most two-dimensional and three-dimensional designs are made up of both *positive* shapes and *negative* shapes. The figure in a painted portrait is the painting's positive shape. The pieces of fruit in a still-life drawing are the positive shapes in the drawing. The background or areas surrounding these objects are the negative shapes. The dark, solid shape of a statue is a positive shape. The area around and inside the forms of the statue make the negative shapes. Artists often plan their work so that the viewer's eyes move back and forth between positive and negative shapes.

Color and Value

Without light, you cannot experience the wonderful world of **color.** The wavelengths of light that we can see are called the color spectrum. This spectrum occurs when white light, such as sunlight, shines through a prism and is split into bands of colors. These colors are red, orange, yellow, green, blue, and violet.

In art, the colors of the spectrum are re-created as dyes and paints. The three *primary hues* are red, yellow, and blue. *Primary* means "first" or "basic." *Hue* is another word for "color." You cannot create primary colors by mixing other colors. But you can use primary colors, along with black and white, to mix almost every other color imaginable.

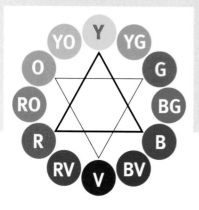

Fig. F3–7 Locate the primary and secondary colors on the color wheel. Why do you think the intermediate colors are also called tertiary colors? (See also page 308.)

Key to the Color Wheel

Y=yellow	V=violet
G=green	R=red
B=blue	O=orange

Fig. F3–8 Australian artist Roy de Maistre was fascinated by the way music could suggest different colors. What type of music is suggested by the colors and shapes in this painting? Roy de Maistre, *Rhythmic Composition in Yellow Green Minor,* 1919.
Oil on paperboard, 33 5/8" x 45 3/8" (85.3 x 115.3 cm). Purchased 1960, The Art Gallery of New South Wales (photo: Jenni Carter for AGNSW).

Fig. F3–10 How does American artist Grant Wood use value to suggest the forms of a midwestern landscape? Notice the smooth transition between the light and dark areas of this drawing. Grant Wood, *In the Spring,* 1939.
Pencil on paper, 18" x 24" (45.7 x 61.0 cm). Courtesy of The Butler Institute of American Art, Youngstown, Ohio.
© Estate of Grant Wood / Licensed by VAGA, New York, NY.

The *secondary* hues are orange, green, and violet. You can create these by mixing two primary colors: red and yellow make orange; yellow and blue make green; red and blue make violet.

To create *intermediate* hues, you mix a primary color with a secondary color that is next to it on the color wheel. For example, mixing yellow and orange creates the intermediate color of yellow-orange.

Value refers to how light or dark a color is. A light value of a color is called a *tint*. A tint is made by adding white to a color. Pink, for example, is a tint made by adding white to red. Artworks made mostly with tints are usually seen as cheerful, bright, and sunny.

A dark value of a color is called a *shade*. A shade is made by adding black to a color. For example, navy blue is a shade made by adding black to blue. Artworks made mostly with dark values are usually thought of as mysterious or gloomy.

The intensity of a color refers to how bright or dull it is. Bright colors are similar to those in the spectrum. You can create dull colors by mixing complementary colors. *Complementary* colors are colors that are opposite each other on the color wheel. Blue and orange are complementary colors. If you mix a small amount of blue with orange, the orange looks duller. Many grays, browns, and other muted colors can be mixed from complementary colors.

When artists plan an artwork, they often choose a *color scheme*—a specific group of colors—to work with. An artist might use a primary, secondary, intermediate, or complementary color scheme. Or the artist might choose any of the color schemes illustrated in the chart below.

Common Color Schemes

warm: colors, such as red, orange, and yellow, that remind people of warm places, things, and feelings.

cool: colors, such as violet, blue, and green, that remind people of cool places, things, and feelings.

neutral: colors, such as black, white, gray, or brown, that are not associated with the spectrum.

monochromatic: the range of values of one color (monochrome means "one color").

analogous: colors that are next to each other on the color wheel; the colors have a common hue, such as red, red-orange, and orange.

split complement: a color and the two colors on each side of its complement, such as yellow with red-violet and blue-violet.

triad: any three colors spaced at an equal distance on the color wheel, such as the primary colors (red, yellow, blue) or the secondary colors (orange, green, violet).

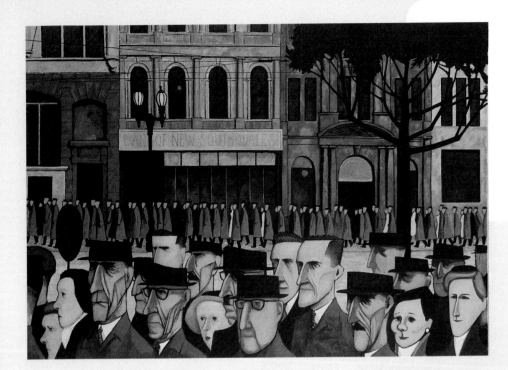

Fig. F3-11 Australian artist John Brack mixed different amounts of yellow, brown, and black to create a monochromatic color scheme. What qualities of a neutral color scheme does this painting have? John Brack, *Collins Street, 5 PM,* 1955. Oil on canvas, 45 ¼" x 64 ⅛" (114.8 x 162.8 cm). Purchased, 1956. National Gallery of Victoria, Melbourne, Australia.

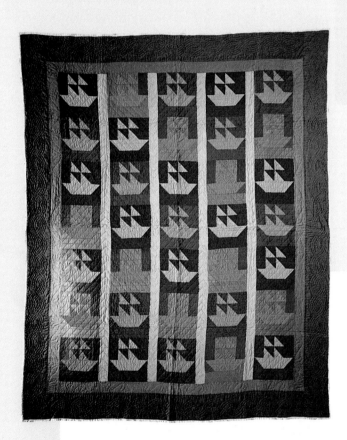

Fig. F3-13 Prudence Heward uses mainly primary and secondary colors to suggest the time of year in her landscape. How would the painting be different if she had used blues, grays, and whites? Prudence Heward, *Autumn Landscape,* c. 1932-46. Oil on plywood, 14 ¼" x 12" (36.2 x 30.5 cm). National Gallery of Canada, Ottawa. Gift of the Heward family, Montreal, 1948.

Fig. F3-12 What cool colors do you see in this quilt? Would you consider this an example of an analogous color scheme? Why or why not? Amanda Lehman, *Sailboats Quilt,* 1955-65. Cotton, 86 ¼" x 72" (219.1 x 182.9 cm) framed. Collection of the Museum of American Folk Art, New York. Gift of David Pottinger. (1980.37.26)

Space

Sculptors and architects work with actual **space.** Their designs occupy three dimensions: height, width, and depth. *Positive* space is filled by the sculpture or building itself. *Negative* space is the space that surrounds the sculpture or building.

In two-dimensional (2-D) art forms, artists can only show an illusion of depth. They have simple ways of creating this illusion. For example, in a drawing of three similar houses along a street, the one closest to the viewer appears larger than the middle one. The house farthest away appears smaller than the middle one. Artists can also create the illusion of depth by overlapping objects or placing distant objects higher in the picture.

Artists working in two dimensions also use linear perspective, a special technique in which lines meet at a specific point in the picture, and thus create the illusion of depth.

Fig. F3–14 **The figure of the Hindu god, Shiva, and the circle of fire that surrounds him fill the positive space of this figure. Where do you see negative space?** India, Tanjore district, Chola-Dynasty (846–1173 AD), *Shira Nataraja,* 11–12th century.
Bronze, height: 32 ¼" (81.9 cm). Museum Rietberg Zurich, Eduard von der Heydt collection.

Fig. F3–15 **In this picture, the artist has used linear perspective to create the illusion of space. If you were to extend the outlines of the lumber, they would meet in the upper left corner area. In what other ways has the artist created the illusion of space?** Alfredo Zalce, *Lumber,* 1946.
Color lithograph, 11" x 14" (28 x 36 cm). Metropolitan Museum of Art, The Elisha Whittelsey Collection, The Elisha Whittelsey Fund, 1950. (44.46.653) Photograph © 1977 The Metropolitan Museum of Art.

Fig. F3–16 **Notice how carefully this artist carved the details and textures of an eagle. If you could run your hands over this bird, what would it feel like?** American, *Eagle* (architectural ornament), ca. 1810.
Pine with gilt and gesso, 37" x 26 1/2" x 60" (94 x 152.5 x 67.3 cm). Smith College Museum of Art, Northampton, Massachusetts. Gift of Dorothy C. Miller, class of 1925 (Mrs. Holger Cahill), 1969.

Fig. F3–17 **Where do you see real and implied textures in this mask? How did this student use art materials to create texture?** Charde Powers, *Mask*, 1997.
Mixed media, paper. West Tatnuck School, Worcester, Massachusetts.

Texture

Texture is the way a surface feels or looks, such as rough, sticky, or prickly. *Real* textures are those you actually feel when you touch things. Sculptors, architects, and craftspeople use a variety of materials to produce textures in their designs. These textures can range from the gritty feel of sand to the smooth feel of satin.

Artists who work in the two-dimensional art forms can create *implied* textures, or the illusion of texture. For example, when an artist paints a picture of a cat, he or she can create the look of soft fur by painting hundreds of tiny fine lines. What kinds of implied texture have you created in paintings or drawings of your own?

Try This

Create a quick sketch focusing on two elements of art described in this lesson. Next, choose two other elements of art. Use the new elements to redo the same composition. How do your two drawings compare? Which works better and why?

Foundation Lesson 3.1

Check Your Understanding
1. How do artists use the elements and principles of design?
2. Select a piece of art in this book that has a monochromatic color scheme. Are its colors warm or cool? Describe the mood of this piece in one or two words.
3. Describe implied textures in a piece of art in this lesson.
4. What is the difference between positive and negative space?

Principles of Design

Balance

Artists use **balance** to give the parts of an artwork equal "visual weight" or interest. The three basic types of visual balance are symmetrical, asymmetrical, and radial. In *symmetrical* balance, the halves of a design are mirror images of each other. Symmetrical balance creates a look of stability and quiet in an artwork.

In *asymmetrical* balance, the halves of a design do not look alike, but they are balanced like a seesaw. For example, a single large shape on the left might balance two smaller shapes on the right. The two sides of the design have the same visual weight, but unlike symmetrical balance, the artwork has a look of action, variety, and change.

In *radial* balance, the parts of a design seem to "radiate" from a central point. The petals of a flower are an example of radial balance. Designs that show radial balance are often symmetrical.

Try This

Create a 2-D or 3-D artwork that shows unity and variety. When you are finished, gather together with classmates who created the same kind of artwork as you. Discuss the challenges you faced when you created your artwork. Which examples of unity and variety work the best? Why?

Computer Option
Choose a drawing or painting of your own that shows unity. Scan and import a copy of your work to an image-editing program. Save the document. Change the artwork electronically so that it shows variety. Save this new work as a separate document, and print. Return to your original document. Add some of your variety ideas to make an artwork that shows both unity and variety. Save and print this new design.

Fig. F3–18 **What kind of balance did Franz Kline create in his composition? How did he create it?** Franz Kline, *Hazelton*, 1957.
Oil on canvas, 41 ¼" x 78" (104.8 x 198.1 cm). The Panza Collection. Museum of Contemporary Art, Los Angeles. © 2000 The Franz Kline Estate / Artist Rights Society (ARS), New York.

Unity

Unity is the feeling that all parts of a design belong together or work as a team. There are several ways that visual artists can create unity in a design.

- repetition: the use of a shape, color, or other visual element over and over
- dominance: the use of a single shape, color, or other visual element as a major part of the design
- harmony: the combination of colors, textures, or materials that are similar or related

Artists use unity to make a design seem whole. But if an artist uses unity alone, the artwork might be visually boring.

Fig. F3–19 **In what ways has this student artist created unity? What kind of balance do you see?** Jenna Skophammer, *Stella's Dream*, 1999.
Marker and tempera, 12" x 18" (30.5 x 46 cm). Manson Northwest Webster, Barnum, Iowa.

Variety

Variety adds visual interest to a work of art. Artists create variety by combining elements that contrast, or are different from one another. For example, a painter might draw varying sizes of circles and squares and then paint them in contrasting colors such as violet, yellow, and black. A sculptor might combine metal and feathers in an artwork or simply vary the texture of one material. Architects create variety when they use materials as different as stone, glass, and concrete to create the architectural forms of a building.

Fig. F3–20 **In this sculpture, generations of family members surround the main figure of an ancestor. In what ways has the artist created unity? Where do you see variety?** Makonde, Tanzania, *Family Group,* 20th century.
Wood, 31" (78.7 cm). Gift of Nancy Gray, Collection Bayly Art Museum of the University of Virginia, Charlottesville. (1981.94.75)

Fig. F3–21 To help create emphasis, this artist has exaggerated the limbs of the ballplayers. How does the placement of the mitt add to the feeling of emphasis? Nelson Rosenberg, *Out at Third,* undated.
Watercolor and gouache on paper, 15" x 21 7/8" (38.1 x 55.5 cm). Acquired 1939, The Phillips Collection, Washington, DC.

Emphasis

Look at *Out at Third* (Fig. F3–21). What is the first thing you see? You might say you see the baseball and mitt first. Now see if you can explain why you notice them first. Here are some clues.

When artists design an artwork, they use **emphasis** to call attention to the main subject. The size of the subject and where it is placed in the image are two key factors of emphasis. Sometimes artists group certain objects together in the design. In this case, however, the artist created emphasis by arranging other elements in the picture to lead the viewer's eyes to the subject. What elements lead your eyes to the ball and mitt?

Pattern

An artist creates a **pattern** by repeating lines, shapes, or colors in a design. He or she uses patterns to organize the design and to create visual interest. You see patterns every day on wallpaper, fabric, and in many other kinds of art.

Patterns are either planned or random. In a *planned* pattern, the element repeats in a regular or expected way. A *random* pattern is one that happened by chance, such as in a sky filled with small puffy clouds or in the freckles on a person's face. Random patterns are usually more exciting or energetic than planned ones.

Fig. F3–22 **This artist has used pattern to create the look of scales on the lizards. What other examples of pattern do you see in this artwork?** Ann Hanson, *Dancing Lizard Couple,* 1985.
Celluclay, 16 1/2" x 20 1/2" (41.9 x 52.1 cm). The National Museum of Women in the Arts. On loan from the Wallace and Wilhelmina Holladay Collection.

Proportion

Proportion is the relationship of size, location, or amount of one thing to another. In art, proportion is mainly associated with the human body. For example, even though your body might be larger, smaller, or shorter than your best friend's, you both share common proportions: Your hips are about halfway between the top of your head and your heels; your knees are halfway between your hips and your feet; and your elbows are about even with your waist.

Scale is the size of one object compared to the size of something else. An artist sometimes uses scale to exaggerate something in an artwork. In a painting, for example, he or she might place a giant coffee mug in the middle of a busy freeway.

Fig. F3–23 Are human beings actually as stick-thin as those shown in this sculpture? How is the proportion of these figures different from the proportion of the human body? Alberto Giacometti, *Three Men Walking,* 1948–49.
Bronze, height: 29 1/2" (74.9 cm). Edward E. Ayer Endowment in memory of Charles L. Hutchinson, 1951.256. Photograph courtesy The Art Institute of Chicago. © 2000 Artists Rights Society (ARS), New York / ADAGP, Paris.

Fig. F3–24 **When you look at this image, do you get the feeling that the people and animals are moving left to right? What creates that feeling?** India, Rasjasthan, Jaipure, *The Wedding Procession of Prince Bakhtawar Singh,* late 18th century.
Opaque watercolor, gold and silver on paper, 18 9/16" x 11 5/8" (47.1 x 29.5 cm). Cincinnati Art Museum, Gift of Mr. and Mrs. Carl Bimel, Jr. 1982.251.

Sketchbook Connection
Read aloud a piece of poetry that you particularly like. Listen for the rhythm of the words. Create a sketch that conveys the same sense of rhythm. Try to visually communicate the poem's tempo. Discuss with classmates how rhythm in poetry and art are similar and different.

Movement and Rhythm

Rhythm is related to both movement and pattern. Artists use rhythm, like pattern, to help organize a design or add visual interest. They create rhythm by repeating elements in a particular order. Rhythm may be simple and predictable, or it may be complex and unexpected.

For example, look at *The Wedding Procession of Prince Bakhtawar Singh* (Fig. F3–24). The repetition of faces in the lower left area creates a predictable rhythm. The rhythm of the fountain-like object in front of the elephant is more complex. What other examples of predictable and complex rhythm do you see in this painting?

Foundation Lesson 3.2

Check Your Understanding
1. Select a piece of artwork from the foundation chapters that has symmetrical balance and another that has asymmetrical balance. Which one has more movement?
2. How did Giacometti alter proportions in Fig. F3-23?
3. Explain how Rosenberg emphasized his message in *Out at Third*, Fig. F3-21. What is the most important part of the picture?
4. From this chapter, choose a piece of art that appeals to you. Describe the art elements and principles that seem most important in this piece of art.

Connect to...

Careers

Do you have a piece of jewelry that you wear every day, jewelry that has become your own personal "signature"? From prehistoric times, jewelry has been a source of identity and pleasure—and, often, a sign of wealth and rank. People originally made ornaments for body adornment from such materials as shells, feathers, teeth, ivory, and metal. With the development of new tools and techniques, jewelry makers used gems and precious metals, like gold and platinum. A **jewelry designer** today—either working alone or in a jewelry-manufacturing company—must be skilled in drawing and in the use of many specialized materials, tools, and processes. Training for jewelry design is available in art schools, colleges, and technical institutes. Whether making necklaces, earrings, rings, pins, or bracelets, jewelry designers use the elements and principles of design on a miniature scale that requires great care and attention to detail.

F3–25 "For me, jewelry design is a wonderful way to show my love for self-expression and to celebrate everyone by decorating them."
—Heather Skowood, jewelry designer, Philadelphia, Pennsylvania.
Photo © George Costa. Courtesy Heather Skowood.

Daily Life

Many of the **elements and principles of design have parallels in daily life**. Can your family tell the time by the repeated pattern of your daily schedule, especially during the school week? Does your day follow a regular pattern? Do you wake up, eat, go to school, change classes, come home, watch TV, and go to bed? How is your pattern different on the weekend? In visual art, pattern is a principle of design in which the repetition of elements forms a recognizable organization. Does that definition seem to relate to your schedule? What are some other ways that you encounter patterns in your day?

F3–26 As you walk down the street, notice the patterns and designs created by reflections on buildings and in windows. What other elements or principles of design do you see? *Façade, Pacific Design Center, Los Angeles, California.*
Courtesy Davis Art Slides.

Internet Connection
For more activities related to this chapter, go to the Davis website at **www.davis-art.com.**

Language Arts

Do you think **color has an important impact** on your senses and emotions? In theory, colors are considered to be warm or cool; tints or shades; and black or white or neutral. In literature, descriptions—in the form of adjectives and adjective phrases—can convey mood and emotion. "In the pink," "blue mood," "green with envy," "red hot," and "black heart" all carry emotional associations. What are some other examples?

Science

Have you ever observed the visible **spectrum**, or the colors, when white light is passed through a prism? The individual bands of color separate within the prism as the different wavelengths of the white light are bent, or refracted. To make your own rainbow at home, use a sprinkler or water hose on a sunny day. Face away from the sun, and spray a thin mist in front of you. Adjust the position of the spray until you can see the rainbow.

Mathematics

Have you ever tried to create a perspective drawing? **Perspective** is the illusion of three-dimensional depth and space on a two-dimensional surface. The use of perspective developed from Renaissance artists' fascination with math-

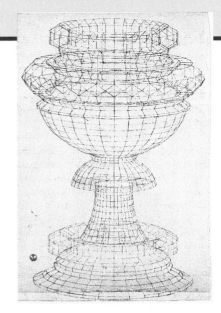

F3–27 **What techniques of perspective has this Renaissance artist used to show a 3-D object on a flat surface? What principles of mathematics must he have known?** Paolo Uccello, *Perspective Drawing of a Chalice,* 15th century. Ink on paper. Gabinetto dei Disegni e delle Stampe, Florence, Italy. Scala/Art Resource, NY.

ematics. Linear perspective uses sets of implied lines that move closer together in the distance until they merge at an imaginary vanishing point on the horizon. One-point perspective uses lines that lead to a single vanishing point, whereas two-point perspective uses lines that lead to two different vanishing points. Why, do you think, do parallel lines converge in perspective drawings, but they do not converge in terms of mathematics?

Other Arts

Theater

Directors of **stage productions** take into consideration **elements and principles** of design, such as space, line, balance, unity, and variety. They also look carefully at the principle of emphasis, which, in theater, is called focus; and the principle of movement, which is called blocking. To block for focus, a director places actors in different areas of the stage and in different body positions.

UP STAGE RIGHT	UP CENTER STAGE	UP STAGE LEFT
STAGE RIGHT	CENTER STAGE	STAGE LEFT
DOWN STAGE RIGHT	DOWN CENTER STAGE	DOWN STAGE LEFT
PROSCENIUM		

F3–28 **The nine basic stage positions are shown here. Notice that the right and left sides of the stage are identified from the actor's perspective. The proscenium (*pro-SE-ne-um*) is the wall that separates the stage from the auditorium.** Courtesy Andrew Harris, The Southeast Institute for Education in Theatre.

Portfolio

"I got the idea to make this drawing from the many 'home style' magazines I read in my spare time. Various times I pretended I was Leonardo da Vinci just to achieve the difficult tasks on the house." **Casey Cahill**

F3–29 Casey Cahill, *Tree Phase*, 1999.
Black marker, 18" x 24" (46 x 61 cm). Laurel Nokomis School, Nokomis, Florida.

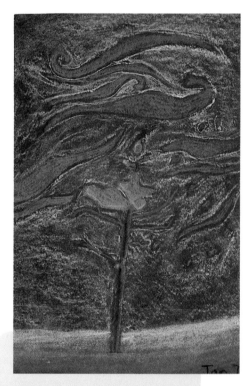

F3–31 Jonathan Davis, *Windy Day*, 1998.
Chalk pastel, 12" x 18" (30.5 x 46 cm). Remington Middle School, Franklin, Massachusetts.

F3–30 Tracy M. Dupuis, *Flaming Dragon Tessellation*, 1999.
Marker, metallic pen, 12" x 18" (30.5 x 46 cm). City View School, Worcester, Massachusetts.

CD-ROM Connection
To see more student art, check out the Community Connection Student Gallery.

Foundation 3 Review

Recall

Define the elements and principles of design.

Understand

Identify two major elements of design in *Autumn Landscape*, Fig. F3–13 *(see below)* and explain your answers.

Apply

Create a bulletin board with visual examples for each of the elements and principles of design.

Analyze

Compare and contrast the way the artists in Figs. F3–16, F3–20, and F3–22 used texture. What do the works have in common in this regard, and how are they different?

Synthesize

Research eagles in science and natural history resources. After, discuss with a partner how the artist of Fig. F3–16 used texture to create a sense of the bird's power. Select another animal to research, and produce an artwork with texture that also conveys something about this creature's qualities.

Evaluate

Choose which artwork—Figs. F3–23 or F3–24—is a better example of emphasis, and write a label for the work defending your selection.

Page 39

For Your Sketchbook

Search through magazines and catalogues for good examples of the use of elements and principles of design. Paste these images on pages in your sketchbook. Make notes about how the elements and principles are used and why you selected these images. Return to these pages when you are arranging design elements in future artworks.

For Your Portfolio

Select an artwork reproduced in your textbook that you think is a good example of the use of elements and principles of design. Write a short essay in which you describe the way the artist has arranged the elements of design to achieve certain results. Your essay will provide evidence that you can analyze the design of artworks.

Approaches to Art

Focus

- What do people want to know about art?
- What kinds of questions do people ask about art?

Imagine finding an object that's unlike anything you've ever seen before. You turn the object over in your hands and ask yourself, "What is this? Who made it? How was it made?" Suppose something about the object suggests that it was made a long time ago. You might wonder why the object was important to the people who lived at that time. What did they use it for? How is it different from objects that you normally see or use?

For thousands of years, people have wondered where objects and artworks come from and why they were made. It's human nature to be curious. We can be as curious about the function of an artwork as we are about its meaning. Asking questions about the artwork helps us understand it. The information we learn about the artwork can also teach us something about the times and cultures of our world and where we fit in.

This chapter will introduce you to the kinds of questions people ask about artworks. As you read the chapter, you will see that the questions fall into four categories: art history, art criticism, the making of art itself, and the philosophy of art.

What's Ahead

- **F4.1 Art History**
  Learn how to find the story behind an artwork.
- **F4.2 Art Criticism**
  Explore ways to find the meaning of a work of art.
- **F4.3 Art Production**
  Learn more about yourself as an artist.
- **F4.4 Aesthetics**

Words to Know

art historian	artist
art critic	aesthetician

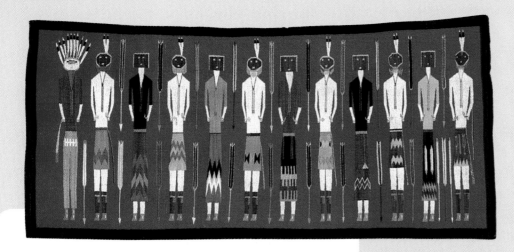

Fig. F4–1 **Notice how the figures on this textile alternate to create a pattern. What might the figures represent?** *Navajo ye ii bicheii (yeibechai)* textile, 20th century.
Wool, 42 1/2" x 91 1/2" (107.3 x 232.5 cm). Collected from Mrs. Fione Warnoff. Photo by Katherine Fogden. Courtesy National Museum of the American Indian, Smithsonian Institution.

Fig. F4–2 **Grandma Moses is probably the most famous American folk artist. What clues suggest that this scene might have been painted in the 1940s?** Anna Mary Robertson Moses, called Grandma Moses, *Summer Party,* 20th century.
Oil on masonite, 23 9/16" x 15 3/4" (59.9 x 40 cm). The Museum of Fine Arts, Houston; Wintermann Collection of American Art, gift of Mr. and Mrs. David R. Wintermann.

Fig. F4–3 **Artists often think about point of view, or the angle from which they will show their subject. How would you describe the point of view in this drawing?** Melissa Reilly, *Patchwork Kitten*, 1999.
Collage, marker, 16" x 20" (40.5 x 51 cm). Laurel Nokomis School, Nokomis, Florida.

Fig. F4–4 **The design of this modern artwork recalls Stonehenge from prehistoric times, or ancient Greek or Roman ruins. When you look at this, do you see it as an artwork or just a bunch of cars? Why?** Jim Reinders, *Carhenge*, Alliance, Nebraska, 1982.
33 cars. © 1999, www.roadsideamerica.com, Kirby, Smith, Wilkins.

Art History

The Stories Behind Art

Art history is just what you'd expect: the history of art. **Art historians**—people who study the history of art—want to know where artworks began. They research the cultures from which artworks spring. They learn about the people, the politics, and the economic conditions at the time and place where artworks were made. They try to figure out why artists created artworks and how the artworks are different from others. And finally, when all of their research is done, they piece together the stories of art.

Do you ever wonder where artworks come from or what their story is? If you do, then you have begun investigating their history.

Looking at Art

There are certain basic questions that will get you started on the search for an artwork's story.

1. What is the artwork? What is it about? What is its purpose?
2. When and where was it made?
3. Has the artwork always looked like this? Or has it changed somehow over time?

Finding the Story

The next set of questions will help you find out what an artwork meant to the artist and to the people who lived at the time it was made. By asking these questions, you can learn how the artwork reflects the cultural traditions of the time. Your answers will also help place the artwork in history.

1. What was happening in the world when the artwork was made? How is the world different now?
2. How do the customs and traditions of the artist's family or culture add to the meaning of the artwork?
3. What other kinds of art did people make at that time?

Fig. F4–5 **What do the figures in this artwork appear to be doing? Why might it have been important for the artist to show this scene?** Yellow Nose, *Ghost Dance,* Cheyenne-Arapaho Reservation, 1891. Deerskin, ink and pigment, width: 50" (127cm). Courtesy the National Museum of Natural History/ Smithsonian Institution.

Fig. F4–6 How did this artist show the importance of the Emancipation Proclamation to the United States? Would everyone living at the time have felt the same way about this artwork? Why or why not? A. A. Lamb, *Emancipation Proclamation*, 1864 or after. Oil on canvas, 32 3/8" x 54" (82.2 x 137.2 cm). Gift of Edgar William and Bernice Chrysler Garbisch, © 1999 Board of Trustees, National Gallery of Art, Washington, DC. (1955.11.10. (1428) / PA)

Fig. F4–7 What decisions do you think artists make when they create seascapes? How does this artwork compare to other seascapes you've seen? Ashley Jacques, *Stormy Night*, 1999. Tempera, 24" x 16" (61 x 40.5 cm). Camels Hump Middle School, Richmond, Vermont.

Introducing the Artist

As the story of an artwork unfolds, questions about the artist begin to surface. Some art historians focus their investigations mainly on the life and work of a single artist. Imagine the challenge of discovering something new and interesting about an artist!

1. Who made this artwork?

2. What role did artists play in the community in which this work was made?

3. How does this artist's style compare to the style of other artists during that time?

4. What decisions was the artist faced with as he or she created this artwork?

You can ask any of these sample questions about a specific artwork or artist. You can also ask similar questions about an entire art period or about the value and use of artworks in general.

See if you can find out what art historians have said about artworks and artists that interest you or about when and where the artworks were created.

Try This

Choose an artwork in this chapter. Investigate the culture and period of time in which it was made. Using the information, re-title the artwork with words that convey what you have learned. Compare your solutions with others by students who chose the same artwork.

Foundation Lesson 4.1

Check Your Understanding

1. What are some questions that art historians ask as they study artworks?

2. Imagine that a committee has asked you to select an artwork to be placed in a public building in your community. Choose a piece from this lesson. Use the questions in "Finding the Story" to help you write an explanation for your choice.

Art Criticism

Searching for Meaning

Art critics want to know what artworks mean. They can help us learn about artworks by describing them and pointing out interesting things to look for. They judge the quality of artworks and suggest why they are valuable or important. Art critics often write about art in newspapers or magazines. Their views can influence the way we look at and think about artworks.

You have already asked questions like an art critic, perhaps without even realizing it. You may have looked at artworks in this book and wondered about their meaning. You have expressed your thoughts and opinions about objects and artworks around you. And you have compared them to other objects or artworks you're familiar with. Your views may have affected the way your classmates or others think about artworks.

Finding Clues

As an art critic, you need to observe certain things about an artwork before you can begin to think about its possible meaning. Here are some questions that will help get you started.

1. What does the artwork look like?
2. How was it made?
3. How are the parts of the artwork arranged?
4. Does it seem to suggest a mood or feeling? An idea or theme?

Making Connections

Once you understand how the artwork is put together, you can focus more on its meaning and ask questions such as these:

1. What is the artwork about?
2. What message does it send? How does it make me think, feel, or act when I see it?
3. How is the artwork related to events in the artist's life? How is it related to events that happened at the time it was made?

Fig. F4–8 **Imagine walking through this landscape. What does the artist show about the relationship between people and nature? What clues do you see that support your ideas?** Qui Ying, *The Emperor Guang Wu Fording a River,* Ming Dynasty (1368–1644 AD). Ink and color on silk, 67 ¼" x 25 ¾" (170.8 x 65.4 cm). National Gallery of Canada, Ottawa. Purchased 1956. Acc. # 6485

Fig. F4–9 William Wegman includes a photograph of Pablo Picasso's famous painting within his own artwork. Wegman's arrangement of the dog and guitar recalls Picasso's style. Why might Wegman have made this visual connection to Picasso's work? William Wegman, *Blue Period*, 1981.
Color Polaroid, 24" x 20" (61 x 50.8 cm). Courtesy of the artist.

Judging Importance

Suppose you have learned enough about the artwork to decide that it is important. Next, you need to support your judgment. Ask yourself:

1. What aspects of the artwork—such as artist, culture, message, or function—make it important? Why?

2. What sets this artwork apart from similar artworks?

3. How is my response to this artwork different from my response to similar artworks?

You can see the kinds of things art critics say about art when you read a review of an art exhibit in your local newspaper. Try to visit the exhibit yourself. Do you agree with what the critic says about it? Why or why not?

Try This

Be a critic of one of your own artworks. Ask yourself the four questions in "Finding Clues." After writing your responses, read over what you have said. Describe to a partner what new ideas you learned about your own art or thinking process.

Sketchbook Connection
Sketch an idea for a painting or sculpture that you would like to create. Then exchange sketches with a classmate. Write comments about the sketch you receive. What good qualities do you see in the sketch? How might your partner change the sketch to make the artwork better?

Foundation Lesson 4.2

Check Your Understanding

1. How does an art critic help us understand works of art?

2. Why might you consult an art review?

Fig. F4–10 What makes this artwork interesting? How would you describe it to someone who is about to see it for the first time? Lisa Rivoir, *Conviviality*, 1999.
Cardboard and silver spray paint, 36" x 28" x 16" (91.5 x 71 x 40.5 cm). Mount Nittany Middle School, State College, Pennsylvania.

Art Production

Making Art

Artists all over the world make artworks for decoration, to celebrate important events, and to communicate ideas or feelings. When artists plan a work of art, they think about its purpose and meaning. As they create the work, they explore their ideas and sometimes test the limits of the materials they use. In the end, they create a work that satisfies their personal and social needs, interests, values, or beliefs.

You think like an artist every time you explore the things you can do with pastels, a lump of clay, or any other art material. You might have an idea when you start, or your exploration might lead you to one. When you are finished expressing your idea, you have a work of art that is all your own.

Reflecting on Your Art and Yourself

As you create art, you will begin to realize what art and making art mean to you. Asking questions about your art-making experience will help you uncover that meaning.

1. What artworks are important to me? How do they affect the way I make art?

2. What feelings or ideas do I like to express in my artwork? What does my art say about me?

3. What process do I go through when I make art?

Considering Your Art and the World

When you have a better understanding of your own art, you can think about how it fits into the big picture. Ask yourself:

1. What does my artwork tell others about the place and time in which I live? What special events, people, or things does it suggest?

2. What do my choices of materials and techniques tell others about my world?

3. How is my artwork similar to or different from art that was made in other times and places?

Fig. F4–11 **This sculpture shows family members waiting for news of loved ones after a mine disaster. How does the artist show the fear and anxiety felt by the families? Would the work have the same feeling if the fence were made with rounded edges or the people stood apart?** Berta Margoulies, *Mine Disaster,* 1942.
Bronze, 23" x 29 1/2" x 12 1/2" (58.4 x 74.9 x 31.8 cm). Collection of the Whitney Museum of American Art, Purchase. Acq. #45.10.

Fig. F4–12 **Why might this student have chosen ceramic clay and glazes to make this sculpture? How would the work look different if it were carved from wood?** Jeff Warner, *Hedgehog*, 1999.
Ceramic clay, 8" x 4" x 3" (20 x 10 x 7.5 cm). Colony Middle School, Palmer, Alaska.

Fig. F4–13 **Notice how simple this image is. It is mainly made with areas of pure color. There is no detail in the background. Why might the artist have created the painting this way? How might the feeling of the painting be different if it were filled with intricate detail?** Khem Karan, *Prince Riding an Elephant,* ca. 1600.
Ink, opaque watercolor and gold on paper, 6 7/8" x 7 5/8" (17.4 x 19.4 cm). The Metropolitan Museum of Art, Rogers Fund, 1925. (25.68.4) Photograph © 1988 The Metropolitan Museum of Art.

Comparing Your Art to Other Art

As an artist, you are probably aware of ideas and concerns that other artists have. When you compare your work to theirs, you might see a connection.

1. How is my artwork similar to or different from artworks made by others? How has their work affected my work?

2. If I could create an artwork with another artist, whom would I choose to work with? Why?

3. What materials and techniques have other artists used that I would like to explore? Why?

The next time you create a work of art, ask yourself the questions in this lesson. See what answers you come up with. You'll probably learn something surprising about the artist in you!

Try This

Select one of the images in this lesson and consider why the artist might have chosen to work in that particular medium. Next, create your own art on the same subject, using a different medium. Answer the questions posed in the section "Comparing Your Art to Other Art." What is the most fascinating thing you learned from this comparison?

Foundation Lesson 4.3

Check Your Understanding

1. Why do artists create art? List some of the common reasons.

2. Use the questions in this lesson to write about a piece of your art. How do you feel about it? How does it fit into the world? How does it compare to other art?

Aesthetics

Investigating Art

Aesthetics is the philosophy, or investigation, of art. **Aestheticians** (*es-the-TI-shens*) can be called art philosophers. They ask questions about why art is made and how it fits into society. They're interested in how artworks came to be.

Every time you wonder about art or beauty, you think like an aesthetician. The questions that come to your mind about art are probably like the questions that aestheticians ask. All you need is a curious mind and probing questions to be an art philosopher yourself.

Thinking About Artworks

At some time or another, you have probably wondered what artworks are. Like an aesthetician, you can ask certain questions that will help you think more carefully.
1. Are all artworks about something?
2. In what ways are artworks special? What makes some artworks better than others?
3. Do artworks have to be beautiful or pretty? Why or why not?
4. What makes one kind of artwork different from another?

Thinking About Artists

As an aesthetician, you might wonder about the people who make art, why they make it, and why some people, but not all, are called artists. You might ask:
1. What do artworks tell us about the people who made them? What do they tell us about the world in which they were made?
2. What do people express through making art? Do artworks always mean what the artist intends them to mean?
3. Should there be rules that artists follow to make good artworks?

Thinking About Experiences with Art

When you talk about art, you probably discuss whether you like an artwork or not. And you probably talk about how an artwork makes you feel. These questions will help you dig deeper into your experience with an artwork.
1. How do people know what an artwork means?
2. Is it possible to dislike an artwork and still think it is good?

Fig. F4–14 Deborah Butterfield is best known for her skeletonlike horses. She creates them from scrap metal, wire, tree branches, clay, and twigs. Butterfield sees the structures as vessels for the horses' spirit. Why might some people find this artwork beautiful? Why might others be disturbed by it? Deborah Butterfield, *Eclipse,* 1986 (standing).
Rusted metal, steel, 80" x 110" x 24" (203.2 x 279.4 x 61 cm).
Mardi, 1986.
Rusted metal, steel, 32" x 103" x 65" (81.3 x 261.6 x 165.1 cm). Both works courtesy SOMA Gallery, La Jolla, CA.

Fig. F4–15 If you saw this image in a photo album, would you guess that it's a building? How is it unlike any other building you've seen? Frank Gehry, *Guggenheim Museum*, Bilbao, Spain, 1997. Courtesy Davis Art Slides.

3. How is the experience of looking at an artwork like the experience of looking at a beautiful sunset? Or are these experiences completely different?

4. How do beliefs about art affect the way people look at and explore artworks?

The questions that aestheticians ask do not necessarily investigate a specific artwork. Instead, they investigate the larger world of art in general.

Computer Option

Have a volunteer begin an artwork on the computer by drawing a few lines. Then transfer the file from student to student. Have each person add to the artwork. After everyone has contributed, discuss how the artwork changed as it was passed along. Did the computer drawing gain a sense of unity? Why or why not?

Try This

Show one of your finished artworks to a partner. Ask what she or he thinks it might be about. Have your partner point to specific details to support the answer. Does your partner understand the work in the way you wanted? Or does the piece mean something else to your partner? Do you think it's okay for people, including the artist, to have different interpretations of the same artwork? Discuss your answers to these questions with your partner.

Foundation Lesson 4.4

Check Your Understanding

1. Explain what aesthetics is. What type of questions do aestheticians ask?

2. Why is it important to learn about art?

Approaches to Art

Connect to...

Careers

One approach to art is art therapy. In this field, **art therapists** encourage people with certain emotional or physical problems, who are in counseling or psychotherapy, to express their emotions through drawing, painting, or other forms of artwork. The art is then used as a way to diagnose and treat the problems. Art therapists try to encourage their clients' self-awareness and personal growth. These art specialists work with people of all ages in hospitals, clinics, community centers, drug and alcohol treatment centers, schools, and prisons, and through individual or family counseling. Art therapists must understand a wide range of art forms and visual expression, psychology, and psychiatry; and must train extensively in specialized art-therapy programs, which are offered by a small number of colleges and universities.

F4–16 **Art therapists can work with people of any age. They use art materials for painting, sculpting, and drawing as a way for people to express and communicate their feelings and emotions about difficult situations and problems.** An art therapist with artwork by patients.
Photo courtesy Milissa Hicks.

Daily Life

Do you think you come across **artistic criticism in your daily life**? Do you ever read movie, music, or software reviews in magazines or newspapers? If so, you are reading journalistic criticism, written for the general public about newsworthy subjects. Some newspapers publish reviews that target a student audience. Do you find such reviews to be generally positive? Or negative? Most people think of criticism as negative, but journalistic criticism is more likely to present both pros and cons. Through the approach of persuasive writing, the critic wants to convince you to share his or her opinion, whether good, bad, or indifferent. A good review might convince you, for instance, to go to a particular movie or buy a certain CD or piece of software; a bad review may convince you to stay home and save your money!

F4–17 **What would convice you to see a movie or buy a CD? When you give a friend your opinion about a movie or a song, are you acting like a critic?** Gene Siskel and Roger Ebert.
Photograph © David Allen/CORBIS.

Internet Connection
For more activities related to this chapter, go to the Davis website at **www.davis-art.com.**

Dance

In this chapter, you learned about the types of questions people ask about a work of visual art. The same questions can be asked about a work of dance. Dance communicates our questions and ideas about who we are and how we can understand our relationship to others and to the world. **People dance for many reasons:** to communicate cultural identity, to provoke discussion, to tell a story, and so on. Think about the role that dance plays in your life. What kind of dance do you do? Why do you dance? Why does dancing feel good?

F4–18 Traditional Thai dance dates back to 650 AD and is still performed today. Each dance tells a story and the characters in the story have special costumes worn by the dancers. Why do people keep these dances alive by performing them? Classic Thai dance performed in Thailand.
Courtesy Davis Art Slides.

Other Subjects

Social Studies

As an approach to research, historians use **primary and secondary sources**. Do you know the difference between them? Primary sources are original materials, like diaries, letters, artifacts, artwork, photographs, and personal interviews. Secondary sources, such as your textbooks, are considered to be interpretations of primary sources. Which do you think would be more reliable? Why?

Language Arts

Literary criticism is writing that explains or judges works of literature. Such criticism is written for a scholarly audience and appears in published, professional reviews of literature, such as academic journals. **Literary criticism** may also be published in other print media or online, or shared with colleagues through presentations at conferences and seminars. Critics of literature are often college or university professors with knowledge about a particular style, period, form, or writer. Can you find examples of literary criticism in your language-arts book? If you have ever written a book review, you have engaged in literary criticism.

Mathematics

Have you ever wondered why we tell time in increments of 60? More than 5000 years ago, the ancient Babylonians used a **system of numbers** based on the concept of 60. This is the origin of our familiar 60-second minute and 60-minute hour. Although you may never have thought about math as having a history, it does have one—and it still affects us. Have approaches to math changed over time? How could you learn more about the history of math?

Science

The **comprehensive approach** to art presented by this text actually developed, in part, from the launching of a Russian satellite. In 1957, the Russians launched the first *sputnik*, an artificial satellite. In America, the sputnik launchings heightened fears of world communism and nuclear war. In response, American schools put a **new emphasis on learning**, and encouraged hands-on approaches, instead of memorization of facts and figures. This approach was also used in art classes. For instance, students no longer studied only artists, but also the **roles and ideas of art historians, art critics, and aestheticians**.

Portfolio

"This assignment revolved around a jazz theme my art teacher chose. While creating my composition, I concentrated on keeping it clean and in proportion. I had fun creating it, and it gave me a chance to work on some different techniques." **Shaun Berhow**

F4–19 Shaun Berhow, *Untitled,* 1998.
Stippled ink, 6" x 9" (15 x 23 cm). T.R. Smedberg Middle School, Sacramento, California.

"My pot symbolizes my freedom more than my Hispanic culture. I picked an object I liked and designed it like Mexican pottery. I chose colors that would catch a person's eye. Our culture is important, but with wings you can fly away from your troubles." **Veronica Martinez**

F4–20 Kaare Patterson, *Just Chill,* 1998.
Colored pencil, 12" x 18" (30.5 x 46 cm). Plymouth Middle School, Plymouth, Minnesota.

F4–21 Veronica Martinez, *Fly Away,* 1999.
Clay and acrylic, 4" x 5" x 3" (10 x 13 x 7.5 cm).
Sweetwater Middle School, Sweetwater, Texas.

CD-ROM Connection
To see more student art, check out the Community Connection Student Gallery.

"I thought it would be cool and weird to see penguins on a beach instead of in the arctic. While I was drawing, I was thinking of how I wanted the penguins to act on the beach. The part I like the most is the colors and how I shaded different parts. Also, I like the penguin in the center lying down with his glass in one flipper and his other one sprawled out." **Kaare Patterson**

Foundation 4 Review

Recall

Define art history, art criticism, art production, and aesthetics.

Understand

Explain the major difference between an art critic and an art historian.

Apply

Make a list of questions you might pose for *Carhenge*, Fig. F4–4 (*see below*), if you were an art critic, and then try answering them.

Analyze

Compare and contrast the message the artists of Figs. F4–11 and F4–14 wanted to convey. How did their choice of materials help communicate their ideas? Although both works are constructed from metal, how did the artists use the medium differently?

Synthesize

Research the two works and the societies that produced the Native American art in Fig. F4–1 and Fig. F4–5. Prepare a display with photographs, maps, illustrations, and explanatory labels that compares and contrasts the two pieces—their meaning, use, and relationship to the cultures from which they stem.

Evaluate

Consider the different approaches to art discussed in Foundation 4 and select the one that you think is most important. Alternatively, create an argument for the necessity of combining all the approaches when examining any work of art.

Page 53

For Your Portfolio

Select one of your completed artworks to insert in your portfolio. Using your own artwork as the focus, write what you think an art historian, a critic, a philosopher, and an artist might wonder about when looking at it. What would they look for? What questions might they ask? Date your writing and your artwork and put both into your portfolio.

For Your Sketchbook

Select an artwork from any chapter in your textbook. Write at least fifty questions about your selected artwork. Review your list of questions and indicate those that might be asked by an artist, a critic, an art historian, and a philosopher of art (aesthetician). Create a symbol for each of these four art professionals as a way of marking your questions.

Page 74

Art Is a Community Connection

If someone were to ask you to talk about your community, what would you say? First of all, what is your community? You may be surprised to learn that you have more than one!

Do you live in a city neighborhood, a town, or a village? One way to identify a community is by its geographical boundaries—that's probably the kind of community you think of first. But community can mean more than the return address on your letters. Think about the things you like to do. You might belong to a sports team, go to church or a synagogue, or be a part of a club at school. All those groups are communities, too.

People everywhere like to tell others about their communities. They like to celebrate what is special about where they live or what they do. They like to let other people know about their heroes, their history, and the things they believe. All over the world, art helps people tell these things.

In this part of this book, you'll learn about the many different ways that communities have used art to communicate. You'll learn that throughout recorded history, people everywhere have used art to teach each other, to keep records of their lives, to celebrate during good times and express feelings in times of sorrow.

As you look at and read about the artworks on these pages, think about the communities you belong to. How is art a part of those communities? How can art help connect your communities to other communities around you? And why is that community connection so important to human beings?

Telling

Fig. 1–1 On any day at the *Vietnam Veterans Memorial* in Washington, DC., you can see someone slowly touching a name, remembering a loved one, and perhaps leaving a token—a flower, a poem, or other special object. Maya Lin, *Vietnam Veterans Memorial,* Washington, DC., 1982.
Black granite, 493' long (150 m). Constitution Gardens, Washington, DC. Photo by Robert Hersh.

- How do people communicate their ideas and feelings to others in a community?
- How is art a way to express ideas and feelings?

From the air, it looks like a large V-shaped gash in the ground. As you approach it on foot, you see a gently sloping walkway beside a smooth dark wall. Up close, you can read the names of all the Americans who died or were reported missing in the Vietnam War. The *Vietnam Veterans Memorial* (Fig. 1–1) has become a national symbol for the loss of human life due to war of any kind. As of 1997, there were 58,209 names on the wall. Artist Maya Lin designed the memorial in 1982 to communicate a message about war. Visitors read the names engraved in the wall. Some people touch the names. They see their own reflections in its surface. What message might the wall give them? Visitors may think that ordinary people like themselves are not only affected by wars, but are also responsible for them. Do you agree?

Artworks play meaningful roles in communities because they communicate important ideas. The message of the *Vietnam Veterans Memorial* has been sent throughout this nation and around the world. Messages from artworks are also sent within smaller areas. Artworks can tell about the interests and concerns that community members share. They can tell about what is important to the community.

What's Ahead

- **Core Lesson** Learn more about how people use art to send important messages.
- **1.1 Art History Lesson** Discover how early Native North American people used art for communication.
- **1.2 Forms and Media Lesson** Focus on ways that craft traditions began and continue within communities, with special attention to jewelry.
- **1.3 Global View Lesson** Explore how early cultures in Mesoamerica and South America used art to tell about what was important to them.
- **1.4 Studio Lesson** Investigate ways to tell about your community through handmade paper.

Words to Know

communication	craft
collage	pre-Columbian
geometric	codex
organic	slurry
pueblo	pulp

Community Messages

Understanding Meaning

Communication is the exchange of information, thoughts, feelings, ideas, opinions, and much more. It can be spoken, written, or take an artistic, visual form. To communicate, you need a sender (someone who expresses ideas or feelings) and a receiver (someone who understands the message). As you have grown up, you have learned how to speak and write the language of your community. You have also learned how to understand visual messages. Messages are usually understood when the sender and receiver use the same spoken, written, or visual language.

Many of the artworks we see were made in communities that flourished hundreds and even thousands of years ago. Some of these artworks were made in faraway places. Because of this, we may never know the full meaning of the artworks. However, we might understand an artwork better by looking at its details and learning about the community in which it was made. Sometimes it helps to see other artworks from the same place or made by the same artist. For example, an object or symbol that is repeated in the artworks might mean something special to the community. We interpret the meaning of an artwork by finding such clues. They help us connect what we see to what we have learned from other sources.

Fig. 1–2 **The main design of this quilt is a pattern of squares, triangles, and rectangles. If you look closely, however, you will also see several stitched designs of stars, flowers, and leaves. Which of the quilt's designs represent the Amish ideas of simplicity? Of quality?** Anonymous Amish quiltmaker, member of the Zook family, American, *Ninepatch*, Lancaster County, Pennsylvania, ca. 1930. Pieced wools, 80" x 80" (203.2 x 203.2 cm). Private Collection, Photo courtesy The Quilt Complex, Oakland, CA.

Fig. 1–3 **Artists from Native-American cultures often use natural materials to create objects. They also decorate their objects with symbols that represent elements of nature. What might this suggest about the beliefs of Native-American cultures?** Canada, *Thompson Indian River Shield,* no date. Deer skin stretched on a wooden hoop. Peabody Museum, Harvard University, Photograph by Hillel Burger.

Communicating Beliefs and Values

Artworks often tell about a community's beliefs and values. The quilt in Fig. 1–2 was made by members of the Amish community in North America. The Amish are a religious group whose members often live close by each other. They believe in living simple, quiet lives. This is reflected in their quilt-making traditions. Amish quilts are beautifully crafted. They communicate the ideas of simplicity and quality through the use of solid colors and geometric shapes.

It is sometimes easy to see the connection between the artwork and the beliefs of a community. In artworks such as the Native-American shield (Fig. 1–3), the meaning of the materials and images is not as clear. We might guess what the symbols mean, but we need to know more about the community to understand the artwork's message.

Teaching and Telling

Communities rely on artworks to show how their members work and play during their daily lives. People use art to tell stories about heroes, historical events, and special places. These stories are often told and retold in the community. Artworks can teach people different ways to think about the world around them. People depend on artists to observe life and, through their artworks, show others what they see.

People also use artworks for inspiration. An artwork might inspire them to reach for goals, to be quiet and reflective, or to do good deeds. Or an artwork might prompt

Fig. 1–4 The name of this artwork is *Southwest Pietà*. "Pietà" can mean mercy or pity. The word often brings to mind Michelangelo's sculpture of the Virgin Mary cradling the body of Christ. How is the subject of this sculpture different from Michelangelo's? What legend might this sculpture represent? Luis Jiménez, *Southwest Pietà*, Albuquerque, New Mexico, 1983. Fiberglass. Photograph by Bruce Berman. © 2000 Luis Jimenez/Artist Rights Society (ARS), New York.

people to rally around a cause. Artworks such as the *Vietnam Veterans Memorial* (Fig. 1–1, page 68) teach community values, such as peace. Some teach or tell about the religious beliefs of a community. Ancient cultures, such as the Aztec, used picture writing on painted animal hides to communicate important messages (Fig. 1–5). Other artworks, such as Luis Jiménez's *Southwest Pietà* (Fig. 1–4), show figures from a community's legends.

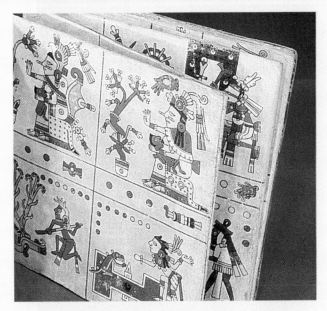

Fig. 1–5 **We can learn a great deal about the Aztec culture from its visual language and its books, called** *codices.* **In what way is Aztec picture writing like the pictures you see in comics?** Mexico, Mixtec style, *Codex Fejervary-Mayer* (shown partially unfolded). Beaten deer skin and limewash. Liverpool Museum, Liverpool, Great Britain. Werner Forman/Art Resource, NY.

A Telling Collage

In this studio experience, you will use collage techniques to tell about the communities you know best. Think about the communities to which you belong. They might be geographical communities, or clubs and groups. Ask yourself: Which of these communities influence the decisions I make? Which ones affect my behavior, my clothing, or the way I spend my time? Rank the communities in terms of their importance. This will help you plan your collage.

Fig. 1–6 **This collage shows the artist's love of running, and her connection to others who run.** Kristina Sacovitch, *Cross-Country Runners,* 2000. Collage, 10" x 15" (25.5 x 38 cm). Notre Dame Academy, Worcester, Massachusetts.

Fig. 1–7 **Romare Bearden's artworks show his interest in his own African-American culture. What thoughts and feelings might he be expressing in this collage? Why do you think so?** Romare Bearden, *Pittsburgh Memories,* 1984. Collage on board, 28 ⅝" x 23 ¼" (72.7 x 59.7 cm). The Carnegie Museum of Art, Pittsburgh (Gift of Mr. and Mrs. Ronald R. Davenport and Mr. and Mrs. Milton A. Washington) © Romare Bearden Foundation/Licensed by VAGA, New York, NY.

Studio Background

Collage Techniques

Collage is a French word for pasted paper. In a collage, flat materials such as paper, fabric, newsclippings, or photographs are pasted on a background. Collage artists may also use pieces of natural materials (twigs, seashells) and other odds and ends. They might add details, shapes, and colors with markers, crayons, or charcoal. Artists use collage to express thoughts, feelings, and ideas about a subject.

Romare Bearden created many collages about life in big cities. In *Pittsburgh Memories* (Fig. 1–7), he remembers his grandmother's boardinghouse in Pittsburgh, Pennsylvania. With shapes, colors, and details, he shows a picture of the community there. For *Cloak of Heritage* (Fig. 1–8), artist Kevin Warren Smith chose photographs of American Indians to help express ideas about his heritage.

You Will Need

- magazines
- drawing paper
- pencils
- glue
- markers
- paint (optional)

Try This

1. Look for and cut out magazine images that symbolize your membership in multiple communities. You may wish to include your own drawings or cut-paper designs. Do not use letters or words.

2. Arrange the images on a background using the principles of design: balance, rhythm, proportion, emphasis, pattern, unity, and variety. Try different arrangements before pasting the images. Choose an arrangement that expresses a message about your community memberships and their rank.

3. Glue the images to the background. Use markers, colored paper, or paint to add meaning to your collage.

Check Your Work

Display your completed collage with those of your classmates. Take turns describing what you see in each other's artworks. Can you name the communities to which each student belongs? Discuss how each artist has arranged pictures to express a message.

Sketchbook Connection

In your sketchbook, write about your experience of creating a collage. Describe the process you used to select images. Tell how you organized the images. What did you think about as you organized your collage? When you create another collage, what might you do differently?

Core Lesson 1

Check Your Understanding

1. What can artworks tell about a community?
2. How can we learn about artworks created long ago or far away?
3. How do people in a community use artworks?
4. What materials do artists use to create collages?

Fig. 1–8 **The subject matter of Kevin Warren Smith's work often focuses on Native-American themes. Why might the woman who wears the cloak be important?** Kevin Warren Smith, *Cloak of Heritage,* 1991. Acrylic and collage on canvas, 24" x 36" (61 x 91.4 cm). © 1991 Kevin Warren Smith.

Art in Early North America

ca. 1000–1200 AD
Anasazi pitcher

ca. 1100 AD
Classic Pueblo
Period pottery

ca. 1100–1400 AD
Hohokam red-on-
buff bowl

Prehistory

Ancient North America

Colonial North
America
page 102

ca. 400–500 AD
Anasazi woven
objects

ca. 1100 AD
Cliff Palace

1200s
Lizard Bowl
Mimbres People

History in a Nutshell

North America includes Canada, the United States, and Mexico. During the Ice Age, between 30,000 and 10,000 years ago, small groups of people began populating the North and South American continents. Most historians believe these people came from Asia across the frozen Bering Strait. They migrated slowly eastward into what are now Canada and the northern United States. Eventually, people moved further south. The ancient southwestern part of the United States became the home of three Native-American cultures—the Hohokam, the Mogollon, and the Anasazi—each with its own special way of life.

Fig. 1–9 **This painted bowl shows a lizard. How is the decoration on this vessel different from the others shown in this lesson?** Mimbres People, *Lizard Bowl,* 13th century.
Polychrome. Peabody Museum, Harvard University, Photograph by Hillel Burger.

Community Messages

Archaeologists and art historians can often tell where an ancient pottery jar or bowl or woven basket came from by studying its form and decoration. Each ancient Native-American community used colors, lines, shapes, and patterns in unique ways. The designs and patterns meant something special to the people who lived at the time. They were often symbols of nature.

The Hohokam lived in what is now Arizona. They created red-on-buff painted designs that showed symbols of animals, masked dancers, and gods (Fig. 1–10). The Mimbres were a Mogollan people who lived in the high mountains of what is now New Mexico. They created elegant black-on-white designs on pottery bowls. These designs were both **geometric** (using shapes

such as squares and triangles) and **organic** (using shapes from nature) (Fig. 1–9). Anasazi potters lived in large apartment-like complexes in the Four Corners region of Utah, Colorado, Arizona, and New Mexico. The Anasazi also used black-on-white patterns, but they were very different from the patterns of the Mimbres (Fig. 1–11).

Fig. 1–11 **The Anasazi painted their pottery with a dye made by boiling shoots of woodland aster. The pattern surrounds the pot. What repeated elements can you see in this pattern?** Native American, Tularosa, *Black-on-White Pitcher*, ca. 1000–1200 AD.
Ceramic, h. 7 1/8" (18 cm) x d. 6 7/8" (17.5 cm) x circum. 23" (58.4 cm). Courtesy the Maxwell Museum of Anthropology, University of New Mexico, Albuquerque, NM.

An Early Community

The Anasazi, or the "ancient ones," were some of the first people in the southwestern United States to live in caves and rocky cliffs. After living in pit houses, they established communities along the canyon walls of a huge plateau in southwestern Colorado. Some of their buildings are still standing after almost 1000 years (Fig. 1–12). The structures, called **pueblos**, are much like a modern apartment building with sections two, three, and four stories high. One dwelling contains more than 200 rooms and probably housed 400 people.

The Anasazi were skillful weavers and sophisticated potters (Figs. 1–13 and 1–14). They also made beautiful turquoise jewelry. Anasazi art forms are highly decorated. Most of the decorations are based on symbols and patterns used on baskets. Some are similar to pictographs that people painted on cliff walls long ago. To the Anasazi, these symbols told about identity, status, or group membership. Early artworks were used to tell stories, to teach young children about adult roles, and to communicate with the spirit world.

Fig 1–12 The Anasazi pueblo had rounded ceremonial rooms, called *kivas,* which were decorated with murals. What do you think this structure might have looked like when it was first built? How easily could this structure have been seen from a distance? Do you think the design of the structure made it easy for people to communicate with one another? Colorado, Mesa Verde National Park, *Cliff Palace,* ca. 1100 AD. © David Muench Photography.

Fig 1–13 **This collection of Anasazi pottery was made during the classic Pueblo Period (ca. 1100–1400). What does the variety of pottery forms tell you about the cooking and eating habits of the Anasazi?** American, New Mexico, Anasazi, Pueblo Period (1100–1400 AD), *Mug, pitcher, large bowl, effigy vessel, large dipper, pottery jar.*
Courtesy Department of Library Services, American Museum of Natural History.

Fig 1–14 **Early archaeologists called the early period of Anasazi culture the "Basket Maker" phase. In addition to baskets, these artists wove sacks, sandals, and other useful objects. Do you see any similarities between these woven designs and the painted decorations on the pottery vessels?** American, New Mexico, Anasazi, *Bruden band, silver basket, sack, cliff dwellers sandal, and sandal made of unsplit yucca blades,* ca. 400–500 AD.
Courtesy Department of Library Services, American Museum of Natural History.

Studio Connection

Design a fiber artwork that shows group membership (such as a class banner or school flag), or a small art-work that reveals your own membership in a community (such as a patch or badge). You might use *appliqué* (fabrics stitched to a back-ground), or combine stitchery and appliqué techniques with beads, buttons, old jewelry, faucet washers, or other found materials. Plan your design by sketching the main shapes first and then adding details.

1.1 Art History

Check Your Understanding

1. Who were among the early settlers in the southwestern United States? How did they build their communities?
2. How were early messages communicated through art?
3. How did the Anasazi use art in their community?
4. What do the artworks on this page tell you about the materials that were available to the Anasazi?

Crafts

Since the earliest times, people have needed shelters, various types of supports, and containers to help them survive. Early people used caves and cliff overhangs for shelters, tree branches or large rocks for supports, and gourds or birds' nests for containers. Eventually, they learned to use natural materials, such as grass, wood, and clay, to make containers, furniture, and other useful objects.

When people make useful objects out of natural materials, they are working in the **craft** traditions. Craft traditions vary from community to community depending on the needs of the people and the materials available. One generation often teaches a craft to another and passes along ideas about how handmade objects should look and work. The Cuna Indians of the San Blas Islands are known for their colorful blouses, or *molas*. Molas show scenes from nature, daily life, and traditional legends of the Cuna community (Fig. 1–15).

Experimenting for Beauty

People in almost every community decorate useful objects, such as clothing and pottery, so that they are pleasing to see and touch. These artists make careful decisions about form, color, texture, and pattern. Sometimes they decorate objects with designs and symbols that mean something to their community. Such designs might reflect religious beliefs or tell about other important community ideas. Artists also explore different ways to use craft materials to create new, or nontraditional, forms.

Fig. 1–15 **The Cuna Indians live on the San Blas Islands off the coast of Panama. Cuna women are famous for their molas. Molas are blouses with brightly colored panels on the front and back. Each panel is made of many rectangular pieces of fabric of different colors and textures sewn together.**
Octopus Mola (back view), 1997. Cotton reverse applique. Carti Suitupo Chapter Cooperative, Carti Suitupo Islands, San Blas Islands. Courtesy of Raul E. Cisneros.

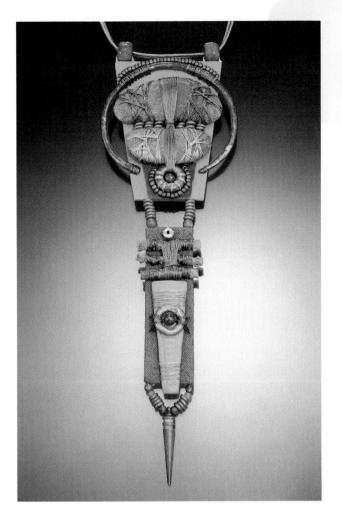

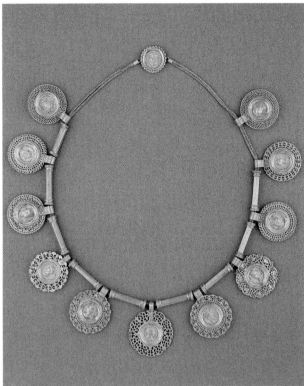

Studio Connection

Jewelry-making is one of the many craft forms that people use to express ideas. In places where people live close to nature, shells, beads, feathers, and other natural objects are valued for jewelry-making (Fig. 1–16). Jewelry is often made from precious gems, silver, gold, and other costly materials. Try to make your own jewelry with inexpensive materials, such as clay, paper, wood, wire, or leather. You can combine the materials or use only one. You might even recycle parts of old jewelry, toys, or other objects. What can your piece of jewelry say about you? What materials will best express your ideas?

1.2 Forms and Media

Check Your Understanding

1. How do people in communities learn to make useful objects? What materials do they use?

2. Why do people decorate useful objects?

The Art of Mesoamerica and South America

Mesoamerica & South America

Global Glance

Mesoamerica extends from present-day Mexico south to Honduras. Further south lies the vast continent of South America. Over 3000 years ago, the people in these areas developed communities. Some of the world's great civilizations developed here. Between 1492 and 1521, much of Mesoamerica and South America was conquered by Spain. Art historians use the term **pre-Columbian** (meaning before Columbus) to describe the art of this region that was made before the Spanish conquered it.

Fig. 1–18 The surfaces of this Mayan platform pyramid are carved with decorations representing Quetzalcoatl, the sun god. What do the decorations suggest about the purpose of the pyramid? Pre-Columbian Mexico, *Chichen Itza Castle,* from Northeast, ca. 12th–13th century. Courtesy Davis Art Slides.

Planned Communities

Beginning around 1500 BC, the people in the Mesoamerican region built a civilization based on agriculture. Throughout history, several different cultures or groups formed within this area. The Mesoamericans were skilled in city planning and architecture. They designed cities with markets, plazas, and temples. They also developed skills in sculpture, painting, pottery, and jewelry-making.

Each of these groups built planned communities that met the specific needs of their belief systems and daily lives. People of the Olmec culture created ceremonial centers with large sculptures of warriors, priests, and athletes. The Mayans built cities, such as Chichen Itza, with pyramids, palaces, courts, and many dwellings. Paintings and relief sculptures on buildings tell stories of animals, people, plants, and gods. The Aztecs, the last group to control the region before it was conquered by Spain, borrowed many ideas from Mayan art. One of their largest cities, Tenochtitlán, was destroyed in 1521. Present-day Mexico City was later built on this site.

In South America, the Andean cultures of Peru also developed large public architecture and sculpture. Their planned communities filled the needs of their military rule, and provided space for their religious and agricultural ceremonies.

Fig. 1–19 **The Inca city of Machu Picchu was built as a royal estate and religious center. The techniques used to create its buildings were as sophisticated as the techniques used by the ancient Egyptians. The carefully cut stones fit together so well that mortar was not necessary.** Pre-Columbian Peru, *Machu Picchu* (General View), 15th century. Photograph by David DeVore.

Communicating with Symbols

Imagine a time when there was no such thing as paper. How would you communicate your ideas and thoughts? How would you keep track of those things you now record on calendars? For the Aztec farming communities of Mesoamerica, calendars were important for determining planting and harvesting cycles. They developed complex stone calendars with unique forms of picture writing (Fig. 1–20). The Aztec people had a written language of symbols and pictures, but no easy means of using this language. So, they learned to make paper.

The Aztecs made paper from the bark of trees. Scribes wrote on strips of this paper that were folded to form a **codex**. Unlike the kind of book we're familiar with, a codex does not have a spine. The bark-paper pages are hinged at both sides, like an accordion. Trained scribes used signs and pictures in these books to keep religious, historical, and government records. Much of what we know about the Aztecs comes from what remains of these early codices (Fig. 1–21).

Fig. 1–20 **This calendar is thirteen feet in diameter and weighs twenty-four tons. Notice the complex picture writing on its surface. If you found an object like this, would you guess that it's a calendar? Why or why not?** Mexico, Aztec, *Calendar Stone*, 1325–1521 AD.
Weighs 24 tons and is 13' (33 cm) in diameter. National Museum of Archaeology, Mexico City. Photo Researchers, Inc. © George Holton.

Studio Connection

Mesoamerican groups built structures that helped show what they thought was important. How can you use repeated forms to make a sculpture that communicates some of your ideas, dreams, or feelings? Gather objects or create forms that can be joined together. Your found objects might be craft sticks, small cups, or pine cones and acorns. Create forms such as cubes, pyramids, cones, or cylinders from construction paper. How can the objects and forms help you express your idea? Try to arrange the forms to create a visual path that leads your eyes from one form to the next.

1.3 Global View

Check Your Understanding

1. What features did Mesoamericans include in the design of their communities?
2. What group is considered to be the oldest culture in Mesoamerica?
3. How did Aztec communities record important information?
4. Imagine your own world without paper. What would you use as a surface to write on?

Fig. 1–21 On this page from an Aztec codex, you see the death god back-to-back with the lord of life. The symbols around them represent the twenty thirteen-day weeks that make up the Aztec calendar. Can you find any of these symbols on the calendar shown in Fig. 1–20? Mexico, Aztec, *Codex Borgia,* ca. 1400 AD.
Pigments on deer skin, 10 5/8" x 3 15/16" (27 x 10 cm). Courtesy Davis Art Slides.

Fig. 1–22 Tonatiuh was the Aztec sun god. What features of this figure suggest symbols of the sun? Mexico, Aztec, *Tonatiuh* (Aztec Sun God), 15th–beginning of 16th century.
Painted volcanic stone, height: 11 13/16" (30 cm). Museum der Kulturen, Basel.

Crafts in the Studio
Making Paper

A Handmade Message

Studio Introduction
Have you ever thought about what you could do with all the scraps of paper that people throw away every day? When paper was invented, it was a precious item because it was made by hand in small quantities. Today, many people take paper for granted.

In this studio lesson, you will make your own paper from recycled paper scraps. The paper you make will communicate something about your community. Pages 88 and 89 will tell you how to do it. Paper is made with a **slurry** (watery mixture) of the soft, moist, formless **pulp** that comes from wood and plant fibers. After the slurry is strained through a wire screen, the pulp that remains is carefully spread and shaped on blotters. Areas of the pulp can be stained with ink or paint. Natural materials such as leaves and flowers can be mixed or pressed into the damp pulp. Torn pieces of candy bar wrappers, newspaper, or images from comic strips can also be dipped in water and pressed into the molded pulp. When the pulp is completely dry, it is a sheet of paper.

Think about the paper you create as a kind of collage of found materials. How can the materials you choose to put in your paper help tell about your community?

Studio Background

Inventing Paper
When paper was invented, communication among people was greatly improved. People could keep records of their history. With paper, people could send messages to each other more easily and carry information with them. Eventually, paper allowed people's language to travel far beyond their communities.

Fig. 1–23 **You have to look very carefully at this sculpture to see that it's made of paper. How has the artist used paper to create the look of stones and twigs?** Jeanne Petrosky, *Untitled*, 1999. Handmade paper, 36" x 20" x 10" (91.4 x 50.8 x 25.4 cm). Courtesy the artist.

Fig. 1–24 **Five students worked together on this large, horizontal strip of hand-made paper. One of them commented, "As I was helping make it, I was thinking how weird it was to turn this 'glop' into a pretty collage. Gathering the 'glop' onto screens and molds was easy, but transferring it to the base sheet was very hard to do. I like how we did the tree and the grass with the border."** Bailey Isgro, Jessica Lynema, Lisa Poszywak, Leslie Savage, and Betty Shreve, *In Touch with Nature*, 2000. Recycled paper made into a collage, 12" x 40" (30.5 x 101.5 cm). Bryant Middle School, Dearborn, Michigan.

The Egyptians made a writing surface by joining together thin strips of papyrus. The process of making paper from chopped up plant fibers was invented in China about 2000 years ago. This same process is used around the world today.

Mesoamericans developed their own kind of paper by soaking and pounding the inner bark of certain trees. Similar traditions of making paper, sometimes called bark cloth, can be found in parts of Africa and Oceania.

Today, artists create and use handmade papers in artworks such as original books and greeting cards, molded relief sculptures, and prints. Think about things made from paper that you see every day. How many different kinds of "messages" can paper send?

Making Your Paper

You Will Need

- scrap paper
- a blender
- water
- fine strainer and dishpan
- old nylon stocking
- cardboard
- felt or blanket scraps
- paint, ink, or dyes
- natural and printed materials
- paper towels
- an iron

Try This

1. To make pulp, soak bits of scrap paper in water overnight.

 **2.** Mix two cups of pulp in a blender half-filled with water. Run the blender for about thirty seconds. After blending the pulp, carefully mix in leaves, petals, and other natural materials by hand, if you wish.

 3. Line a fine strainer with a nylon stocking and hold it over a dishpan. Pour the pulp into the strainer.

 4. Choose a shape for your new sheet of paper. Cut a cardboard stencil in this shape. Place the stencil on top of several layers of felt or blanket scraps.

 5. Press the pulp flat inside the stencil. Add color with ink, paint, or dyes. Press newspaper clippings or other materials that tell about your community into the paper form.

6. Cover the form with paper towels and allow it to dry. Remove towels, stencil, and blanket carefully.

7. Place the newly formed sheet of paper between paper towels and press with a warm iron.

Check Your Work

Discuss your work with your classmates. What materials did you add to your hand-made paper? What message does your paper communicate about your community? While you were creating your paper, did you think about it as a collage?

Computer Option
Make a collage of images about your community by using paint or image-editing software. Create "texture" and "patterns" that simulate various paper surfaces, and then apply selected texture filters to the images.

Sketchbook Connection
Observe your community's environment and note colors, fibers, and shapes that you could use in your handmade paper. Attach samples of natural materials to your sketchbook pages. Experiment with colors and designs that say something about your community. After your handmade paper is dry, slip a small sheet inside your sketchbook or use it to make a new sketchbook cover.

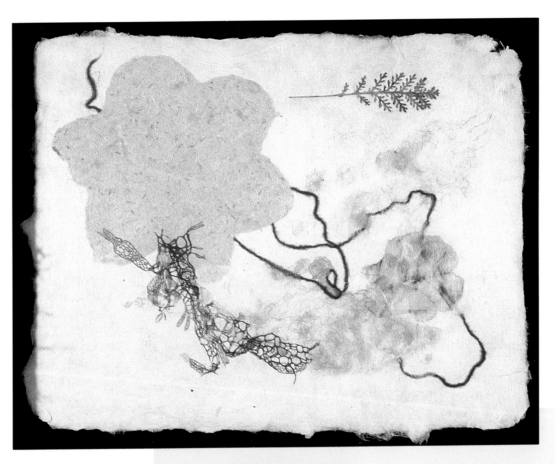

Fig. 1–25 **This artist used natural materials to add texture and interesting shapes to her paper work.** Kelsey Shuhart, *Spring.*
Handmade paper, 7" x 4 1/2 " (17 x 11 cm).
Kutztown University Lab School, Kutztown, Pennsylvania.

Fig. 1–26 **Architectural shapes were cut from old photographs and added to handmade paper in this abstract artwork.** Sam Billingslea, *My Neighborhood's Different!*
Handmade paper, 4" x 7 " (10 x 20 cm).
Kutztown University Lab School, Kutztown, Pennsylvania.

Connect to...

Careers

Imagine making a scene from the past or future "come alive." The world of theater presents many opportunities for a visual artist who is interested in drama. One of the careers in theater arts is that of scenic designer. The **scenic designer** is responsible for the appearance of the stage, and ultimately creates a convincing reality.

To achieve what are often extremely elaborate stage sets, much planning is required. Lighting and the use of space are important considerations. The scenic designer reads the script, and makes sketches and models to present to the production's director. When final designs are decided upon, the designer provides working plans for the set-construction crews. Set design includes not only the backdrop and walls, but all furniture and other objects within the space. How might a scenic designer become aware of the ways actors would move throughout the stage area? How important would it be to have this information before making final design decisions?

Daily Life

What are your favorite **television programs**? Do you prefer factual shows or fictional ones? Humor or drama? Through both programs and commercials, television presents a **view of contemporary life** that may or may not be true. Much of what we see on TV is directed at a teenage or young-adult audience. How accurately do such shows tell stories that reflect your life and the life of your community? Do you think television can create unrealistic expectations of you and your peers? How might that be a danger?

Fig. 1–27 **Many cultures use music and dance as a way to tell stories. The Balinese dance called** *Barong* **tells the story of good versus evil. The witch** *Rangda* **represents evil, while the half-lion, half-dog creature called** *Barong* **represents good.** Bali, Indonesia, Barong Play: *Rangda, the Witch, Appears.*
Courtesy Davis Art Slides.

Other Arts

Theater

You know that visual art communicates important messages about communities. The same is true of theater and the theatrical **tradition of storytelling**. Within the Cherokee culture of the Southeast, stories are used to educate children in the values of the Cherokee culture and to review those values for adults. Stories are told at family gatherings, community events, and during everyday conversation.

Other Subjects

Social Studies

Outdoor sculpture and monuments may take the form of statues made of stone or metals, relief sculptures, painted murals, or commemorative plaques. Americans build monuments to tell and honor our nation's history. Are the monuments in your community well preserved, or are they in need of repair? What stories do they tell? How could you find out? What could your school do to "adopt" a monument?

Fig. 1–28 **This sculpture was made from melted down cannons from the War of 1812. Jackson was a hero of this war. What does this sculpture say about Andrew Jackson?** Clark Mills, *Andrew Jackson Equestrian Statue,* 1853. Courtesy Davis Art Slides.

Language Arts

Have you ever attended a family reunion or holiday gathering of several generations of your family? Do the older members of your family like to tell stories about their life? To maintain these **oral traditions of storytelling**, ask an older relative for permission to record his or her memories on audio- or videotape. Record and then write down their stories, and share them with the rest of your family.

Fig. 1–29 **This Amish quiltmaker chose the primary colors and geometric shapes to create a powerful work of art. What type of symmetry do you see in this quilt?** Rebecca Fisher Stoltzfus, *Diamond in the Square Quilt,* 1903. Wool with rayon binding added later, 77" x 77" (195.6 x 195.6 cm). Collection of the Museum of American Folk Art, New York; Gift of Mr. and Mrs. William B. Wigton. 1984.25.1

Mathematics

Have you seen **patchwork quilts** that are based on geometric shapes? Amish quilts, for example, contain only the most basic geometric shapes—squares, triangles, and rectangles. Amish quilters are restricted, by their religious beliefs, to the use of only simple shapes and solid colors. The use of printed fabrics or too many pieces of patchwork is considered "too worldly." Despite the restrictions, Amish quilts are powerful in their simplicity. The quilts' design characteristics—distinctive patterns, the width of borders and bindings, the size of blocks—"tell" their origins to fellow Amish by revealing the community from which they came. How intricate a geometric design could you make by using only squares, rectangles, and triangles?

Internet Connection
For more activities related to this chapter, go to the Davis website at **www.davis-art.com.**

Portfolio

"We were given the assignment to create an identity pennant. I sketched many different ideas about which of my interests would truly identify me. I finally settled on an outline of Martha's Vineyard island and goggles: the island because it's probably my favorite place on earth, and goggles since swimming is my favorite sport." **Katherine McCord**

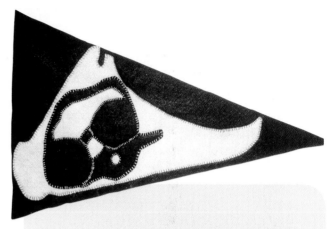

Fig. 1–30 Katherine McCord, *Representing Me,* 1998.
Felt, 8" x 14" (20 x 35.5 cm). Winsor School, Boston, Massachusetts.

Fig. 1–31 **Each student in a California art class colored and cut out a cube from a template, taking inspiration from the brilliant colors in artwork by Victor Vasarely. The colors, lines, and textures interact in different ways depending on how the cubes are arranged.** Students from Los Cerros Middle School, *Collaborative Sculpture,* 1999.
Markers, 3 3/4" (9.5 cm) cubes. Danville, California.

Fig. 1–32 **When asked to create wearable art that represented something she liked about Alaska, this student chose the sun, stars, and moon that are out on clear nights during the winter. For most of the school year Alaskan students go to school in the dark, and it's dark soon after they come home. Thus, the night sky is a favorite topic.** Kelsey Johnson, *Moon and Stars,* 2000.
Egyptian paste, 2" x 2" (5 x 5 cm). Colony Middle School, Palmer, Alaska.

CD-ROM Connection
To see more student art, check out the Community Connection Student Gallery.

Chapter 1 Review

Recall

Identify two of the many ways that artworks can be used for communication in a community.

Understand

Describe what viewers can do when they wish to "receive" an artworks message.

Apply

Imagine that you and a friend are exploring an old barn, hoping to learn about the people who owned it. Suppose you find a trunk filled with quilts. Your friend dismisses these as "just a bunch of blankets" and moves on in search of other evidence. Would you agree with your friend? Why?

Analyze

Compare the codex in the Core Lesson (Fig. 1–5) to the sculpture fragment (Fig. 1–22) in Lesson 1.3. In what ways are these similar? How are they different?

Synthesize

Create a worksheet that someone could use to identify membership in various communities. Your worksheet might include questions, sentences with blank spaces, diagrams and/or charts to complete.

Evaluate

Of the two pieces of jewelry shown in Lesson 1.2 (Figs. 1–16 and 1–17, *shown below*), which do you believe communicates the clearest message? Why?

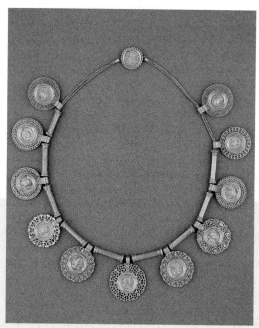

Page 81

For Your Portfolio

You can keep your artworks, essays, and other work you have accomplished in a portfolio. Your portfolio can help you reflect on how you have developed as a maker and viewer of art. For an artwork you made in this chapter, create an artist's statement form. Include a place for your name and date, the media and techniques used, how your artwork sends a message, how satisfied you are with this completed artwork and why. Remember to include similar forms when you insert artworks into your portfolio in the future.

For Your Sketchbook

Your sketchbook is a good place to explore the themes studied in each chapter of your book. This chapter explored the theme of art and communication. Fill some sketchbook pages with different visual ways you can tell about the communities of which you are a member. You might, for example, develop a symbol for each geographical and shared interest community.

Living

Fig. 2–1 **This scene of children going to school is three stories high. It is displayed on the outside wall of a building in the middle of the South Bronx. Each figure is a plaster cast of a community member. Would you like to see art like this in your town or city?** John Ahearn, *Back to School*, 1985.
Permanent outdoor mural at Walton Avenue and 172nd Street, Bronx, NY. Courtesy Alexander and Bonin, New York.

- How do the members of a community work and play?

- How is daily life reflected in art?

When you go to your local grocery store, do you often see the same people working there? Do you recognize your local mail carrier or librarian? You probably know many members of your local community. You may not know their names, but you recognize their faces. Perhaps you also know about the daily work they do.

The life and energy of any community come from the many different people who live, work, and play there. These people have talents and interests to share with each other. They also have certain roles. Some of them protect us, help build our homes, or care for us when we are ill.

Some people work within the community as artists. The artists John Ahearn and Rigoberto Torres worked together in the South Bronx in New York. They made plaster casts of residents at work and play. Many of the sculptures are displayed on the outside walls of local buildings (Fig. 2–1). Through their artworks, Ahearn and Torres called attention to the important roles people have in the South Bronx. Their artworks remind viewers that each person in the neighborhood is important. They send a message that says, "A celebration of daily life in any community is a celebration of the people who live there."

What's Ahead

- **Core Lesson** Learn about the roles artists play in the daily life of communities.
- **2.1 Art History Lesson**
  Discover how people living in North American colonies between 1500 and 1776 included art in their daily lives.
- **2.2 Forms and Media Lesson**
  Explore ways that artists use drawing skills to record daily life.
- **2.3 Global View Lesson**
  Examine the role that art plays in the daily life of communities in India.
- **2.4 Studio Lesson**
  Create a group portrait of people you see at school every day.

Words to Know

portrait	contour drawing
designer	gesture drawing
bisqueware	whole-to-part
dry media	drawing
wet media	miniature
mixed media	proportions

Daily Observations

Artists Show Us at Work and Play

We look to artists to observe and record our daily life in the community. Artists often show who we are, what we do, and what we care about. In the sculpture *The Steelmakers* (Fig. 2–2), artist George Segal shows people who have been important in the daily life of Youngstown, Ohio. The steelworkers' union chose two of its members to be models for this sculpture. They represent all the steel-workers who have worked in Youngstown.

Artists observe people at work and play, and then create images of them. They might show close-up views of how children or adults spend their leisure time. Some artists observe and record an entire community at play. Artist Jacques Callot created the print *Great Fair at Imprunita* (Fig. 2–3) in 1620. The print shows people gathered together for a community event. In artworks such as these, artists can show us how people lived at other times. These works can also show us how similar our daily life is to life in the past. How is the fair you see in this artwork similar to state or county fairs that you know about?

Fig. 2–2 **This artist often creates sculptures dedicated to the idea of people and their daily work. If you were to celebrate workers in your community, who would they be?** George Segal, *The Steelmakers,* Youngstown, Ohio, 1980.
Open hearth furnace contributed from Jones and Laughlin Steel Co., and bronze castings. Courtesy The Youngstown Area Arts Council. © George Segal/Licensed by VAGA, New York, NY.

Artists Create Portraits

A **portrait** is an artwork that shows a specific person or group of people. *Portraiture,* the art of creating portraits, is another way that artists observe and record daily life. People cherish painted, sculpted, and photographed portraits of their leaders, family members, and other loved ones from the past and present. Portraits provide us with a glimpse into the daily lives of their subjects.

Portrait artists might show one person or a group of people in the community. Charles Willson Peale is known for his portraits of Andrew Jackson, John Quincy Adams, and other early American leaders. He painted this group portrait of his own famous family of artists (Fig. 2–4). Here he shows himself giving his brother a drawing lesson.

Living

Enriching Community Spaces

Have you ever wondered how the street-lights, signs, benches, and landscaping that you pass by every day were created? Do you know who designed these things? Artists design and create places and objects that we see in our neighborhood every day. Some of these objects, such as the streetlights in Victoria, Canada (Fig. 2–5), are beautiful as well as functional. In the past, the people who made objects for daily use were well known in the community. This is still true today in some parts of the world.

Fig. 2–5 **These streetlights are in front of the parliament buildings in Victoria, Canada. What does their beauty suggest about the local community?** *Street lamp from Victoria,* Vancouver Island.
© 1999 Reimut Lieder/Image Makers.

Fig. 2–6 **How is the design of this garden different from the design of a public garden you know? How does the design of your community's garden reflect the garden's function?** India, *Brindavan Gardens at Mysore,* Karnataka.
© M. Amirtham/Dinodia Picture Agency.

Fig. 2–7 Notice how this mural helps the underpass blend in with the local architecture. Why might the community have wanted this wall to be painted? David S. Gordon, *Unbridled* (Ocean Park Boulevard at the 4th Street Underpass, Santa Monica, CA), 1984–86. Keim paint (silica based) on concrete, 25' x 600' (7.62 x 182.9 m). Courtesy the artist.

Designers help plan and lay out buildings and outdoor spaces used in the community's social, religious, civic, and economic life. For example, public gardens, such as the Brindavan Gardens in India (Fig. 2–6), offer places for people to relax and enjoy the quiet beauty of nature. Plazas and malls that lead visitors to the entrances of important public places are often designed like this garden. As you look around your town or city, note the homes, gardens, parks, meeting halls, churches, courthouses, libraries, and shopping districts. How were they designed to be both functional and beautiful?

Group Artworks for the Community

Sometimes, groups of artists work together to create community places and objects. They divide tasks among themselves and work side-by-side to finish the project. All around the world, people work together to create large-scale sculptures, murals, monuments, parks, and other public projects.

Many artists learn their skills from family members. Others learn from local experts who share their skills. This teaching might take place in schools or within social groups. Sometimes artists get together with local people who have similar interests, such as stone carving or landscape design. In groups such as these, members share their ideas and skills with each other.

Create Your Own Pottery

Think of how often you use boxes, bags, and plastic storage bins at home and at school. What do you think people living in earlier times used for containers? Many made clay pots in hundreds of different shapes and sizes. They added decorative features to make the pots both functional and beautiful. The forms and features of the pots varied depending on where the people lived, what they needed, and how they passed along their culture's traditions.

In this studio experience, you will create a clay container that can be used in daily life. Like generations of pottery makers, you will explore the coil method to make a decorated and functional object. What uses will your container have? How will you decorate it? What local pottery traditions might you follow?

You Will Need

- clay
- rolling pin
- two flat sticks
- water
- slip
- paintbrush
- clay tools, such as a fork, spoon, wooden dowel
- sheet of plastic or large plastic bag

Try This

1. Cut a 3/4"-thick slab of clay into a shape for the base of your pot. Roll out coils of clay about 3/4" (2 cm) thick. These will be used to build up the sides of the container.

2. Scratch the edge of the clay slab with a fork. Apply slip (a thick liquid made of clay mixed with water) on top of the roughened clay. Press the first coil to the base. Blend the coil to the base. Continue building, coil upon coil. Scratch the clay and use slip before you blend the coils together.

Studio Background

Techniques and Traditions in Pottery

For thousands of years, people all over the world have made beautiful clay pots for cooking, storing food and water, and other everyday purposes. They form the pots with their hands and allow them to

Fig. 2–8 Traditional Pueblo pottery is decorated with simplified shapes of animals, birds, or other elements of nature, and geometric shapes. What words can you use to describe the form, color, and decorative elements of this pottery? Maria Martinez of San Ildefonso Pueblo, New Mexico, April 1976.
Photo by Jerry Jacka.

3. As you work, look at the pot often from all sides. Try to keep its shape symmetrical.

4. Decorate your pot before firing. You can add small balls or coils of clay for a relief design. You might also carve a design directly into the surface of the clay.

5. Cover your finished pot loosely with plastic. Allow it to dry slowly. When your pot is dry, you may wish to smooth the surface with the edge or back of a spoon.

Fig. 2–9 "This pot was inspired when I looked out the window of our art class and saw a tree with no leaves." Danielle Zoe Rivera, *Untitled*, 2000.
Clay, glaze. 5" x 6 ½" (12.7 x 16.5 cm). Mount Nittany Middle School, State College, Pennsylvania.

Check Your Work

Display your completed work. Think about the form and decoration of your pot. Does the form fit its intended use? Why? How do your decorative features add to the pot? What changes would you make, if any?

Sketchbook Connection
Carry your sketchbook with you and pay attention to the shapes and designs of the pottery you see in your community. Make sketches of these shapes and designs to refer to later.

Core Lesson 2

Check Your Understanding
1. Name two ways artists contribute to daily community life.
2. What is a portrait?
3. Identify a skill that is taught within your family or local community, much like the pottery skills that are taught within the Pueblo community.
4. Suppose that traditions of making objects were not passed along to future generations. What would people need to do to set up a new tradition for making a particular kind of useful object for their community?

dry, creating what is called *greenware*. Greenware is fragile and must be handled with care. It is often baked in a fire or a kiln until the clay is hard and strong. The once-fired clay is called **bisqueware**. Bisqueware can be made waterproof by applying glaze with a brush and firing again.

Techniques and traditions in making clay pots are often passed down through generations in a family. Maria Martinez, a Native-American artist, learned to make pottery by watching and imitating her aunt in the pueblo of San Ildefonso, New Mexico. Maria learned the ancient method of building pots and plates from coils of clay. She is known and honored for having revived the finest traditions of pottery among the Pueblo community.

Art in Colonial North America: 1500–1776

1585
White, *Indians Fishing*

1674
Mrs. Freake and Baby Mary

1768
Revere, *Sons of Liberty Bowl*

Ancient North America
page 76

Colonial North America

American Neoclassicism
page 128

1565
Le Moyne, *Rene Goulaine de Laudonniere and Chief Athore*

1630
Bradford Chair

1716
Burgis, *View of New York*

History in a Nutshell

During the sixteenth century, Europeans made important progress in navigation. As a result, many Europeans boarded ships and crossed the oceans to establish new communities in Asia, Africa, and the Americas. In North America, three major colonies began: New Spain, New France, and New England.

The colonial period in North America began in 1521, when the Spaniard Hernando Cortes conquered the region of present-day Mexico. A century later, the first English, Dutch, and French colonists settled along the east coast region of what are now the United States and Canada.

Fig. 2–10 **Jacques Le Moyne used watercolor to record the early settlement of colonies in Florida. What does this painting suggest about the relationship between European settlers and Native Americans in the Florida colonies?** Jacques Le Moyne, *Rene Goulaine de Laudonniere and Chief Athore* (detail), 1565.
Gouache and metallic pigments on vellum, with traces of black chalk outlines. Prints Collection, Miriam and Ira D. Wallach Division of Art. Prints and Photographs, The New York Public Library, Astor, Lenox and Tilden Foundations. Bequest of James Hazen Hyde.

Fig. 2–11 **In the early 1700s, when this engraving was created, New York was the third largest city in the colonies. What does this image tell you about daily life in New York at that time? How is it different today?** William Burgis, *View of New York from Brooklyn Heights* (detail: section one), 1716–18. Engraving after drawing, 20 7/8" x 17 15/16" (53 x 44.7 cm). Collection of the New York Historical Society.

Fig. 2–12 **This watercolor painting shows one glimpse of what life was like in Virginia during Sir Walter Raleigh's colonial venture there. What details from daily life do you see?** After original watercolor by John White, *Indians Fishing*, Virginia, 1585. Watercolor touched with gold. Courtesy the Trustees of the British Museum. © Copyright The British Museum.

A Common Art Heritage

Meeting basic needs in their new land challenged North American colonists. They had to make the things they could not bring from Europe. Those who knew a craft tradition helped by making things that were needed. Artworks by European printmakers, engravers, and painters are visual records of the colonists' early settlements. The artworks shown in Figs. 2–11 and 2–12 are scenes of daily life in early communities in New York and Virginia.

Colonial art owes much to the memories and experiences of the first settlers. The people who built the colonies were familiar with art created during the European Renaissance. Some were also familiar with art from ancient Greece and Rome. This common heritage is one reason why we can see similarities in the crafts, painting, sculpture, and architecture created by different North American communities.

Living

Art for Living

Colonists along the east coast created decorative items for daily use in wood, silver, and other metals. Women created fine quilts, needlework, and homespun weaving. The major influences on art in the thirteen colonies came from England. The silver bowl in Fig. 2–13 was made by the same Paul Revere who warned that the British were coming in the Revolutionary War. Paul Revere was a silversmith as well as a hero in his community. The form of the bowl is similar to Chinese porcelain bowls that traders brought to America by ship.

In these New England colonies, portraits for the home were popular. Many portraits show settlers in fine clothes, posed as if they were European aristocrats. Although the portrait in Fig. 2–15 was painted by a trained artist, most painters were self-taught. *Limners* traveled from one town to another to paint signs and houses. In their spare time, they painted portraits of the colonists. Eventually, some artists moved beyond portrait painting and created historical paintings as well.

Fig. 2–13 **This punch bowl is one of the most famous pieces of American silver. The artist, Paul Revere, was an important figure in the Boston community. For whom might he have made this bowl? On what occasions might a bowl like this be used?** Paul Revere, *Sons of Liberty Bowl*, Boston, 1768. Silver, 5 1/2" x 11" (14 x 27.9 cm). Gift by Subscription and Francis Bartlett Fund. Courtesy Museum of Fine Arts, Boston. Reproduced with permission. ©1999 Museum of Fine Arts, Boston. All Rights Reserved.

Fig. 2–14 **Chairs were luxury items in many early New England homes. Would you consider this a luxury chair? Why or why not?** Massachusetts Bay Colony, *Bradford Chair*, 1630. Black ash, seat: wood, 46" x 24" x 19" (116.8 x 61 x 48.3 cm). Pilgrim Society, Pilgrim Hall Museum, Plymouth, MA.

Studio Connection

Observe and draw an arrangement of objects, such as dishes, chairs, or tools, that are an important part of your everyday life. Choose drawing media and arrange the objects to bring out the main visual differences between them. Study the objects carefully before making your decisions.

Plan your composition by using the principles of design. What will you emphasize? Are there rhythms you can show? Will you use normal, ideal, or exaggerated proportions? Why? How can you use other principles of design to create a definite mood or feeling?

Check Your Understanding

1. How did art play a part in the daily life of the North American colonists?
2. What is the common artistic heritage of colonial communities?
3. What decorative items were made for the homes of the early colonists?
4. What are limners and what role did they play in colonial life?

Fig. 2–15 **In this portrait, the artist uses the elegant, embroidered style of the Tudor period in England (1485–1603). The delicate treatment of lace and fabric help soften the stiffness of the figures. Anonymous,** *Mrs. Elizabeth Freake and Baby Mary,* **portrait, ca. 1671–74.**
Oil on canvas, 42 1/2" x 36 3/4" (108 x 93.4 cm). Worcester Art Museum, Worcester, Massachusetts, Gift of Mr. and Mrs. Albert W. Rice.

Living

105

Drawing

Add drawing to your daily life! Drawings can be quick records of things you see and want to remember. They can be a way to explore and try out ideas for other kinds of artwork, such as paintings or sculptures. Drawings can also be finished works of art.

Before they draw, artists think about the medium they will use. They choose the medium that will help them express their ideas and feelings. **Dry media** include pencils, charcoal, pastels, and crayons. **Wet media** include inks applied with a pen or a brush. In a **mixed-media** artwork, artists combine drawing with painting, collage, or printmaking.

Once artists choose their medium, they experiment with it to find the techniques they like best.

Fig. 2–16 **This artist created a still life of everyday objects. Notice how carefully he has drawn the shapes and forms. What drawing technique do you think he used?** Robert Kogge, *Untitled*, 1989.
Graphite on canvas, 20" x 30" (50.8 x 76.2 cm). Courtesy O.K. Harris Works of Art, New York, NY.

Fig. 2–17 **Would you consider this a contour drawing or a whole-to-part drawing? Why?** Joseph H. Davis, *The Tilton Family*, Deerfield, New Hampshire, 1837. Watercolor, pencil and ink on wove paper, 10" x 15 1/16" (25.4 x 38.3 cm). Abby Aldrich Rockefeller Folk Art Center, Williamsburg, VA.

Drawing Techniques

Most artists prefer one particular drawing technique over another. Here are three techniques that you might try. Which one feels best to you?

• **Contour drawings** show the edges (contours) of objects. To make a contour drawing, keep your eyes on your subject. Imagine that you are tracing it.

• **Gesture drawings** are done quickly, without attention to details. Try drawing only the main "action lines" of your subject.

• **Whole-to-part drawings** are those in which the largest shapes are drawn first. Details are added afterwards.

To get ideas for drawings, artists look at things, depend on their memories, or tap their imaginations. Sometimes they get ideas from art that was created by other artists.

2.2 Forms and Media

Check Your Understanding

1. Why might an artist want to mix media in a drawing?

2. What are the main differences between contour drawings and gesture drawings?

Studio Connection

Experiment with the three drawing techniques. Choose an object that you see every day. First, make a contour drawing. Focus carefully on the edges of your object, and draw slowly. Next, make a gesture drawing of the same object. This time focus on the direction of its parts. Finally, make a whole-to-part drawing. Sketch the large shapes first. Refine them with lines and shading. Then fill in the details. Use a pencil or marker for the first two drawings and a pencil and eraser for the third.

Sketchbook Connection

Use your sketchbook every day to draw or sketch objects, people, and places around you. Drawing every day will help you strengthen your skills. Carry your sketchbook with you or plan time in your daily schedule to draw.

Painting Life in an Indian Empire

India

China

Pakistan

Indus River

Nepal

• Malwa

India

Bangladesh

Sri Lanka

Daily Life in Miniature

The art of India is rich and varied. Artworks are greatly different from one part of the country to another and from one time period to another. The Hindu and Buddhist religions had a strong influence on Indian art. The Hindu figure Shiva, the destroyer, is shown in many artworks. Buddha, the founder of Buddhism, is the subject of many sculptures. Buddha is often shown seated in

Fig. 2–18 Many miniature paintings were created as illustrations for manuscripts. What does this image tell you about farming practices in India? Miftah al Fuzula, *Oxen Ploughing*, 15th century.
Gouache on paper. British Library, Oriental and India Office Library.

Global Glance

About 5000 years ago, the first known civilization developed in the Indus Valley, the area now known as India. Over the centuries, many different people settled in this vast land for different periods of time. Aryans, Persians, Greeks, and Muslims each blended elements of their civilizations with the original Indian culture. For thousands of years, Hinduism and Buddhism were the native religions in India. Then, in the sixteenth and seventeenth centuries, the Mughal Empire came to rule most of India. The Mughal rulers were Muslim. They developed a distinctive culture that blended Middle Eastern and Indian elements.

meditation with large "all-hearing" ears and a third "all-seeing" eye. The positions of his hands have special, symbolic meanings for Buddhists.

Miniature painting is detailed and very small. It became especially popular in the fifteenth century. Islam, the religion of the Muslims, did not allow artists to create religious art that showed people. So, wealthy Muslims encouraged Hindu artists to illustrate stories and sell their paintings in street markets or bazaars. Subjects for the paintings came from Hindu legends and everyday life. The colors used to create the paintings were bright. Look closely at Figs. 2–18, 2–19, and 2–20. They were created in sixteenth-century India. What do they tell you about everyday life in India then?

Before the Mughal Empire was established in 1526, paintings were created in small commercial studios. Soon after the empire was established, the production of paintings shifted to royal court workshops.

Fig. 2–19 This is a page from a sixteenth-century cookbook. Notice how drawings of grass and vegetation decorate the page. Why, do you think, did the sultan want this book illustrated for his son? Ni'mat-nama, *The Preparation of Hare Soup*, 1500–10. Gouache on paper. British Library, Oriental and India Office Library.

Fig. 2–20 There are many things going on in this camp scene. What features of daily life in sixteenth-century India do you see? M. Ali, *Camp Scene*, Khsa of Nizami, 1539–43. Gouache on paper. British Library, Oriental and India Office Library.

The Court Workshop

Emperor Akbar ruled the Mughal Empire in India from 1556–1605. At the start of his reign, Akbar the Great set up a workshop for court artists. He employed Muslim artists from Persia to instruct Hindu artists from India. The workshop community grew to more than 100 artists. It produced images of daily court life and garden scenes that told the story of Akbar's reign (Figs. 2–21 and 2–22).

Muslim and Hindu artists often worked together on paintings. One artist might create the general outline. Another might create the portrait heads, another the landscape, and yet another the coloring. The paintings of this workshop are a blend of beautiful color, perfect calligraphy, and detailed realism. The artists developed a unique style that combined Hindu ideas, European realism, Persian composition, and Muslim discipline.

The court workshop tradition continued during the reigns of the next two emperors, Jehangir and Shah Jahan. But the famous workshop was abolished at the end of Shah Jahan's rule in 1658. After that, the artists had to make their livings selling their art on the streets and in the marketplaces of large cities.

Fig. 2–21 **Akbar paid his workshop artists to record daily events. Notice the detail and the rich decoration in this painting. Do you think the artists might have glorified or exaggerated the reality of this event? What makes you think so?** Farrukh Beg, *Akbar's Entry Into Surat,* Akbar-nama, ca. 1590.
Gouache on paper, 14 7/8" x 9 9/16" (37.9 x 24.3 cm).
Trustees of the Victoria & Albert Museum.

Fig. 2–22 **In this scene, Akbar is shown greeting an old friend in a garden pavilion. Do you think daily life in Akbar's court was formal or informal? What makes you think so?** Manohar Das, India, *Akbar Receives Mirza 'Aziz Koka,* 1602. Opaque watercolor and gold on paper, 7 1/4" x 4 3/4" (18.4 x 12.1 cm). Cincinnati Art Museum, Gift of John J. Emery 1950.289a.

Studio Connection

Organize a workshop community of artists in your classroom. Plan a series of paintings together that tell about daily life at your school. Talk about the images you will show. For example, you might include morning bell, homeroom, first period, and the like. Assign parts of the paintings to different artists in your workshop. Who likes to draw or paint portraits? Who likes to draw or paint landscapes or indoor scenes? Who likes to add details? Set up work stations and work together to create your paintings.

2.3 Global View

Check Your Understanding

1. How did the religions of India's communities influence art?
2. What outside influences changed the direction of art in Indian painting?
3. How did art relate to daily life during the Mughal Empire?
4. How was art created in the royal court workshops?

Drawing in the Studio

Drawing a Group Portrait

A Picture of Daily Life

Studio Introduction

Portrait artists observe the way people sit, stand, and move. They notice the position and placement of their subjects' arms and legs, hands and heads. They study facial expressions and characteristics that are unique to the people they portray. **In this studio experience you will observe classmates or people in your school community and draw a group portrait of them.** Pages 114 and 115 will tell you how to do it.

When artists create portraits, they pay special attention to their subjects' **proportions,** or the relation between one part of the body and another. People are surprisingly alike in their proportions. A good portrait captures a person's general proportions and individuality. (See the diagrams on page 114 to learn about proportions in a face or figure.)

Come up with a plan for your portrait. Do you want your subjects to stand or sit? What view of them will you choose: front, three-quarter, or profile? You may want to observe your subjects in their daily activities. Make sketches of them in your sketchbook to use later in your final drawing. Think about details you will include that will tell about the daily lives of these people.

Studio Background

The Importance of Portraits

Portraits play an important role in the daily lives of people all over the world. They help people remember loved ones and honor great leaders and heroes (Fig. 2–23). They can give us an idea of what life was like for their subjects. For the North American colonists, having their portraits painted was a sign of success in a growing community. Usually, the style of these portraits was based on what was popular in Europe at the time (Fig. 2–25).

Fig. 2–23 During the American Revolution, Paul Revere made a "midnight ride" to warn his community that the British were coming. What does the artist of this portrait show us about Paul Revere's daily life as a silversmith? Notice the three-quarter view of Revere's face. John Singleton Copley, *Paul Revere,* 1768.
Oil on canvas, 35 1/8" x 28 1/2" (89.2 x 72.4 cm). Gift of Joseph W. Revere, William B. Revere and Edward H. R. Revere. Courtesy Museum of Fine Arts, Boston. Reproduced with permission. ©1999 Museum of Fine Arts, Boston. All Rights Reserved.

Fig. 2–24 "I drew this of my shop teacher. I was experimenting with shading." James Mast, *Many Talents*, 1999. Pencil, 16" x 10 1/2" (40.5 x 26.5 cm). Penn View Christian School, Souderton, Pennsylvania.

Fig. 2–25 This artist painted full-figure portraits of children in formal garden scenes. Parents wanted these portraits to show their children's pleasures. The backgrounds recall the communities that parents had left behind in Europe. Justus Engelhardt Kuhn, *Eleanor Darnall* (Mrs. Daniel Carroll—1704–96), ca. 1710. Oil on canvas, 54" x 44 1/2" (137.2 x 113 cm). Courtesy Maryland Historical Society, Baltimore, Maryland.

Portraits were also important to the rulers of the Mughal Empire. Formal portraits of the ruling class and scenes of daily court life show a blend of Persian, Hindu, and European elements. Most portraits include a garden or landscape scene. Notice the details in the portrait of Emperor Aurangzeb (Fig. 2–26). What does this portrait tell you about the daily life of an emperor in India?

Fig. 2–26 Notice the simple composition of this portrait. It does not include the garden or landscape scene that many Indian portraits have. Why might the artist have chosen not to include a detailed background? India, Mughal School, *The Emperor Aurangzeb*, ca. 1690–1710. Color on paper, 12" x 8 13/16" (30.5 x 22.3 cm). © The Cleveland Museum of Art, Andrew R. and Martha Holden Jennings Fund, 1971.81.

Drawing in the Studio

Drawing Your Portrait

You Will Need

- drawing paper
- charcoal, pencil, or pastels

Try This

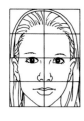 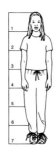

1. Observe the people you want to draw. Notice the shape and features of their faces. Notice whether your subjects are tall, thin, short, or plump. Then set up guidelines for proportion in your portrait.

2. Decide which view of each person you want to show. Will you show any profile or three-quarter views?

3. Draw your portrait. Work on the character or special qualities of your subjects. For example, you might use thin, wiry lines for a thin, nervous person. Capture important details. These might include the shape of the eyebrows, a dimple in the chin, a sparkle in the eyes, or a unique hair style.

4. Remember to include backgrounds and props that tell about the daily lives of the people in your portrait. Think about the mood or feeling you want to show. Are the lives of the people in your portrait serious or joyful? How can you show this detail?

5. Try shading your drawing. Imagine shining a strong light on your subjects. Where would you see the highlights and shadows?

Check Your Work

What guidelines for proportions did you use to start your drawing? Did they help you? Were you able to capture the mood and unique characteristics of your subjects? What details from their daily lives did you show?

Sketchbook Connection

The sketches you make of things you observe are one of the best sources of ideas for artworks. Sketch the most important or interesting elements of your community. Draw the people you know and see regularly. Sketch scenes of daily life in your neighborhood. Try filling a page with *thumbnail sketches,* or small drawings. Sketch your subject from different views or with different amounts of detail.

Computer Option

Look at some artists' self-portraits on the Internet. Then use paint or draw software to create your self-portrait. Add symbols that represent your interests, community, and/or culture.

Fig. 2–27 "The picture that I have drawn is of a girl on the school basketball team. Drawing her hair, the basketball, and her uniform was easy. The difficult parts were drawing her face (mostly her eyes) and shading." Mackenzie Granger, *Warrior in Waiting*, 2000.
Pastel, 12" x 9" (30.5 x 29 cm). Thomas Prince School, Princeton, Massachusetts.

Connect to...

Careers

Were you the one to choose the color scheme and furniture in your bedroom? Are you allowed to paint and decorate your room as you choose? Many teenagers serve as their own interior decorators; but professional **interior designers** work with clients, and generally on a much larger scale. Interior designers are responsible for planning and coordinating the design, decoration, and functionality of interior spaces—spaces where we live, work, and play. They may work with either residential or commercial clients to select furniture, fabrics, wall and floor coverings, accessories, and art elements appropriate for each client's individual characteristics and needs. Interior designers have to be skilled at working with color, fabric, and furniture, and

Fig. 2–28 **Do certain rooms make you feel calm or happy? Have you ever thought about why? Is it the color of the walls or the way things are placed? This woman thought about these kinds of things when she decorated the living areas for NASA astronauts on a space station.** NASA space station decorator, 1988.
Photograph ©Roger Ressmeyer/CORBIS.

they must have good communication and budgeting skills. Interior design is demanding—and fulfilling—especially for those who do it well.

Fig. 2–29 **During a perfomance of** *STOMP*, **cast members create music using a variety of everyday objects such as brooms, sink plugs, and plastic containers. What object do you use every day that could be transformed into a musical instrument?** *Cast members of the musical* STOMP.
Photo ©Junichi Takahashi. Courtesy Takahashi Studios, New York.

Other Arts

Dance

Visual art may depict scenes of daily life or may be directly involved in daily activities or rituals. Likewise, **dance can be a part of daily life**. What movements can you associate with specific activities you participate in every day? Is it possible that those movements could be considered dance? Why or why not?

Think of some chores or other responsibilities you have. If you were to create a dance to help you with your daily work, what would it look like? Would your dance involve other people, or would you dance alone?

Social Studies

What are some everyday outdoor activities that take place in your neighborhood after school or on the weekends? Perhaps people sit on the front steps and chat, walk their pet, mow their yard, or play games on the sidewalk. Did you know that such **ordinary subjects** are found in art? In art, a representation of a scene from everyday life is called a **genre scene**. How could the daily life of your neighborhood be depicted through art? What subject would you choose for a genre painting?

Language Arts

Have you read any **books that were told from several perspectives**, or points of view? Perhaps two narrators took turns telling interlocking stories of their lives. Perhaps the book was about a community in which a number of people had individual versions of the same story, as is common in many mysteries. How might this be possible in the visual arts?

Science

Each **Native-American pueblo** in New Mexico traditionally uses a particular **color of clay for its pottery**. For example, the pueblo San Ildefonso is famous for its heavy-walled black pottery, and Acoma is known for its creamy-white clay. What are the reasons, do you think, for differences among pueblos? Each pueblo gathers the natural materials—gypsum, sand, and clay—only from its own reservation, which individualizes their pottery.

Fig. 2–30 **Maria Martinez invented the technique of black-on-black pottery you see pictured here. She made the pots and her husband, Julian, decorated them.** Maria and Julian Martinez, *Bowl*, n.d.
Clay, height: 7" (17.8 cm). National Museum of American Art, Smithsonian Institution, Washington, DC/Art Resource, NY.

Internet Connection
For more activities related to this chapter, go to the Davis website at **www.davis-art.com.**

Portfolio

Fig. 2–31 Ben Lewis, *Staetler Scatter*, 1998.
Colored pencil, 9" x 12" (23 x 30 cm). Samford Middle School, Auburn, Alabama.

"My teacher taught me a lot of methods to shade with colored pencil. When I had to come up with an idea for a final drawing I looked by my sketchbook and saw all my pens scattered over the table. I thought that would make a neat design. The hardest part was making it look real and coming up with a background." **Ben Lewis**

Fig. 2–32 A'lise Havemeister, *Athletes Only*, 1999.
Tempera, 12" x 18" (30 x 46 cm). Colony Middle School, Palmer, Alaska.

"This is a self-portrait because I love sports. Basketball is my favorite sport, and that is why it is the largest. I like to compete and practice with my friends."
A'lise Havemeister

CD-ROM Connection
To see more student art, check out the Community Connection Student Gallery.

Fig. 2–33 Stacey Fong, *Contemplation*, 1999.
Papier- mâché, wire, tape, tempera, 8" x 6" x 6" (20 x 15 x 15 cm). Los Cerros Middle School, Danville, California.

Chapter 2 Review

Recall

Name at least two ways that artists contribute to the daily life of communities.

Understand

Explain why the artworks produced in widespread North American colonies have a similar look.

Apply

Produce a visual aid that you could use for teaching a younger child or an older adult how to observe and capture the proportions in a human figure at work and play.

Analyze

Compare the way artists worked in the royal studio workshops of the Mughal emperors in sixteenth-century India (described in Lesson 2.3; *see example below*) with the group artworks for communities today as discussed in the Core Lesson. Note similarities and differences.

Synthesize

Propose an idea for an artwork that you would like to see designed for your community based on a perceived need or to send an important message to community members. Look to the artworks and ideas presented in this chapter as a springboard for your sketch and written description of what you think the finished piece should look like.

Evaluate

Select one artwork from this chapter that you think would be the best cover image for a book entitled "Art in Community Life." Select a second image as an alternate. Give reasons for your choices and justify your number-one choice by describing features of the work.

For Your Sketchbook

Design a page in your sketchbook for writing visually descriptive impressions of daily life scenes in your community. Refer to these poetic descriptions for the development of ideas for future artworks.

For Your Portfolio

Select an artwork in this book that sends a clear message about daily life in a community. Describe the work in detail. Tell how the arrangement of the parts helps to convey the message. Date your written response and add it to your portfolio.

Page 113

Belonging

Fig. 3–1 **The many different faces in this flag say to viewers, This is who we are as a nation— people from every kind of background joined together as Americans. We belong to this community. Does your community have an artwork that suggests the idea of belonging?** Pablo Delano (photographer of faces), Installation designed by MetaForm/Rathe/D&P (The Liberty/Ellis Island Collaborative), *Flag of Faces*, Ellis Island, 1990.
8' 8" x 16' 6 3/4" x 2" (264.2 x 504.8 x 5.1 cm). Exhibit installation at the Ellis Island Immigration Museum, National Park Service / Statue of Liberty National Monument.

Focus

- What does it mean to belong to a community?
- How does art help us belong?

Do you know where your ancestors are from? Ireland? Jamaica? Poland? China? Spain? Iran? India? Italy? South Africa? Peru? How did your family arrive in America? In the late 1800s and early 1900s, millions of people from around the world came to live in the United States. These people came from many different places and for lots of reasons. The one thing they all had in common was a belief that life in America would be better than it was in the country they came from.

People who move from one country to another are called *immigrants*. At the turn of the twentieth century, most immigrants to the United States arrived in New York City, America's busiest port. One of their first sights was the Statue of Liberty. The *Flag of Faces* (Fig. 3–1) is on display at the Statue of Liberty National Monument/Ellis Island Immigration Museum, a museum that tells how new citizens arrived in America. The *Flag of Faces* shows people whose ancestors journeyed here seeking a new home. The faces are seen through the stars and stripes of the American flag, our national symbol.

Artworks can express what it means to belong to a community, whether that community is as large as a country or as small as a neighborhood. Although the Statue of Liberty and *Flag of Faces* send messages about a whole nation, other artworks tell about belonging to local communities throughout the world.

What's Ahead

- **Core Lesson** Discover how art can express the idea that we belong to a national community of people from all over the world.
- **3.1 Art History Lesson**
  Learn how art helped new nations in North America establish their own identities and a sense of belonging.
- **3.2 Forms and Media Lesson**
  Learn about sculpture and how it can symbolize the idea of belonging.
- **3.3 Global View Lesson**
  Explore how Polynesian art shows people's individual importance within their communities.
- **3.4 Studio Lesson**
  Make a plaster model of a large sculpture that honors an event, person, or group.

Words to Know

monument	found objects
commemorate	earthworks
Neoclassical	motif
sgrafitto	maquette

Art Shows Community Values and Beliefs

Public Monuments

Look around your town or city. Do you see artworks in public places that mean something special to the local people? Perhaps there is a sculpture that reminds people of an event in the area's history. Is there a statue or a plaque on a building that honors a person or group? Many artworks are created for public places—places where people gather or pass by every day. These artworks are public **monuments**. They represent ideas that are important to the people who live in the area. The Statue of Liberty is such a monument. Public monuments remind us that we belong to communities because we share certain beliefs and values.

Fig. 3–2 **The Qin Dynasty lasted only 15 years—from 221 BC until 206 BC. During this time, the Chinese people living north of the Yellow River were united for the first time. How does this sculpture commemorate this important event in China's history? The monument is over 300 feet long and was made by over 100 stone carvers.** Wang Tianren, Ge Demao, Meng Xiling, *Emperor Qin Unifying China,* Xi'an, 1993. Granite. Reprinted by permission of the University of Washington Press. Photo by John T. Young.

Public Tributes

Public monuments can also remind us of events, time periods, or people that are important to the community. They allow people to express their sense of belonging. They **commemorate**, or honor, the events and people that have shaped the histories of towns, cities, and even countries. The monument *Emperor Qin Unifying China* (Fig. 3–2) reminds the people of China about an important event. Under the rule of Emperor Qin, all the people of China were first united as one country. This large sculpture was created in 1993. It is located on an important road between the city of Xi'an and third century BC tombs from the Qin dynasty. The sculpture sends a message about the people's sense of pride in their community.

Some public monuments express thanks to groups of people who have helped a community. The sculpture of *The Burghers of Calais* (Fig. 3–3) was created for the town of Calais, France. The burghers, or leaders, of the town offered their lives in exchange for the town's safety during the Hundred Years' War. The sculpture shows the six men facing death. It tells us that the people of this town value bravery and feel bound together by their beliefs.

Fig. 3–3 **Are these men heroes?** Auguste Rodin, *The Burghers of Calais,* 1884–85. Bronze, 81 7/8" x 55 1/8" x 74 3/4" (208 x 140 x 190 cm). Musee Rodin, Paris, France. Courtesy Art Resource, New York.

Fig. 3–4 **This monument honors African-American soldiers of the Civil War. How does it compare to Fig. 3–3?** Augustus Saint-Gaudens, *Shaw Memorial* (Final Version), 1900. U.S. Department of the Interior, National Park Service, Saint-Gaudens National Historic Site, Cornish, NH.

Art Honors Heroes and Leaders

Who are your heroes? Professional basketball players? Actresses? Someone in your neighborhood? Heroes and leaders are people who do things that represent the values and beliefs of a community. People look to them as examples of strength and courage. Local heroes are an important source of pride for the people who live in the area. They help create a sense of belonging because everyone honors or respects them for the same reasons. What do you admire most about your heroes?

Stories of heroic actions and deeds are often told and retold within a community. Artworks help record these stories. The painting of Molly Pitcher tells the story of an American Revolutionary War heroine (Fig. 3–7). Molly Pitcher's birth name was Mary Ludwig McCauley. She earned the nickname Molly Pitcher because she carried pitchers of water to soldiers during the Battle of Monmouth.

Fig. 3–5 **This sculpture commemorates George Washington Carver, who developed agricultural products that could be grown in the South. What commemorative sculptures have you seen?** Richmond Barthe, *George Washington Carver,* 1977.
Hall of Fame, Bronx Community College, New York City. Bronze. Photo © 1999 Frank Fournier.

Fig. 3–6 **Quetzalcoatl is a cultural hero in Mesoamerican history. The limestone sculpture stands about five feet tall. What cultural hero in your community would you like to be remembered hundreds of years from now?** Mexico, Mayan, *Head of Quetzalcoatl* at the Temple of Quetzalcoatl, Teotihuacan, ca. 150–200 AD.
Limestone. Photograph © 1999 Entrique Franco Torrijos

Fig. 3–7 **How does this painting commemorate Molly Pitcher's bravery? Can you name other important women in history? How might they be shown in commemorative artworks?** Dennis Malone Carter, *Molly Pitcher at the Battle of Monmouth*, 1854.
Oil on canvas, 42" x 56" (106.7 x 142.2 cm). Gift of Herbert P. Whitlock, 1913. Courtesy Fraunces Tavern Museum, New York City.

All kinds of communities have heroes and leaders. For example, groups of scientists, politicians, writers, and artists each have their own heroes. These heroes represent ideas and beliefs that each group values most. Artists sometimes create artworks to help people remember and honor their leaders and heroes. We can relate to great individuals through these artworks. They help us feel that we belong together. For example, the sculpture of George Washington Carver (Fig. 3–5) commemorates his importance as a great scientist.

Other public artworks remind us of people, such as firefighters and nurses, who have served a community with heroic deeds. The sculpture of Quetzalcoatl was created many years ago by the Toltec community of Mexico (Fig. 3–6). Quetzalcoatl was a Mesoamerican prince who supported art and learning. Legend says that he was banished from the community but promised to return at the dawn of a new golden age. Whether he did or not is a mystery, but the sculpture reminds us of him. Are there sculptures of heroes in your community? What stories do you know about them?

Drawing in the Studio
Recording a Community Story

Many towns and cities have an interesting and unique story that tells about the place's history. Sometimes these stories describe an exciting event or involve a local hero. **In this studio experience, you will make a drawing that shows the main event from an important community story.** What stories are important to your town or city? What characters or heroes are in the stories? Brainstorm ideas with your classmates about the main event from a story you might show and the heroes who are involved. Find out as much as you can about the event. How did it affect the people in your community? What does the story tell about your community's beliefs and values?

Try This

1. Determine what the main event of your story is. This will be the focus of your drawing. What people will you include? Will you create a particular setting? From what point of view will you draw the scene?

2. Sketch your ideas. Think about how you will organize your work. Where will you place the figures and objects? What action will you show? What details will help viewers identify the community, event, and people in the story?

3. Select your best sketch and use it to create your final drawing. Sketch the large areas first. Then add smaller features and details. Think about the lines and colors you can use to create mood or add meaning to the work.

Fig. 3–8 A clergyman named Mason Weems invented the story of George Washington and the cherry tree. He wanted to convince people of the value of telling the truth. What is the irony, or funny part, of the story you see in this painting? How did artist Grant Wood use point of view to show the main idea? Grant Wood, *Parson Weems's Fable*, 1939. Oil on canvas, 38 3/8" x 50 1/8" (97.5 x 127.3 cm). Courtesy Amon Carter Museum, Fort Worth, Texas. © Estate of Grant Wood / Licensed by VAGA, New York, NY.

Studio Background

Artworks that Tell a Story

Not all artworks that reflect the stories and beliefs of a community were created for public spaces. Smaller artworks, such as paintings and sculptures, help create a strong and positive image of the early Americans.

With photography, video, and film, we view historic events almost immediately as they occur. In the past, many stories were passed along by travelers telling one person, who then told another, and so on. The stories probably changed each time they were retold. Artists who recorded important events

4. If necessary, use your eraser to lighten pencil marks before using your colored pencils or markers.

Check Your Work

Show your drawing to a small group of classmates. Ask them to describe what they see. Ask them which parts of the drawing help them recognize the community, event, or hero you have shown. Is your point of view about the story clear?

Fig. 3–9 **"My picture represents my town. It shows the story of 'Mary Had a Little Lamb,' which actually took place in Sterling. The apples represent all the orchards found in the area."** Nicolette Schlichting, *Its Fleece Was White as Snow*, 2000.
Colored pencil, 12" x 18" (30.5 x 46 cm). Chocksett Middle School, Sterling, Massachusetts.

Sketchbook Connection
Experiment with your colored pencils or markers before you use them in your final drawing. Make different kinds of marks with them: thin, thick, curved, jagged, light, and dark. Which marks will express the point of view you want to show in your drawing?

Core Lesson 3

Check Your Understanding

1. Use examples to explain how public monuments can show ideas about belonging to a community.
2. Select one artwork from this lesson and tell how it honors or gives tribute to an individual who has promoted the ideals of a community.
3. Name one of your heroes and tell how you might show this person in a sculpture.
4. Do you think it is ever a good idea to "stretch the truth" when showing historical events that are important to a community? Why or why not?

had to rely on the information available to them, whether it was accurate or not.

Artists also have their own points of view or opinions about events. *Parson Weems's Fable* (Fig. 3–8) shows a unique point of view on the story of George Washington and the cherry tree. *Penn's Treaty with the Indians* (Fig. 3–10) records a true story that is important to people from Pennsylvania. Look at artworks in your own community. What events do they show? From what point of view do they tell a story?

Fig. 3–10 **William Penn was guided by his Quaker belief that all people should be treated fairly and with respect. He paid the Lenape and Delaware Indians for their land and made a treaty of friendship with them. Do you think this artwork accurately depicts the way this event took place? How has the artist expressed a point of view?** Benjamin West, *Penn's Treaty with the Indians*, 1771–72.
Oil on canvas, 75 1/2" x 107 3/4" (191.9 cm x 273.7 cm). Courtesy of the Pennsylvania Academy of the Fine Arts, Philadelphia. Gift of Mrs. Sarah Harrison (The Joseph Harrison, Jr. Collection)

Art and Independence: 1776–1820

1770
Jefferson, *Monticello*

1788
Marriage Chest of Margaret Kernan

1817
Waner, *Sampler*

Colonial North America
page 102

American Neoclassicism

Realism and Romanticism
page 154

1786
Huebner, *Earthenware Plate*

1815
Krimmel, *Election Day in Philadelphia*

1840
Greenough, *George Washington*

History in a Nutshell

The years between 1776 and 1867 gave birth to three nations within North America: the United States, Canada, and Mexico. In 1776, the United States declared its independence from England. In 1821, Mexico became a nation, and the region of New Spain north of the Rio Grande became part of the United States. Canada set up its national government in 1867.

A Classical Nation

When people form new groups, they often try to create a style that identifies the group. For example, when the new nation of the United States formed, artists tried to capture the spirit of its national identity. Portraits of leaders and paintings about historical events became popular subjects. In their artworks, artists recorded the nation's fight for independence. Many artists looked to the classical art and architecture of ancient Greece and Rome for

Fig. 3–11 **Thomas Jefferson designed his own house. Most Neoclassical-style buildings are symmetrical and have the same number of windows on each side of a center door. What other elements of classical architecture can you identify?** Thomas Jefferson, *Monticello*, Charlottesville, Virginia, 1769–84.
44.7' x 87.9' x 110' (13.6 x 26.8 x 33.5 m). Photograph by Robert Llewellyn.

Fig. 3–12 **This painting is a celebration of community. It is crowded with figures representing several social classes. In this picture of an election, what important ideal of government is being celebrated?** John Lewis Krimmel, *Election Day in Philadelphia,* 1815. Oil on canvas, 16 3/8" x 25 5/8" (41.6 x 65.2 cm). Courtesy The Henry Francis Du Pont Winterthur Museum.

Fig. 3–13 **Can you explain why the sculptor portrayed a national leader in a Roman toga?** Horatio Greenough, *George Washington,* 1840. Marble, 133 7/8" (340 cm) from back to front of base. National Museum of American Art, Smithsonian Institution, Washington, DC./Art Resource, NY.

inspiration. A new style in art, known as **Neoclassical**, became popular in the United States. The sculpture of George Washington (Fig. 3–13) reflects the nation's adoption of Greek and Roman ideals.

The Neoclassical style included painting, sculpture, and architecture. Some sculptures of human figures express ideals such as truth and justice. Other artworks show important historic events. Artworks such as *Election Day in Philadelphia* (Fig. 3–12) document the workings of democracy in the United States. As large cities developed, sculptures appeared in community parks and public buildings for all to see.

Buildings in the Neoclassical style include features of Greek and Roman architecture. Some have the large Doric, Ionic, or Corinthian columns seen in Greek structures. These buildings are sometimes called *Greek Revival style*, which is a fancier version of the Neoclassical style of architecture. Large Greek Revival homes became popular in the southern United States. Thomas Jefferson promoted the Neoclassical style through the design of his own home in Virginia (Fig. 3–11).

Signs of Belonging

A nation is made up of many different smaller communities, each with its own unique style and identity. Designs seen in local art are often connected to the region's weather or to the background of the people who live there. For instance, winter scenes are common in the art of New England. What designs do you think identify the Southwest? Why? What designs identify the region where you live?

In the years following American independence, rural Pennsylvania was home to a rich folk art tradition. The European settlers in Pennsylvania were called Pennsylvania Germans or, sometimes, Pennsylvania Dutch. They made furniture, pottery, and glassware based on the traditions of their homelands. In their craft, they used a decorative style that goes back to the Middle Ages. Their style continues to identify this region of the United States today.

Wooden chests were painted in vivid colors with simplified tulips, birds, and prancing unicorns (Fig. 3–14). Marbleized effects were produced by rubbing wet paint with a corncob. The same rich floral patterning is also seen in pottery and glass. Potters used the **sgrafitto** technique to decorate plates and jars (Fig. 3–15). In sgrafitto, designs are scratched onto a clay object through a thin layer of colored slip. Then the pottery is glazed and fired. In Pennsylvania, unfired pottery is called *redware* because of the red color of the natural clay in this region.

Fig. 3–14 **Chests of this kind are decorated with icons, lettering, and calligraphy. What do the decorations on this chest suggest about the Pennsylvania Germans?** Pennsylvania German, *Marriage Chest of Margaret Kernan,* 1788.
Painted tulipwood, 28 3/8" x 50" x 24" (72.1 x 127 x 61 cm). Courtesy The Henry Francis Du Pont Winterthur Museum.

Fig. 3–15 **The inscription on this plate reads, "Catharine Raeder, her plate. Out of the earth with understanding the potter makes everything." Can you see the heart shape that is formed by the bodies of the two doves?** George Huebner, *Plate*, inscribed to Catharine Raeder, 1786.
Earthenware, 2" x diam. 12 5/8" (5 x 32 cm). Philadelphia Museum of Art: Gift of John T. Morris.

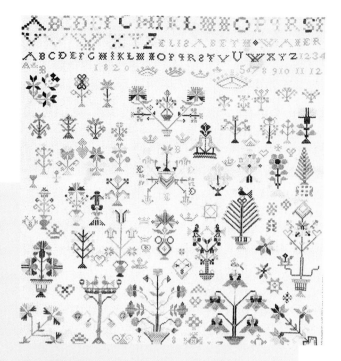

Fig. 3–16 **Notice the simplified plant and bird designs on this sampler. What elements and principles of design do you think the Pennsylvania Germans were interested in?** Elisabeth Waner, *Sampler*, 1817–20.
Linen, silk, and cotton, 17 1/4" x 16 3/8" (43.8 x 41.6 cm). Courtesy The Henry Francis Du Pont Winterthur Museum.

For the Pennsylvania Germans, the home was valued as a special place. Sharing and working together as a family were important ideals. This was reflected in framed "blessings" or sayings for the home. These richly decorated sayings were often painted or embroidered by young women to show off their handwriting and needlework skills.

Studio Connection

Make your own house blessing. Look at the embroidered sampler shown in Fig. 3–16 and then write a saying for your home. Decide how the words will look best. Using pencil and drawing paper, write the letters in your best handwriting. Trace your letters in marker. Decorate the letters, especially the first letter of the first word. Create a border. Think about visual symbols you might include. What design elements and principles will help you express your idea?

3.1 Art History

Check Your Understanding

1. How did art in the decades following independence reflect the identity of the United States?
2. How did sculptures call attention to ideals in the new United States communities?
3. What are the characteristics of the Neoclassical style of architecture?
4. How did Pennsylvania German folk art reflect the identity and ideals of that region of the country?

Sculpture

Have you ever picked up a rock or a piece of wood because you liked its shape or texture? Nature creates beautiful forms. Since the earliest times, people have used their own methods and tools to shape materials into beautiful forms. Forms have three dimensions: height, width, and depth. Artworks that have three dimensions are called *sculpture*. Traditional materials for sculptures include stone, wood, clay, ivory, and cast metal, such as bronze. Traditional ways to create sculpture involve carving, modeling, and casting. Today, many sculptors combine discarded materials, called **found objects**, to create sculptures. Some use construction equipment to create sculptural forms from the environment. These forms are called **earthworks**. Sculptures can be made to last for centuries or for only a short time.

Communities throughout history have created sculptures for different reasons.

Fig. 3–17 **What ideals do you think are represented by this tribute to community workers? How does the form of this sculpture convey these ideals?** Miere Laderman Ukeles, *Ceremonial Arch Honoring Service Workers in the New Service Economy*, 1988.
Steel arch with materials donated from New York City agencies, 11' x 12' 4" x 9' 1" (335.3 x 148 x 109 cm). Courtesy Ronald Feldman Fine Arts, New York.

Ancient people created sculptures of their gods and ancestors. These were used in community rituals, worship, or celebrations. More recent sculptures often show leaders or individuals and groups that people admire. The ceremonial arch in Fig. 3–17 honors the people who work for the city of New York. Each city agency donated materials related to the services they provide. What items do you recognize in the sculpture?

Some sculptures are requested by a city or town to show something special or unique about the community. These sculptures can also be useful, such as fountains or shelters. The sculpture of a fountain in Fig. 3–18 is at the center of an eight-acre plaza in Detroit. The artist designed the plaza downtown next to the Detroit River. It includes restaurant and performance facilities, a large outdoor amphitheater, walkways, green areas, and, in the center, the fountain.

Studio Connection

Create a clay sculpture of one of your heroes. Think about a person you admire. Your hero might be someone who lives in your community or someone who lives elsewhere in the nation or world. You may choose to depict a hero from the past or present. Give your finished sculpture a title that indicates what you admire about your hero.

3.2 Forms and Media

Check Your Understanding
1. How is sculpture different from paintings and drawings?
2. What materials and methods are commonly used to create sculpture?

Fig. 3–18 **The flow of water in this fountain is computerized and creates patterns that change constantly. How does the look of the fountain convey the importance of the city as the home of the automobile industry?** Isamu Noguchi, *Horace E. Dodge and Son Memorial Fountain*, 1978.
Stainless steel with granite base, height: 24' (7.3 m). Philip A. Hart Plaza, Detroit, Michigan. Courtesy Balthazar Korab Ltd.

Art of Polynesia

Oceania

Global Glance

The term *Polynesia* comes from the Greek *polus* (many) and *nesos* (island). The waters of the South Pacific Ocean surround thousands of diverse and isolated islands. The South Pacific Rim, as it is sometimes called, includes six major cultures. One of these cultures is Polynesia.

Polynesia is a vast triangle about 5000 miles along each side with corners at New Zealand, Hawaii, and Easter Island. Tahiti, in the Society Islands, marks the geographic center of Polynesia. Polynesian art reflects the people of the South Pacific. Many of these people were explorers who set out on unknown seas to find and settle new lands.

Fig. 3–19 **Carved relief patterns appear on all old clubs like this. The patterns in the lower half are different on each club. They probably identified the owners. What do you think the tattoos of the owner of this club might have looked like?** Marquesas Islands, *Head detail of war club,* late 18th century. Hardwood, length: 63" (160 cm). Peabody Essex Museum, Salem, Massachusetts.

Fig. 3–20 The Hawaiians, who originally came from the Marquesas and Society islands, crafted beautiful objects, including spectacular featherworks. Men and women of the privileged noble class wore feather capes such as this one. Why might feathers have symbolized importance in this community? Hawaii, *Starbuck Cape,* ca. 1824. Red, yellow, and black feathers, length 16.5" x front 14.5" x neck 21.5" x base 85" (42 x 36.8 x 54.6 x 216 cm). Courtesy Bishop Museum, Seth Joel.

Art and Community Life

People around the world have different ways of showing that they belong to a community. Many have also found ways to show their status, or importance, in that community. In the South Pacific region, people show their importance through the objects they use and things they give to others.

Much of the art in Polynesia is created for ceremonial use. Decorations can symbolize a person's status or identity. In some island cultures, people wear jewelry and body tattoos to show identity and status. Figure 3–19 shows the head of a war club from the Marquesas Islands. Notice its tattoo pattern. This pattern identifies the owner of the club.

Traditionally, the quality and craftsmanship of a Polynesian man's weapons, clothing, and tattoos reflected his place in the community. So did the size and height of his house. Women didn't have as much need for status symbols. However, if they owned certain fans and ornaments, they were important in the community.

Polynesian artworks were originally made from natural materials without the use of metal tools. Local materials such as raffia, bark cloth, tusks, shells, and feathers are often combined in dramatic ways. Look at the Hawaiian feather cape in Fig. 3–20. Feathers are highly valued in Hawaiian culture. Feather capes were one way people showed that they belonged to this community.

Studio Connection

Make a list of your characteristics. What's your astrological sign? What talents do you have? What are your favorite things? Think about yourself as a shape, a color, a line, a flower, an insect, or an animal. Plan a cut-paper collage in the form of a manuscript page with figures and a patterned background. Use colored and textured papers to create a collage that teaches others something about yourself.

Fig. 3–21 **Precise tattoo markings on the face show that Raharuhi Rukupo, the man in the sculpture, belongs to the Maori community. What else might the tattoo pattern say about him?** New Zealand, Gisborne, Manutuke, *Carved figure of Raharuhi Rukupo,* from the carved house Te Hau ki Turanga, ca. 1835–42.
Wood, red and black paint, and paua shell, 42 ⅛" (107 cm). Photography Museum of New Zealand Te Papa Tongarewa, Wellington, New Zealand. (B.15448)

Fig. 3–22 **There are two masks at the peak of this house. Where else do you see masks?** Maori, New Zealand, *Maori Meeting House,* 1881. 56'x 22'(17 cm x 6.7 m). The Field Museum of Natural Histroy, Chicago, Illinois. (# A11518C)

Maori Master Carvers

Some areas of Polynesia are famous for artworks created in particular art forms. The Maori of New Zealand are excellent carvers. A great master carver is called *tohunga,* meaning craftsman-priest. Tohungas have high social rank and special status in the community.

Some of the most spectacular works by tohungas are prow and stern ornaments used to decorate their canoes. Notice the open spiral **motif**, or pattern, that is skillfully carved on the example in Fig. 3–23. These elegant and open shapes help the canoes move swiftly through water.

Master carvers are also skilled at carving house decorations. Among the Maori, houses indicates the status of their owners. The size, height, and decoration of the house are related to the owner's importance in the community. The wood carving in

Fig. 3–21, for example, portrays the carving master Raharuhi Rukupo, who built the ceremonial house in which the sculpture is located.

All houses of importance have a name and are highly respected as symbols of living beings. Community meeting houses, in particular, are symbolic of a community ancestor. The ridge beam of the house represents the ancestor's backbone, and the rafters stand for his ribs. The face boards on the front of the house represent his outstretched arms. A mask at the peak of the face boards symbolizes his face. Notice the many pairs of eyes on the Maori house shown here (Fig. 3–22). What might they symbolize?

Studio Connection

How can you create a richly patterned design that symbolizes your membership in a group or community? Think of all the communities you belong to. Select one and design a motif that represents your membership. Cut a stencil from tag board or stencil paper. You can use both positive and negative stencils. Try outlining and decorating a repeated pattern on paper. Try different ways of repeating the basic pattern. Think about various ways you can use your motif: on a skateboard, as a backpack label, or stitched onto a shirt or jacket.

3.3 Global View

Check Your Understanding

1. How does Polynesian art show ways that people belong to their communities?
2. What kinds of materials are used by artists in the South Pacific island groups?
3. What do tattoo patterns symbolize?
4. What is a tohunga?

Carving a Plaster Maquette

Teaching with Symbols

Studio Introduction

Imagine building a monument or sculpture to honor a special event, person, or group within your community. Where might such a sculpture stand? How big might it be? What materials could you use to create it?

Traditionally, large sculptures are carved from stone or wood. Artists must plan their sculptures carefully before they actually create them. They sketch their ideas first and often make small-scale models, called **maquettes**, of the larger sculpture. **In this studio lesson, you will carve a plaster maquette for a large sculpture that honors an event, person, or group in your community.** Pages 140 and 141 will tell you how to do it.

Visit a large sculpture or monument that already exists in your town or city. Spend some time walking around it. Look at every side of the sculpture and notice how each side flows into the next. When you think about your own sculpture, imagine it from every side.

Studio Background

Planning Large Sculpture

Carving and cutting are called *subtractive processes* in sculpture, because you take away material with cutting tools. Large monuments and sculptures are often carved from blocks of stone or wood. Sometimes they are cut from cast metal. The planks of wood and corrugated iron works used to create *City to Sea Bridge* (Fig. 3–24) were shaped with tools before they were assembled.

Fig. 3–24 **This contemporary sculpture in New Zealand includes the forms of birds, a whale, and the ribs of a ship. Poles bearing hearts and stars stand over these forms. How might these forms relate to life in this Maori community? What might the sculpture symbolize?** Paratene Matchitt, *City to Sea Bridge,* Wellington, New Zealand, 1993.
Museum of New Zealand Te Papa Tongarewa. Photograph by Michael Hall.

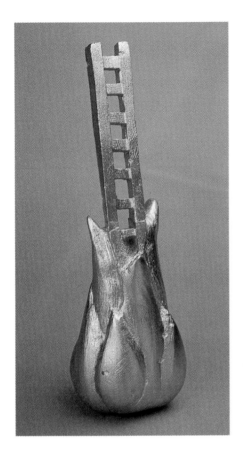

Fig 3–25 **In December, 1999, a tragic fire in Worcester, Massachusetts, resulted in the death of six firemen. A procession to honor those men was seen across the country on television. The plaster maquettes in this lesson represent ideas for sculptures to honor the bravery of firemen everywhere.** Julian Wade, *Untitled*, 2000.
Plaster, gold spray paint, 9" (23 cm) high. Forest Grove Middle School, Worcester, Massachusetts.

Large sculptures must be carefully planned, because mistakes in carving or cutting are difficult or impossible to correct. Maquettes allow artists to try out and develop their ideas first. Artists carve maquettes from inexpensive material, such as plaster or Styrofoam™. Then they refer to their maquettes when they create the actual sculpture.

Artist Augustus Saint-Gaudens created many monuments in his lifetime. The *Robert Gould Shaw Memorial* (Fig. 3–4, page 123) in Boston, Massachusetts, is considered to be his finest work.

Fig. 3–26 **This maquette is called a sketch. How does this remind you of sketches you have made when planning a two-dimensional artwork?** Augustus Saint-Gaudens, *Maquette for the Robert Gould Shaw Memorial*, 1883.
Plaster, 15" x 16" (38.1 x 40.6 cm). U.S. Department of the Interior, National Park Service, Saint-Gaudens National Historic Site, Cornish, NH.

This monument of the Civil War honors African-American soldiers. How might the maquette for this monument (Fig. 3–26) have helped the artist shape his ideas?

Sculpture in the Studio
Carving Your Maquette

You Will Need

- sketch paper
- pencil
- waxed carton
- plastic bucket
- plaster powder
- rubber gloves and dust mask
- water
- carving tools
- paint and paintbrush

Safety Note

Always wear rubber gloves and a dust mask or respirator when mixing plaster. Wear protective goggles and a dust mask while carving plaster. Always carve away from your body. Hold the work securely.

Try This

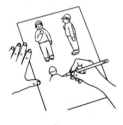

1. Sketch your ideas on paper. The idea for your sculpture must be suitable for carving. Think about a basic shape that you can use for your maquette. Imagine all sides of your sculpture and sketch each one. Keep your idea simple.

2. Cut a waxed container to the basic dimensions you want for your maquette. Will it be tall and thin? Or short and stout? What other dimensions can you think of?

3. Fill a plastic bucket about halfway with warm water. Sift the plaster powder through your fingers into the water until an island forms in the middle of the bucket. After a few minutes, stir the mixture slowly with your hand. Break up any lumps. If your mixture is too thick, add a little more water.

4. Pour the plaster into the prepared carton. Gently tap the carton to pop any air bubbles that may have formed. Let the plaster harden; then remove the carton.

5. Use a chisel to carve the rough forms first. Then use a rasp or file to smooth and define the edges of your forms. To carve small details, use a paint scraper or sandpaper. Remember that your sculpture will be seen from all sides. Every view should be interesting and flow into the next view. Work slowly and carefully. Look at your work often as you carve.

6. You might choose to paint your maquette. Imagine how a large sculpture made from your maquette would look. Choose colors that will best represent your subject.

Check Your Work

Display and discuss your work with your classmates. Are all sides of your work interesting? What does your sculpture tell about the event, person, or group that you wish to honor? What messages about your community's values and beliefs do the sculptures convey?

Sketchbook Connection

Study and draw the light and shadow areas of three-dimensional forms. Include different values or shades from white to black. How can you change the values gradually to suggest forms, textures, and space? Sharp contrasts in value will create a dramatic effect.

Computer Option

Use a 3-D program to create a model of a sculpture. Print out different angles or views of the sculpture, and then use the model as a reference for creating the sculpture in another medium.

Studio Collaboration

Work with your classmates. Use objects and materials found in your community to construct a monument representing your community. Your monument might be an assemblage made by attaching found materials to an armature or base. Or it might be planned as an installation.

Fig. 3–27 **"My artwork is a sculpture of an axe used by a fireman. Before I started carving, I brainstormed to come up with the idea. It was fun to make!"** A layer of gold spray paint gives the impression of a gold or bronze metal. What material would your sculpture be made of? Michael J. Gasperski, *Fireman Axe*, 2000. Plaster, gold spray paint, 6" (15 cm) high. Forest Grove Middle School, Worcester, Massachusetts.

Tips for Safe Carving

Students: If you are unsure about any of the tips listed below, ask your teacher for help.

• Learn how to use sharp tools properly.
• Make sure you are using the right tool for the job.
• Sharpen your tools, if necessary. Dull tools slip more easily and cause painful cuts.
• Hold or clamp your form tightly to prevent it from slipping as you work.
• Always carve away from your body. Keep your fingers and hands clear of the carving tool.
• Wear goggles to protect your eyes.
• Keep a safe distance from other students to avoid injury from flying chips.
• Properly clean and store tools when they are not in use.

Connect to...

Careers

Do you know who designed the Statue of Liberty? How do you think such monumental works are created? Frédéric-Auguste Bartholdi, one of the foremost sculptors in France in the late 1800s, designed Liberty Enlightening the World (Liberty's original name) and worked within a process still used by sculptors today. Like Bartholdi, most **sculptors** design a public work to fit a specific place for a particular purpose. Sculptors develop initial sketches into small-scale models, and then into larger fabrications. Sculptors need the services of many other people to complete monumental works. For instance, Bartholdi enlisted Gustave Eiffel to design Liberty's interior structure, and he employed a legion of workers to build, pack, ship, unpack, and install Liberty.

STATUE OF LIBERTY.—VIEWS SHOWING THE METHOD OF ERECTION AND PRESENT CONDITION OF THE WORK.—[See page 100.]

Fig. 3–28 **Sculptors often have many details to work out when creating "site-specific" sculptures. To help them find potential problems, many build small-scale models first before undertaking the final sculpture.** *Statue of Liberty Under Construction,* 1886.
Illustration from "The Scientific American," August 14, 1886. Courtesy the Statue of Liberty National Monument, New York.

Other Arts

Dance

Like art, **dance can also tell about communities** of many cultures and periods. Through dance, we can explore who we are and the communities we belong to.

Dance can represent different aspects of belonging to a community. For instance, an Italian tarantella, during a wedding celebration, is sometimes performed by the older women of the community as a way to honor the newlyweds. Dance can define membership in a specific generation: young people of the 1920s danced the Charleston; those of the 1930s through the 1950s danced the jitterbug. Dance can educate people about a community: during Native American powwows, both younger members of the community and outsiders can learn certain cultural traditions through dance.

Fig. 3–29 **The Native-American powwow is a celebration of culture and shared history. You can see many different styles of dance at a powwow. Each dance has special regalia (costumes) that the dancers wear and often make themselves.** Native American, Pueblo (New Mexico), *Deer Dancers Inter-tribal Ceremony.*
Courtesy Davis Art Slides.

Choreographers combine dance elements (time, the body, space, and energy), and sometimes music and costumes, to communicate a message symbolically. If you were to create a dance that defined your generation, what would it look like?

Language Arts

Do you think **Parson Weems's Fable** *(see page 126)* is based on fact or fiction? Grant Wood painted it in 1939, during the Great Depression, to "help awaken interest in the cherry tree and other bits of **American folklore** that are too good to lose." *Parson Weems's Fable* was the first painting in a series of American myths and stories the artist wanted to create. Wood had planned the second painting to be the legend of Pocahontas, but he died before he could produce it. Why, do you think, did the artist show Parson Weems pulling back a curtain? What do you think George's father is saying? Why, do you think, did Wood put the head of the adult George Washington on the body of a young boy?

Science

Do you know the biological classification to which human beings belong? Thanks to Carl Linnaeus, a Swedish botanist who lived from 1707 to 1778, the modern scientific world still benefits from his **biological classification system** of plants and animals. Linnaeus developed binomial nomenclature, in which each species

Fig. 3–30 **Notice details this botanical artist includes in her paintings of flowers. She also has a background in biology, or the study of plant and animal life. How do you think this knowledge helps her in her art?** Carol Wickenhiser-Schaudt, *Blc. Malworth D'or "Pinkie" (Hybrid Orchid),* 1992. Transparent and iridescent watercolor on paper, 28" x 35" (71.1 x 89 cm). ©1992 Carol Wickenhiser-Schaudt. Courtesy the artist.

has a two-term biological name. The terms are in Latin, the universal language of science. The first term identifies the genus or class to which a living thing belongs; the second term names the species itself. In part because Linnaeus classified plants by their flowers and system of reproduction, botanical illustrators began to create more realistic and accurate drawings, depicting all parts of a plant, including the stalk, leaf, flower, fruit, and seed.

Daily Life

To which groups do you belong? Do you belong to school groups? Religious groups? Community groups? Do you think that you relate well to different generations? Or are you more comfortable being with friends your own age? Young people have an extraordinary impact on popular culture today, but the word teenager was not established in print until about 1941. In earlier times, adults paid little attention to the stage between childhood and adulthood. As a result, teenagers were usually treated like adults. With both good and bad results, teens made their own decisions. Do you think being a teenager is difficult today? For many teens, school can be very isolating and alienating. How might others help teenagers feel that they belong—in their family, in school, and in the community?

Internet Connection
For more activities related to this chapter, go to the Davis website at **www.davis-art.com.**

Portfolio

"I did this for my grandmother because she is always so happy when she can see my drawings." **Aaron Mast**

Fig. 3–31 Aaron Mast, *Proverbs 31:28* (Fraktur), 1998. Watercolor, ink, 11 1/2" x 14 1/2" (29 x 37 cm). Penn View Christian School, Souderton, Pennsylvania.

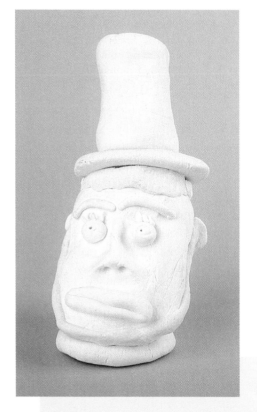

"I was thinking about Abraham Lincoln giving his speech. There were some parts that were easy. The difficult parts were the eyes and the beard. I like that he looks alive." **Julian Wade**

Fig. 3–32 **A portrait doesn't need to be 100 percent realistic to convey the identity of the subject. This work is more like a caricature.** Julian Wade, *Abraham Lincoln,* 1999. Clay, 5 1/2" (14 cm) high. Forest Grove Middle School, Worcester, Massachusetts.

Fig. 3–33 **Belonging can be expressed through a sport, club, or body image. What is important to this artist?** Tyrone Nixon, *Gym Workout,* 1999. Crayon, 12" x 18" (30.5 x 46 cm). Johnakin Middle School, Marion, South Carolina.

CD-ROM Connection
To see more student art, check out the Community Connection Student Gallery.

Chapter 3 Review

Recall

Identify the characteristics of sculpture and the common materials and methods used in making sculpture.

Understand

Explain, using examples, how some artworks remind people that they belong to a community.

Apply

Suppose that the school administration asks students to submit suggestions for ways to create a stronger spirit of community within the school. How might you respond to this request? Make sure that your suggestion demonstrates what you know about how art can promote a sense of belonging.

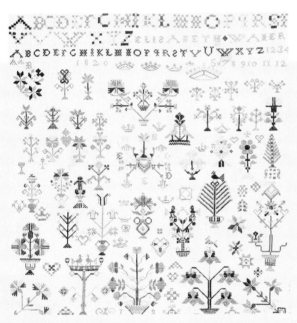

Page 131

Analyze

Select one artwork from the chapter (*see example below*) and tell how its parts are organized to convey an important idea about belonging to a community.

Synthesize

Imagine that you have been asked by a local community group such as an athletic team or a scouting organization to help them brainstorm ideas for a sculpture. They want the sculpture to communicate the ideals and beliefs of their group. What questions would you ask the group members to help them get ideas?

Evaluate

Which do you think would be a better way to communicate what it means to belong to a school community—school uniforms or a sculpture placed in the school lobby? Why?

For Your Portfolio

Look through this chapter and select one artwork from the past. Write a two-part essay. In the first part, describe the work with careful attention to detail. In the second part, summarize how this artwork suggests group membership and ideals. Write your name and date your essay to include in your portfolio.

For Your Sketchbook

Design a page in your sketchbook for generating a list of words that are associated with belonging: words that describe friendship, responsibility, loyalty, ownership, for example. Create visual symbols, or icons, for each of these words.

Connecting to Place

Fig. 4–1 Imagine seeing this gateway, with its sculpted features and decorative tiles. Now imagine designing a gateway to your own town or city. What features would you include to remind people of its history? Andrew Leicester, *Cincinnati Gateway,* 1988. Bronze, steel cast iron, polychrome masonry, stone, water and plant materials 480' x 145' x 65' (146.3 x 44.2 x 20 m). Sawyer Point Park, Cincinnati, Ohio. Photo copyright Andrew Leicester.

Cincinnati Gateway (detail).

Every place has a history. Think about one of your favorite places—maybe a park, a library, or a farm. Who were the people who created that place? What did they do there? How did they feel about the place? There are many ways for you to find out. Artworks can often provide some of the clues.

The people of Cincinnati, Ohio, asked artist Andrew Leicester to create an entrance to Sawyer Point Park, a downtown riverfront park. The artist learned as much as he could about the city's history and the Ohio Valley in which it is located. The completed gateway includes tall riverboat smokestacks topped with sculpted winged pigs. These forms refer to the city's history as a river port and a major producer of pork. The artist also learned that groups of Native Americans once lived where Cincinnati is built. As a reminder of this, he created a wall that includes glazed ceramic "fossils" and reproductions of Native American artifacts found in the Ohio Valley.

Cincinnati Gateway (Fig. 4–1) inspires new ways to think about the city's history. This lighthearted entrance to a riverside park tells all who visit that special places have stories to tell about their past.

What's Ahead

- **Core Lesson** Learn how art celebrates community places and spaces.
- **4.1 Art History Lesson** Discover how mid-nineteenth-century artists recorded the expansion of the United States.
- **4.2 Forms and Media Lesson** Explore ways that artists create the illusion of space in drawings.
- **4.3 Global View Lesson** Learn about Japanese respect for places in nature and the role of art in Japan.
- **4.4 Studio Lesson** Make a pastel drawing of a special place using perspective techniques to show space and distance.

Words to Know

memorial	linear perspective
document	ukiyo-e
Romantic style	two-point perspective
Realistic style	

Common Places

People need places for public meetings, shopping, entertainment, and community celebrations. Artists and architects design and create places such as plazas, town squares, shopping malls, gardens, parks, and cultural centers. Sometimes, the places they design become famous and symbolize the community. The Sydney Opera House (Fig. 4–2) is a cultural center for the performing arts. Does it look familiar to you? It has come to represent the city of Sydney, Australia, much like the Eiffel Tower represents Paris, France, and the Golden Gate Bridge represents San Francisco, California.

Fig. 4–2 Joern Utzon, a Danish architect, designed the Opera House to blend in with Sydney Harbor. The curved roofs look like the sails of boats. What special meaning might the design of the roof have for the residents of Sydney, Australia? Joern Utzon, *Sydney Opera House,* 1973.
Courtesy Woodfin Camp.

Fig. 4–3 Saul Steinberg is known for his humorous style. His drawing is not of a Main Street in a particular place. The title suggests that this is a place where people meet and lots of action takes place. How has the artist used lines to show action in this artwork? Saul Steinberg, *Main Street,* 1972–73.
Lithograph, printed in color, 15 3/4" x 22" (40 x 56 cm). The Museum of Modern Art, New York. Gift of Celeste Bartos. Photograph © 1999 The Museum of Modern Art, New York. © 2000 Estate of Saul Steinberg / Artist Rights Society (ARS), New York.

A Place Called Main Street

Most towns and cities grew up around a place where people gathered to exchange goods and ideas. This central place may have been a crossroads, general store, trading post, or railroad station. It may have been wharves or docks along rivers or seacoasts. Most towns have a "Main" Street, the first street that grew up with the town. Some of the oldest buildings in a town or city might still stand on this first street. What was the first street in your city or town?

When we think of a town or city, we think of its center. Many postcards feature photos of Main Street to show the life and personality of a place. When drawing or painting an image of a city or town, artists often show its center because that's where things happen and people gather.

Fig. 4–4 **The Main Street that Walt Disney designed resembles the main streets found in most small towns in late nineteenth-century America. How does Disney's Main Street look like the main street in your town or city?** *Panoramic view of Main Street, U.S.A.,* in the Magic Kingdom Park at the Walt Disney World Resort.
© Disney Enterprises, Inc.

Showing Places in New Ways

People tend to mark places that mean something to them. Sometimes they erect **memorials**—artworks or other objects that help people remember where important events took place or where famous individuals lived. People have also marked burial sites throughout history. Artists all over the world create grave markers, memorials, and other kinds of artworks that celebrate special places. By doing so, they help people remember the history and significance of these places.

Artists look at our communities carefully, then show us new ways to see them. They think about what makes a place unique and interesting, and use their ideas to create artworks. Andrew Leicester created *Cincinnati Gateway* (Fig. 4–1, page 146) to provide the people of Cincinnati with a historic view of their city.

Artists also make paintings, drawings, prints, and photographs of places. Sometimes, they show what is most common about the place. Wayne Thiebaud's *Downgrade* (Fig. 4–5) shows a steep hill, a landscape feature that is common in the San Francisco Bay area. Thiebaud uses the San Francisco area as subject matter for many of his artworks. In

Downtown (Fig. 4–7), California artist Frank Romero highlights the importance of cars and freeways in the Los Angeles area.

We often think that photographers show us things exactly as they look in real life. But photographers also show us certain views to express ideas about the places they photograph. Berenice Abbott spent several years photographing the city of New York. Sometimes, she photographed New York City from the air at night or during different times of the day. Other times, she focused on details of buildings and bridges. How did she call attention to the awesome strength and size of a city bridge in Fig. 4–6?

Fig. 4–5 **The artist has exaggerated certain parts of this artwork to highlight landscape features of the San Francisco Bay area. How has he used line to convey the idea of a place with long, steep hills?** Wayne Thiebaud, *Downgrade*, 1979. Aquatint and watercolor over hard-ground etching, 20" x 30" (50.8 x 76.2 cm). Image courtesy the Campbell-Thiebaud Gallery, San Francisco, CA. © Wayne Thiebaud/Licensed by VAGA, New York, NY.

Fig. 4–6 In crowded cities, people often look up to the sky to feel a sense of space in their environment. How does this artist capture the feeling of great space in Manhattan? Berenice Abbott, *Walkway, Manhattan Bridge, New York,* 1936.
Silver gelatin print. Museum of the City of New York.

Fig. 4–7 California is known for its many cars and freeways. It was the first state to have drive-through banks, restaurants, and even funeral parlors. In what ways does the artist capture the spirit of Los Angeles? Frank Romero, *Downtown,* 1990.
Oil on linen, 24" x 48" (61 x 121.9 cm). Courtesy of the artist.

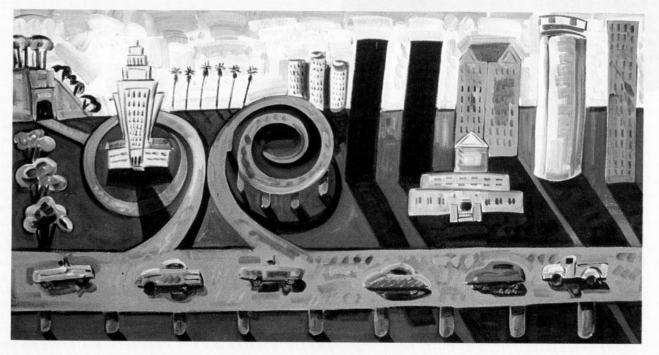

Drawing a Town Center

Think about the center of your town or city. What buildings, streets, parks, and plazas are there? Is your town or city the birthplace of someone famous? Is it known as a vacation resort or place of industry?

In this studio experience, you will create a drawing that shows why your town or city center is special. Decide whether you will include many buildings or just one. Perhaps instead you will focus on an interesting detail, such as a window, sign, doorstep, or chimney. Draw the feature of your town or city that you think expresses why it is special.

You Will Need

- viewfinder
- sketch paper
- pencil
- eraser
- drawing paper

Try This

1. Choose a scene or object that expresses why your town or city is special. Then choose a viewpoint from which to create your drawing. Will you show your subject up close or far away? Use a viewfinder to help you, if you wish.

2. Sketch your ideas. Experiment with different lines and ways to make marks. Think about which marks will work best in your drawing.

3. When you are happy with your sketch, begin your final drawing on drawing paper. Draw the largest shapes first. Then add details and shading.

Check Your Work

Display your drawing. How did you use subject matter, viewpoint, and marks to express why your town or city is special? Talk to your classmates about their drawings. What do all of your drawings together say about your town or city?

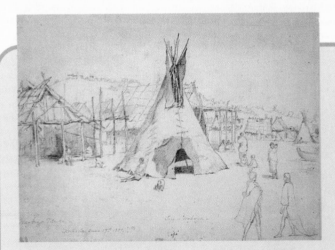

Fig. 4–8 Notice how this artist has used simple marks and lines to show a quiet scene. How many different effects has he created with pencil? How would you describe the textures you see? Blackwell Meyer, *Treaty Site of Traverse des Sioux,* 1851. Pencil drawing, 10" x 13" (25.4 x 33 cm). Edward E. Ayer Collection, The Newberry Library, Chicago.

Studio Background

Making Marks

Drawing begins with making marks. The first marks were probably made long ago by people who scratched the dirt with sticks. You can use many different tools, such as pencils and crayons, to make marks on lots of different papers and other materials. Look at the way you make marks and decide what effects you like.

The objects shown in drawings don't have to look exactly like the real objects. Drawings have personality when certain parts are exaggerated or simplified. Look at the drawings in Figs. 4–8 and 4–9. How many different kinds of lines or marks have the artists used? How do the lines help us see what the artists saw?

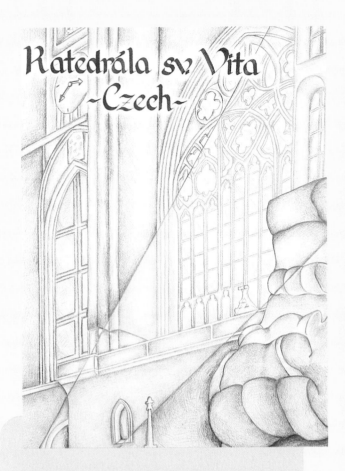

Kateðrála sv Víta
~Czech~

Fig. 4–9 **What features did this student explore in her artwork? How might you describe her viewpoint?** Erisa Dilo, *Katedrala sv. Vita*, 1998.
Colored pencil, calligraphy, 20" x 25 ¾" (51 x 65.5 cm). Burncoat School, Worcester, Massachusetts.

Sketchbook Connection
Experiment with making marks on paper. Use different media, such as crayons, markers, pastels, pencils, pens, and paint. Try using the tips and sides of different media. What kinds of lines can you make? How might you use lines to show texture? Practice shading with the different media. Which medium do you feel most comfortable using? Why?

Core Lesson 4

Check Your Understanding
1. What are some kinds of places that artists and architects create for people in communities to use together?
2. Why is the main street of a town important?
3. What kinds of artworks might mark a place as having a special meaning in a community?
4. Why might an artist make an artwork that shows a close-up view of a place?

Fig. 4–10 **This artist has created a detailed ink drawing of a city street. How does the quality of this drawing compare to the quality of *Treaty Site of Traverse des Sioux* (Fig. 4–8), which was drawn in pencil?** David Schofield, *Wooster Street, North of Canal*, 1997.
Ink on parchment. 36" x 108" (91.4 x 274.3 cm). Courtesy Gallery Henoch.

The Majesty of Place: 1820–1860

1851
Duncanson, *Blue Hole*

CA. 1880–90
Homestead

American Neoclassicism
page 128

Realism and Romanticism in America

Late 19th Century
page 180

1849
Durand, *Kindred Spirits*

CA. 1859
Bierstadt, *Wolf River*

History in a Nutshell

Between 1820 and 1860, the United States grew rapidly in size. Many individuals became wealthy very quickly, but a population of poor people also developed. Communities began to group people into upper or lower classes based on the level of their wealth. Some of the poor moved west to search for their own fortunes. This search for a better life often led to conflict between settlers and Native-American cultures.

Documenting Place

The period between 1820 and 1860 was a time of discovery and exploration for artists in the United States. Much of the North American landscape was still unknown. Yet artists set out to **document**, or record, the place they now called home. They also looked at how artists in Europe were documenting places.

Two major styles of art—Romanticism and Realism—influenced the way American artists created pictures. Art in the **Romantic style** shows foreign or exotic places, myths and legends, and imaginary events. Art in the **Realistic style** shows people, scenes, and events of the artist's own time. Realistic artworks show their subjects clearly, much like the way we see them. American artists blended the two styles. In this way, they tried to show an accurate view of the landscape, yet still inspire a sense of awe.

Photography also influenced American art at this time. It offered yet another way to document places and events. It changed the way artists thought about realism in painting. It also helped set the stage for new styles of painting in the twentieth century.

One new style of painting was developed by a group of American artists known as the Hudson River School. These artists were inspired by the beauty and majesty of the landscapes around them. Many artists traveled west and painted the unknown American landscape. Their artworks document the settlement of western territories (Figs. 4–11 and 4–12).

Fig. 4–11 **Midwestern landscapes, such as this one, encouraged people to visit or move to places west of the Appalachian Mountains. How does this painting call attention to the grandeur and majesty of the landscape?** Robert Scott Duncanson (1821–72), *Blue Hole, Little Miami River,* 1851.
Oil on canvas, 28 1/2" x 41 1/2" (72.4 x 105.4 cm). Cincinnati Art Museum, Gift of Norbert Heerman and Arthur Helbig 1926.18

Fig. 4–12 **What details suggest that this was a relatively new homestead at the time this painting was created? Why might viewers of the time have been interested in this painting?** Sally Cover, *Homestead of Ellsworth L. Ball,* ca. 1880–90.
Oil on canvas, 19 1/2" x 23" (49.5 x 58.4 cm.) Museum of Nebraska History Collections.

Wilderness Places

Do you know where the Hudson River is? Find the state of New York on a map, and you'll see the river moving south from Canada to New York City. The Hudson River Valley is rich in natural beauty and history. It is the area in which fables and folklore, such as Washington Irving's *The Legend of Sleepy Hollow*, take place.

Perhaps you have seen paintings such as those in Figs. 4–13 and 4–14. A group of nineteenth-century artists painted scenes of the Hudson River Valley and Catskill Mountains. These paintings show us the artists' view of the scenery there. The Hudson River Valley area was easy to get to from New York City, where the group frequently gathered and exhibited their work. They called themselves the Hudson River School.

Artists of the Hudson River School strongly believed in the ideals of their country. They wanted to show everyone the beauty of the United States. This nationalistic spirit led them to explore and document wilderness places throughout North America. Their romantic paintings were inspired by nature. They provided national images of majestic landscapes and community centers that most people in the nation recognize.

In what parts of the country were the paintings shown here painted? How can you tell? Do they make you feel proud to be a citizen of this country? Why?

Fig. 4–13 The poet William Cullen Bryant and the painter Thomas Cole are seen here enjoying a breathtaking scene. If you were standing where they are, how would you feel? Does this painting have that kind of feeling? Why do you think so? Asher Brown Durand (1796–1886), *Kindred Spirits*, 1849. Oil on canvas, 3' 8" x 3' (112 x 91 cm). Collection of The New York Public Library, Astor, Lenox and Tilden Foundations.

Studio Connection

Create a realistic painting of a place you know very well. Try to capture what you think is beautiful about this place.

Look carefully at it and note details that others might miss at first glance. Sketch your composition. When you are ready to paint, use light and dull colors to create the largest background areas first. As you work toward the foreground, brighten your colors and add more details.

4.1 Art History

Check Your Understanding

1. What art styles influenced the way American artists interpreted place in the early nineteenth century?
2. What impact did early photography have on the way artists documented place?
3. How did art affect the geographical expansion of North American communities?
4. What kinds of places did the Hudson River School explore for sources of subject matter?

Fig. 4–14 Albert Bierstadt painted romantic pictures of the West. His paintings tempted many people to move from New York City to the western wilderness. Do you think this painting is romantic? Why? Albert Bierstadt, *The Wolf River, Kansas,* ca.1859.
Oil on canvas, 48 1/4" x 38 1/4" (122.6 x 97.2 cm.) Founders Society Purchase, Dexter M. Ferry, Jr. Fund. Photograph © 1987 The Detroit Institute of Arts.

Connecting to Place

Perspective Drawing

Fig. 4–15 **Where do you see changes in line quality in this painting? How does Audubon use line and value to create mood?** John James Audubon, *Mallard* (Anas Playyrhynchos), ca. 1821–25.
Watercolor, graphite, pastel, collage, selective glazing, metallic paint on paper, 25 5/8" x 38 1/4" (65.2 x 97.2 cm.) Collection of the New York Historical Society (1863.17.221).

Drawing is a way to record your ideas, impressions, and feelings about spaces and places. You have probably noticed that most drawings are created with lines and shapes. You can learn to create mood in your drawings by experimenting with lines and shapes.

When you draw lines, hold your pencil in different positions, such as straight up and down, or with the lead on its side. As you draw, try shifting your lines from long to short, wide to thin, rough to smooth, or straight to curved. Notice how a change in line quality can create a change in mood. Next, experiment with shapes. Draw some geometric shapes, such as circles, squares, and triangles. Then draw some organic

shapes, such as leaves, raindrops, or other shapes in nature. What feelings does each group of shapes suggest?

Now, try shading your shapes to make them look three-dimensional. *Shading* is a gradual change in value from dark to light. Notice how use of shading can change the mood of a drawing. You can also use shading to create *texture*—the way something feels to the touch.

Creating the Illusion of Space

As you know, drawings are two-dimensional. You can use perspective techniques to create the illusion of space in drawings and other two-dimensional artworks. For instance, when you overlap shapes, the shapes on the top will appear closer than the other shapes. Draw the shapes that are close up larger than those that are farther away. Also, use brighter colors and more detail in your foreground shapes than the background shapes.

You can also try using **linear perspective** to create the illusion of space. Place a *horizon line*—the line where the earth seems to end and the sky begins—high, low, or in the middle of the paper. Choose one or more points along the line as *vanishing points*. Then draw shapes that recede to the vanishing points.

See pages 166 and 167 for diagrams and more information about perspective.

Studio Connection

Think about animals that live in their own communities. Make a drawing of insects or animals in an underground or underwater environment. Use perspective techniques to create an illusion of space. What will be in the foreground and background of your drawing? Think about where your horizon line will be. Draw a horizon line that will help you create the point of view you want to show. Use linear perspective to make your drawing realistic.

4.2 Forms and Media

Check Your Understanding
1. Identify two ways to change the mood of a drawing.
2. Explain how drawings can show the illusion of space.

Fig. 4–16 **This artist has used at least three methods of perspective. Can you name them and point to examples?** Anonymous, *Coral Reef,* 2000.
Digital 3-D image. Courtesy of the artist.

Japanese Places in Art

Global Glance

Japan is an island country in the Pacific Ocean. The four large islands and many smaller ones that make up Japan are spread out over 1300 miles of ocean. The islands lie along the northeastern coast of Asia and face Russia, Korea, and China. Because of the country's location along major trade routes, Japan's culture has been influenced by Korea, China, the South Pacific, Europe, and the Americas. The Japanese have adapted these influences into a unique artistic style that reflects Japanese culture.

Japan

China
Russia
North Korea
South Korea
Japan
Tokyo (Edo)
Mt. Fuji
Kyoto

A Place in the Sun

Japan is called the "Land of the Rising Sun." The country's flag is a red sun on a white field. Images of the sun, sea, sky, and mountains have always appeared in Japanese art. Japanese artists have a deep respect for nature. They are especially aware of the beauty of places and spaces around them. The places in their art may be the sites of historical events, beautiful views, or places written about in poetry.

The Japanese are well known for their painted scrolls and folding screens, and for their woodblock prints. The pair of six-panel screens in Fig. 4–17 show the four seasons. Screens such as these provide people with a way to bring nature into the home.

Fig. 4–17 Can you see where one season fades into the next?
Sesson Suikei, *Landscape of Four Seasons,* Muromachi period, 16th century.
Ink and light colors on paper (one of pair of six-panel screens), 61 3/8" x 133 1/4" (155.9 x 338.4 cm). Gift of the Joseph and Helen Regenstein Foundation, right side of pair - 1958.167, left side of pair -1958.168. Photograph courtesy The Art Institute of Chicago.

Fig. 4–18 **What qualities of a Japanese landscape do you see in this print? Where do you see patterns?** Sakino Hokusai IITSU, *Fukagawa Mannembashi*, from 36 Views of Mt. Fuji, 1830.
Multiple block wood blockprint, 10 1/4" x 15" (26 x 38 cm). Courtesy The Japan Ukiyo-e Museum.

Fig. 4–19 **What details suggest that the village shown in this print is rural? What mood is expressed by the composition? Why do you think so?** Utagawa Hiroshige, *Night Snow at Kambara* (from the series Fifty-Three Stations on the Tokaido), ca. 1833.
Woodblock print, 9 1/2" x 14 1/2" (24.1 x 36.8 cm). Clarence Buchingham Collection, 1925.3517. Photograph courtesy The Art Institute of Chicago.

Prints of Places

The Japanese made woodblock prints as early as the eighth century. Color prints from woodblocks appeared in the seventeenth century. In the nineteenth century, Japanese landscape and nature prints influenced many artists in Europe and the United States. Western artists were interested in the lines, flat spaces, asymmetry, and close-up views shown in the images.

Two Japanese printmakers of the mid-nineteenth century became masters of the style of woodcut known as **ukiyo-e** (oo-key-OH-eh). They created *folios*, or series, of art-works showing famous places in Japan. Many of Katsushika (Sakino) Hokusai's works show landscapes with clear patterns (Fig. 4–18). Ando (Utagawa) Hiroshige usually looked for rural places where men and women were at work (Fig. 4–19). Both artists tried to capture the moods of the scenic Japanese countryside. Ukiyo-e means "pictures of the floating world." The term refers to woodblock prints that show life in nineteenth-century Japan.

Ukiyo-e: Pictures of the Floating World

Artists Hokusai and Hiroshige brought ukiyo-e to the world's attention in the mid-nineteenth century. But the history of ukiyo-e began long before these two artists lived. In the seventeenth century, when Japan was ruled by a strict military government, merchants and artists had no power in society. The merchant class grew wealthy, but could not buy positions of power in Japan. Instead, they built their own communities centered around the pleasures of money, theater, and worldly possessions. The word *ukiyo*, meaning temporary or floating, was used to describe these communities. This way of life was frowned on by the ruling class.

Many ukiyo-e woodblock prints show life in the ukiyo-e communities. Japanese Kabuki theater was an important part of life there. The theaters needed prints to advertise their plays and actors. The popular themes and elaborate costuming of Kabuki drama made it a rich source of images for ukiyo-e artists.

Throughout the next two centuries, ukiyo-e became more and more accepted. Its subject matter began to include Japanese history, landscapes, and other natural images. Printing techniques also became more complex to allow the use of multiple colors. By the mid-nineteenth century, the woodcuts of ukiyo-e artists presented the world with a view of Japanese life.

Fig. 4–20 **How would you describe the glimpse of Japanese life that you see in this print? How has the artist created mood?** Torii Kiyotada, *Naka-no-cho Street of the Yoshiwara,* Edo period, ca. 1735. Handcolored woodblock print, 17" x 35 ¼" (43.2 x 89.5 cm). Clarence Buchingham Collection, 1939.2152. Photograph courtesy The Art Institute of Chicago.

Fig. 4–21 **This print shows the inside of a theater. How has the artist used line and pattern to create the feeling of busyness in this scene?** Okumura Masanobu, *Interior View of the Nakamura-za Theatre in Edo,* 1740. Handcolored woodblock print, 18 1/4" x 26 3/4" (46.3 x 67.9 cm). Clarence Buchingham Collection, 1925.2285. Photograph courtesy The Art Institute of Chicago.

Studio Connection

Create two relief prints that show different views of a special place in your community. You might choose to show the place in two different seasons, in different weather, or at different times of day.

Sketch your scenes on paper first, then transfer them to Styrofoam™ blocks. On the block, trace over the lines with a ballpoint pen, "carving away" areas that you do not want to print. Spread ink or paint onto the raised areas of the block. Carefully place a piece of paper over the inked block. Rub the back of the paper evenly. Carefully lift the print from the block. The raised areas of the block will have printed, and the carved-away areas will have remained the color of the paper. Repeat the process on the second block.

4.3 Global View

Check Your Understanding

1. How does the art of Japan show connections to place?
2. Who were two famous Japanese printmakers of the nineteenth century?
3. How did Japanese woodblock prints influence artists in the United States and Europe?
4. What can we learn about Japan from its ukiyo-e woodcuts?

Connecting to Place

Perspective in Pastels

A Postcard Scene

Studio Introduction

If you were asked to design a postcard that shows a special place, what place would you choose? What details and qualities of this place would you want to capture? Which method of creating space would you use? You might decide to combine any of the perspective techniques that are described in the next few pages. **In this studio lesson, you will draw a scene in linear perspective.** Pages 166 and 167 will show you how to do it. **Two-point perspective** is a method of creating the illusion of deep space on a flat surface. Artists who use two-point perspective start with a horizon line.

Studio Background

Postcard Tales

Why do you send postcards to your friends? Postcards let you show your friends a picture of where you are. The pictures on postcards are usually drawings, paintings, or photographs. They often show a popular scene or historical sight from a particular region. Sometimes, they document important events and inventions, such as world's fairs and first airplane flights.

Postcards first became popular at the beginning of the twentieth century. They allowed people to send short messages to family and friends without great expense. Many people collect old postcards, because they like their beautiful colors, special details, and historic value. Public libraries often have collections of postcards that show what local buildings, streets, and neighborhoods looked like in the past. These postcards (Figs. 4–24 and 4–25) are from Kansas City, Missouri. They show views of the same area twenty-five years apart. Perhaps your local library or historical society has old postcards or photographs of your town that you can examine.

Fig. 4–22 This artist created a drawing to help her remember a visit to Paris. Would this be a good image for a postcard? Why or why not? Linnea Pergola, *Le Consulat,* Fall 1998. Pastel, 16" x 20" (40.6 x 50.8 cm). Courtesy of the artist.

They place two vanishing points on the horizon line. If the lines that mark certain edges of objects are extended, those that seem to recede into the distance would meet at one of the vanishing points. Other receding lines would meet at the other vanishing point.

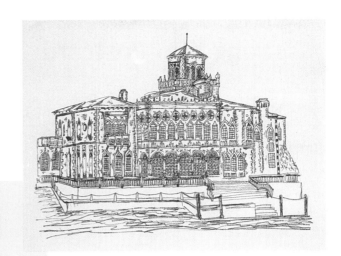

Fig. 4–23 **"This home is part of the Ringling Museum estate on Sarasota Bay. It is very beautiful, large, and elegant. The difficult thing about drawing this picture was all of the detail and perspective. It took a long time. I tried to show shading through lines."** Harrison Henke, *Ca'd'Zan*, 1999.
Pen, ink, 12" x 18" (30.5 x 46 cm). Laurel Nokomis School, Nokomis, Florida.

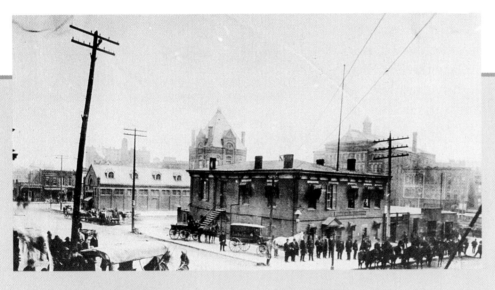

Fig. 4–24 **Compare this postcard to the one shown in Fig. 4–25. What similarities do you see? What differences do you see? Why might these two postcards be valuable for recording the history of Kansas City?** *Old City Hall and Police Station 4th and Main, Kansas City, MO*, 19th century.
Postcard. Special Collections, Kansas City Public Library, Kansas City, Missouri.

Fig. 4–25 **If you were visiting Kansas City, Missouri, in 1913, why might you have chosen this postcard to send to friends?** *The City Market, Kansas City, MO*, 1913.
Postcard. Special Collections, Kansas City Public Library, Kansas City, Missouri.

Drawing in the Studio
Creating Your Postcard

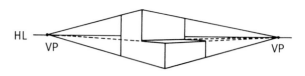

You Will Need

- pencil
- ruler
- erasers
- large white drawing paper
- pastels

Try This

1. Choose a special place that you would like to show on a postcard. The scene you choose should have objects in it that are up close and far away.

2. Decide whether you will draw the scene at eye level, or from above or below. Then figure out where you will place the horizon line (HL). Using a ruler, lightly draw the horizon line. Mark two vanishing points (VP) on it.

3. Sketch the shapes in your scene. The horizontal lines that recede into space should meet at a vanishing point. Fill the page with your drawing. What other methods of perspective can you use to create the illusion of space?

4. Add color to your drawing with pastels. Use bright bold colors for things that are up close. Use light dull colors to show things that are far away. Build up colors gradually and blend them with a tissue or cotton swab.

Fig. 4–26 **"I was looking through pictures of historical buildings, and the Carnegie Library seemed to stand out, so I chose to draw it. It was easy to do a basic sketch or outline of the library. The difficult part was painting the palm leaves."** Kara Nickell, *Carnegie Library*, 1999. Marker, 12" x 18" (30.5 x 46 cm). Laurel Nokomis School, Nokomis, Florida.

What special qualities of your place did you show? How did you use two-point perspective to show space? What other perspective techniques did you use?

Sketchbook Connection

Choose a simple object to draw. Use the object to create an example of each of the perspective techniques described in this lesson. Practice drawing some boxlike forms in linear perspective. Combine them with other forms such as cylinders.

Computer Option

Use a drawing program to create the skeleton of a landscape in one- or two-point perspective. Use lines and shapes to create a framework of buildings, roads, and so on. Group and copy all the elements. Copy and paste the group in a paint program. Paint over the outlines and fill in shapes with color. Consider the use of color and other elements to enhance depth. Think of ways to make your image look like a painting.

Perspective Techniques

Overlap: Draw near objects on top of or partly covering distant objects.

Placement: Place distant objects near the top of the picture. Place near objects at the bottom of the picture.

Linear perspective: Use the rules of linear perspective to draw objects that seem to disappear into the distance.

Focus: Draw sharper edges and more details on close objects. Draw distant objects with few details.

Size: Draw objects that are closer to the viewer larger than those that are farther away.

Color and value: Use light shades and dull colors to suggest distant features. Use bright colors in the foreground.

Foreshortening: Draw the nearest part of a form larger than the more distant parts.

Connect to...

FRAGMENT I.

ON

RURAL ARCHITECTURE.

NOTWITHSTANDING the numerous volumes on Grecian Architecture from the days of Vitruvius to the present time, to which may be added all that have appeared within the last century on the subject of Gothic Antiquities: little or no notice has been taken of the relative effects of the two styles, compared with each other; nor even of those leading principles by which they are to be distinguished, characterised, and appropriated to the scenery of nature. It would seem as if the whole science of Grecian Architecture consisted in the five orders of columns, and that of Gothic in pointed arches and notched battlements.

To explain this subject more clearly, and bring it before the eye more distinctly, I will refer to the following Plate,

B

Careers

What buildings in your community have beautiful grounds or gardens? Do you ever notice people working in these landscapes? Though many people like to do their own gardening at home, large institutions—such as office and apartment complexes, public and governmental agencies, banks, schools, and malls—employ **landscape architects** to design the surrounding outdoor space. Landscape architects prepare site plans and models, select plantings, and supervise implementation for such clients as building contractors, architectural firms, developers, and homeowners. These architects must be knowledgeable about art and design, botany and ecology, climate and weather, and architecture and building codes. What evidence can you find in your community of a landscape architect's work?

Fig. 4–27 **Designers, decorators, and artists often look in books for ideas, information, and inspiration. This nineteenth-century book gave designers ideas about landscape architecture, a popular art form at the time.** *An illustrated page from the* Fragments on the Theory and Practice of Landscape Gardening, 1816.
Photo by Philip de Bay. ©Historical Picture Archive/CORBIS.

Daily Life

Is there a particular place that your family thinks of as home? It might be your grandparents' apartment or a piece of land that has been in your family for generations. In simpler times, families stayed closer together and shared a sense of place—**a sense of home**. In our increasingly mobile society, family members are now more likely to be separated by distance and may not be able to see one another often. Is there a place to which you feel strongly connected? A place that feels like home? If so, why are you drawn to it?

Fig. 4–28 **Sometimes an artwork inspires a sense of community. This group of outdoor sculptures has come to symbolize the Los Angeles neighborhood of Watts where it was built. When the structures were in danger of being torn down, the community worked to stop the demolition.** Simon Rodia, *Watts Towers,* 1921–54.
Photograph ©Marvin Rand.

Internet Connection
For more activities related to this chapter, go to the Davis website at **www.davis-art.com.**

Fig. 4–29 **This artwork, painted in 1860, calls attention to the new technology of the railroad. How has the artist contrasted the uncomfortable, dusty ride of the covered wagon with the smooth travel of the train?** Thomas Otter, *On the Road*, 1860.
Oil on canvas, 22" x 45 3/8" (55.8 x 115.3 cm). The Nelson-Atkins Museum of Art, Kansas City, Missouri (Purchase: Nelson Trust).

Social Studies

Do you know what **Manifest Destiny** was? Manifest Destiny was a nineteenth-century political doctrine that promoted the belief that it was America's national destiny to spread over the entire continent, to control and populate the country while pushing aside the Native Americans and anyone else who got in the way. A number of artists played a role in westward expansion, by painting stereotypical images of Native Americans and other western subjects at the request of the railroads. The paintings were printed as posters and used back East to promote tourism—and, thereby, the use of trains. What ideas about Native Americans do you think these images promoted?

Language Arts

Why, do you think, are **landscapes** so popular? Are you drawn to these art forms? Look through this book to find landscapes that come from different times and cultures. Take a class vote for two of the landscapes. What similarities and differences can you identify? Are the two works more alike than they are different? Or vice versa? Which do you prefer? Why? How could you persuade someone else to agree with you?

Science

You may recall from science class that **biomes** are major ecological communities of plants and animals. The average rainfall and temperature determine the different biomes. There are eight terrestrial biomes: tundra, taiga/evergreen coniferous forest, temperate deciduous forest, temperate grasslands/prairie, desert, dry scrubland/chapparal, tropical grassland/savanna, and rain forest. Can you identify the biome for where you live?

Music

The identity of a culture is expressed through its music—its rhythms, melodies, and vocal styles. Certain instruments identify regions: Caribbean steel drums, Scottish and Irish bagpipes, Japanese bamboo flutes.

Beginning in the nineteenth century, many composers were inspired by nationalism, a sense of national identity, to write music that reflected their particular culture. Aaron Copland (1900–90) composed distinctively "American" music. Heitor Villa-Lobos

Fig. 4–30 **Aaron Copland was one of the great American composers. He also wrote several books on music and music appreciation.** Conductor Aaron Copland.
©Bettmann/CORBIS.

(1887–1959) wrote music infused with the folk and popular music of his native Brazil.

Portfolio

"My great-aunt lives in Denver, Colorado, and we got to visit there. I always think of the mountains and how pretty they are."
Jenna Skophammer

Fig. 4–31 **How has this artist used color and texture to create a mood?** Jenna Skophammer, *Denver, Colorado, View,* 1999.
Oil pastel, 12" x 18" (30.5 x 46 cm). Manson Northwest Webster, Barnum, Iowa.

Fig. 4–32 Keith Bush, *Deep Blue Sea,* 2000.
Markers, 16" diam. (40.5 cm). Sarasota Middle School, Sarasota, Florida.

"I was thinking about tropical fish. I thought of a clown fish—it's bright and looks cool. What I like most about my art is it is colorful and almost real." **Keith Bush**

"My teacher said that this would be a tough picture to do, but I knew that I could make it. The shading is the best part because it makes the house look realistic." **Marti Corn**

Fig. 4–33 **By observing detail, an artist becomes familiar with a place.** Marti Corn, *Architectural Creativity,* 1999.
Watercolor, marker, 18" x 24" (46 x 61 cm). Laurel Nokomis School, Nokomis, Florida.

CD-ROM Connection
To see more student art, check out the Community Connection Student Gallery.

Chapter 4 Review

Recall

Identify two artists whose artworks show the special features of community places.

Understand

How can a photograph that documents the way a place looks also send a message about its special features? *(See example below.)*

Apply

State at least one reason you could offer to try to convince community members to preserve the old buildings in your town center.

Page 165

Analyze

Select an artwork from this chapter and tell how art elements are used to tell about the special characteristics of a place. You might mention the use of color, line, shape, value, texture, form, and/or space.

Synthesize

Imagine that you are a member of the community group asked to select from proposals for a gateway to your town center. What criteria would you use to select the gateway design?

Evaluate

Select an artwork from this chapter and offer at least three reasons why you believe it is successful in conveying the special features of a place. Be sure to state reasons that are based on your careful use of your skills in describing, analyzing, and interpreting art.

For Your Portfolio
Select an artwork in this book that sends a clear message about place. Select one element from that artwork and incorporate it into your own artwork of a special place. Place this work in your portfolio. Include a photocopy of the artwork that inspired you and attach a short statement about why this detail appealed to you and how in contributed to your own artwork.

For Your Sketchbook
Fill a page with thumbnail sketches of gateways to special places and actual scenes that can be associated with human aspirations, such as opportunity, success, freedom, and the like.

Responding to Nature

Fig. 5–1 **Like other Inuit people, Kenojuak has seen many changes in her community because of the expanding modern world. As in other parts of the world, the environment in the northern arctic is in danger. What message about nature does her artwork convey?** Kenojuak Ashevak, *The World Around Me,* 1980.
Lithograph, 22 ¼" x 31 ⅛" (56.5 x 79 cm). © By permission of the West Baffin Eskimo Cooperative Lmtd, Cape Dorset, Numavut, Dorset Fine Arts, Indian and Northern Affairs Canada.

- How are communities affected by nature and its beauty?
- How does art call attention to natural beauty in the world?

Think about the ways nature affects your life. How does the weather influence your activities, the clothes you wear, and the food you eat? How do you relate to wild animals that live in your area? If you think about it, you'll realize that we are connected to nature in many ways. Throughout history, people around the world have made art to show their connection to nature. In artworks dating from the earliest times, nature is seen as powerful and, at times, even ruthless. Artists have also created artworks that show nature as a gentle and nurturing force. They have long used plants and animals as the main subjects of their work and as inspiration for decoration and design.

In *The World Around Me* (Fig. 5–1), Kenojuak Ashevak, an Inuit woman living in Cape Dorset in the Canadian arctic, shows an Inuit person surrounded by birds, fish, and trees. They symbolize this culture's closeness to nature. The Inuit people live in a harsh, frozen land. Animals are very important for their survival. People who live in places like Cape Dorset understand how much people depend on nature.

Today, people all over the world still witness nature's power and beauty in events such as earthquakes, hurricanes, and blizzards. Artworks send messages about nature's power and beauty. They tell us how nature affects our lives.

What's Ahead

- **Core Lesson** Learn how art helps people understand the power and beauty of nature.
- **5.1 Art History Lesson** Discover how nature inspired artists of the late nineteenth century.
- **5.2 Forms and Media Lesson** Explore ways that the work of graphic designers can send messages about nature.
- **5.3 Global View Lesson** Learn how Scandinavian art reflects these communities' connection with nature.
- **5.4 Studio Lesson** Make a relief sculpture that describes a natural environment.

Words to Know

scientific record	Art Nouveau
graphic designer	graphic design
Impressionist	relief sculpture

Natural Wonders

Nature's Power

Does nature sometimes frighten you? Even though we understand much about how nature works, nature's fury can still frighten people or spark their curiosity. Some people brave wind and rain to watch oceans launch huge waves over sea walls. Others tremble under the covers at night during thunderstorms.

Artworks from the past show the awesome power of nature. Ancient communities tried to understand tornadoes, volcanoes, and tidal waves through stories about gods and goddesses. Gods and goddesses often appear in artworks with the sun, moon, and other natural elements. Many artworks show animals with magical powers. For example, the Celtic Cernunnos (Fig. 5–2) is a mythical animal who could change its form. Why do you think this figure is called the stag god?

Investigating Nature

Have you ever watched a line of ants and wondered where they were going? Or have you ever wondered why moths fly around a bright light at night? Can you name the different kinds of clouds you see or the different kinds of trees and flowers in your yard or neighborhood? To learn about nature, you must look carefully and observe its characteristics and habits. Because people tend to be curious, they have looked carefully at natural things and tried to understand how nature works.

Artists help people investigate nature in different ways. People often ask artists to look closely at nature and make accurate **scientific records** of the plants and animals in their community. Other artists observe nature, then express their own ideas and feelings about it in their artworks. Which of the artworks in Figs. 5–3 and 5–4 is an example of scientific investigation? Which expresses more creative ideas?

Fig. 5–2 **Cernunnos, or The Horned One, was an ancient god of the Celtic people. He had ears and antlers of a stag and was thought to be lord of the beasts. He also could change into the form of a snake, wolf, or stag.** Celtic, Gundestrup cauldron, inner plate: *Cerrunnos holding a snake and a torque, surrounded by animals,* 1st century BC. Embossed silver, gilded. National Museum, Copenhagen, Denmark. Erich Lessing / Art Resource, NY.

Fig. 5–3 **Why might some people compare the quality of this painting to that of a photograph? How is the painting different from a photograph?** Martin Johnson Heade, *Cattleya Orchid and Three Brazilian Hummingbirds*, 1871.
Oil on wood, 13 ³/₄" x 18" (34.8 x 45.6 cm). Gift of The Morris and Gwendolyn Cafritz Foundation, © 1999 Board of Trustees, National Gallery of Art, Washington, DC.

Fig. 5–4 **Would you consider this artwork to be an example of a scientific record or an artistic expression of nature? Why?** Joe Walters, *Vignette #6* (butterfly, songbird), 1999.
Aluminum, mesh, polymer clay, resin, glue, sand, paint, 32" x 32" x 10" (81.3 x 81.3 x 25.4 cm). Courtesy Bernice Steinbaum Gallery, Miami, FL.

Natural Beauty

Even though people have feared the power of nature, they have also enjoyed the natural world for its beauty. They have looked for places in nature for quiet thought. Delicate flowers, brightly colored birds, and magnificent scenery have given people great pleasure for thousands of years. People have been inspired by the beauty of nature to write poetry and to capture views in paintings and other artworks.

Many artists find beauty in the natural environment near their homes. The seascape in Fig. 5–5 is by artist Fitz Hugh Lane. It shows a view of nature from a seaside community on Cape Ann in Massachusetts. In *Brace's Rock, Brace's Cove*, Lane captured the peaceful beauty of the rugged New England coastline where he lived.

Fig. 5–5 Many people go to places like the one shown here to sit quietly and enjoy the beauty of nature. Where would you go to enjoy nature? How would you show that place in a painting? Fitz Hugh Lane, *Brace's Rock, Brace's Cove,* 1864.
Oil on canvas, 10 1/4" x 15 1/4" (26 x 38.7 cm). Terra Foundation for the Arts, Daniel J. Terra Collection, 1999.83, Photograph courtesy Terra Museum of American Art, Chicago.

Fig. 5–6 **How is this artwork an expression of concern for the environment?** Agnes Denes, *Tree Mountain—A Living Time Capsule, 11,000 Trees, 11,000 People, 400 Years, 420 x 270 x 28 meters, Pinsio gravel pits*, Ylojarvi, Finland, 1996. Metallic inks on mylar, 34 1/4" x 96 1/2" (87 x 245 cm). © Agnes Denes, 1996.

A Message to Care

Today, many artists reflect our concerns about the environment in their artworks. Environmental groups work hard to protect endangered species of animals and plants. They think about how the extinction of these plants and animals will upset the balance of nature. Many areas of natural beauty in our world could disappear.

Much contemporary art calls our attention to this delicate balance in nature. Artists who create these artworks often use nontraditional art materials and sites. Some of them use plants and other natural materials or place their artworks outdoors. The drawing of Agnes Denes' *Tree Mountain* (Fig. 5–6) shows the artist's plan for creating a living artwork. For *Tree Mountain*, 11,000 trees were planted by 11,000 people from all over the world. The trees were planted in a spiral pattern on a human-made mountain. They will live for 400 years. During that time, the people who planted the trees and the generations of family that follow them are expected to care for the trees. The artist thought of this artwork as a growing "time capsule" representing 400 years of life. The trees were planted in Finland between 1992 and 1996.

Stamps Inspired by Nature

So far in this chapter, we have explored how artists express ideas about nature's powerful forces. Sometimes, artists stand back and view nature from a distance. Other times, they show natural objects close up. **In this studio experience, you will design a set of four postage stamps that sends a message about your natural surroundings.** You may wish to say, "Look closely at the textures and lines in plants." Or "See a tree in every season." Or "Stand back and admire the power of wind." How might you express your own ideas about nature?

You Will Need

- sketch paper
- pencil and eraser
- drawing paper
- colored pencils, markers, or paint

Studio Background

The Nature of Design

If you look around, you will see objects that have designs inspired by nature. **Graphic designers** are artists who design such things as packages, wrapping papers, book jackets, posters, and greeting cards. Some graphic designers simplify the features of natural objects in the designs they create.

Designers also create the postage stamps used in communities around the world. By examining stamps, you can discover what a community cares about. Compare today's postage stamps with those from the past. You can see how graphic design styles have changed. Subject matter for stamps has

1. Choose a subject or theme for your stamps that sends a message about your natural surroundings. Will you choose birds or flowers? The seasons or weather?

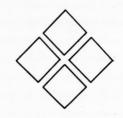

2. Decide what shape you want your stamps to be. Choose the shape that best expresses your ideas about nature. Will they be round or oval? Square or triangular?

Fig. 5–7 Artists and designers in Sweden often look to nature for subject matter. Here we see one designer's representation of flowers found in Sweden. In what other ways do these stamps look like they belong together in a set? Margareta Jacobson, *Swedish Orchids Stamps*, May 20, 1999. © Sweden Post Stamps.

changed over time, too. Some stamps now focus on community heroes or special events. Others, such as those shown in Figs. 5–7 and 5–9, feature the beauty of nature.

3. Sketch your ideas. Remember that the stamps belong in a set and should look good together. Think about the colors you want to use.

4. When you are happy with your sketches, create your finished drawings on drawing paper.

Check Your Work

Share your completed set of stamps with a group of classmates. Try to determine the message sent by each stamp and by the set as a whole. Do the four stamps work together as a set? To answer this, think about both the message and the design.

Core Lesson 5

Check Your Understanding

1. What are two general kinds of messages that artworks send about nature?
2. Use examples to explain how artists investigate nature.
3. Describe an artwork that a graphic designer might make that refers to nature in some way.
4. Suggest an idea for making an artwork that would include a message to care about the natural world.

Sketchbook Connection

Take your sketchbook outdoors and choose a natural object that you think is beautiful. Draw it from a distance and then close up. Focus on drawing the overall form of the object in the far-away view. Focus on details in the close-up view. Think of the messages about nature that each view might help you express.

Fig. 5–8 **"My message is: 'every difference is the same'—all of the stamps are different, but they are all bad weather."** Ted LoDuca, *My Brother's Attitude*, 1999. Colored pencil, each stamp design is 7 1/2" x 5 5/8" (19 x 14 cm). Pocono Mountain Intermediate School South, Swiftwater, Pennsylvania.

Fig. 5–9 **This stamp is older than those in Fig. 5–7. Imagine receiving a letter from Sweden with this stamp on it. What does the stamp tell you about the Swedish landscape? Would you want to go there? Why or why not?** Sven Hornell, *Rapa Valley Stamps*, May 2, 1977. © Sweden Post Stamps.

Responding to Beauty: 1860–1900

1895
Dewing, *Garden in May*

ca. 1900
Tiffany, *Dragonfly Lamp*

1914–15
Tiffany, *Necklace with grape and vine motifs*

Realism and
Romanticism
page 154

Late 19th Century America

Industrial America
page 206

1891
Brown, *Grand Canyon of the Yellowstone from Hayden Point*

1908
Tiffany, *View of Oyster Bay*

1915
Sullivan, *J. D. Van Allen Building*

History in a Nutshell

Between 1860 and 1900, the developing nations of North America saw times of peace and turmoil. In 1867, Canada became the independent nation it is today. Politics in Mexico were stable and the country's economy was growing. The United States, however, was fighting the Civil War from 1861 to 1865. Following the Civil War, cities grew rapidly as the age of industrialism began.

The Appeal of Nature

In the last decades of the nineteenth century, there was a great demand for paintings of the natural environment. People wanted to see the natural beauty of the North American wilderness they had heard about. In the years following the Civil War, there was a need in the United States to find new national symbols. People's interest in nature became something all communities could share. The first national parks in the United States were created at this time.

In response to the people's desire to see the wilderness, artists journeyed into unexplored regions of the United States. They took photographs and made sketches of the plants and features of the land. Back in their studios, they painted landscapes from these photos and sketches. Landscape paintings,

Fig. 5–10 Grafton Brown was one of the first African-American artists to paint mountain scenes in California. Why would people living in late-nineteenth-century America find this image exciting?
Grafton Tyler Brown, *Grand Canyon of the Yellowstone from Hayden Point,* 1891.
Oil on canvas, 24 " x 16 " (61 x 40.6 cm). Oakland Museum of California Founders Fund.

such as the one by Grafton Brown (Fig. 5–10), allowed communities to see the natural beauty of their nation.

Natural Impressions

Impressionist artists painted the seasonal changes and weather in their local regions. They worked outside and painted directly from nature. With rapid brushstrokes, they captured an impression of light and color. They painted what the eye sees at one particular moment. The American Impressionist artists saw this approach as a way to explore color in art. The close-up view of flowers in *Garden in May* by Maria Oakey Dewing (Fig. 5–11) shows the artist's impressionist style.

The theme of nature can also be seen in architecture of this period. Notice the details used by architect Louis Sullivan (Fig. 5–12).

Fig. 5–11 **Maria Oakey Dewing was probably the most important flower specialist of this period. Where do you see impressionistic brush-strokes?** Maria Oakey Dewing, *Garden in May,* 1895.
Oil on canvas. 23 ⅝" x 32 ½" (60.1 x 82.5 cm). National Museum of American Art, Smithsonian Institution, Washington, DC./Art Resource, NY.

Fig. 5–12 **The decorative elements that you see here add beauty to what could have been an ordinary-looking building. How many different plant forms can you find?** Louis Sullivan, *J. D. Van Allen Building,* 1915.
Detail of terra cotta leaf bursts on the 4th story attic. @ artonfile.com.

Design Inspired by Nature

Painters, sculptors, and architects were not the only artists who were inspired by nature. Artists such as Louis Comfort Tiffany, who designed decorative items, also turned to nature for ideas. Patterns created from plant and animal forms, flames, smoke, waves, and other natural elements can be seen in jewelry, stained-glass windows, and home furnishings. Tiffany is known as the American pioneer of the **Art Nouveau** movement (ca. 1890–1918). This design style explores the flowing lines, curves, and shapes of nature.

Tiffany is best known for his designs of stained-glass items, such as windows and lamps, and jewelry. Tiffany hired a great number of craftspeople to produce jewelry and blown-glass designs. He encouraged these craftspeople to be creative in their work. He wanted every piece produced in Tiffany Studios to reflect his unique sense of design. Each piece had to be crafted in the nature-inspired Art Nouveau style. Tiffany also designed and built a home for his family. It was known as the finest example of Art Nouveau architecture in the United States. A stained-glass window from his home is shown in Fig. 5–14.

Fig. 5–13 **Notice how Tiffany created a pattern of dragonflies in this stained-glass lampshade. What other elements from nature do you see on the lamp?** Louis Comfort Tiffany, *Dragonfly Lamp,* ca. 1900. Bronze base with color favrile glass, 28" x 22" (71.2 x 55.9 cm). Collection of the New York Historical Society (N84.113).

Fig. 5–14 **Why might people recognize this stained-glass window as a work of Tiffany?** Louis Comfort Tiffany, *View of Oyster Bay,* Window from the William C. Skinner House, New York City, ca. 1908. Leaded favrile glass, 72 3/4" x 66 1/2" (184.8 x 168.9 cm). The Metropolitan Museum of Art, Lent by the Charles Hosmer Morse Museum of American Art, Winter Park, Florida, in memory of Charles Hosmer Morse. (L.1978.19) Photograph © 1993 The Metropolitan Museum of Art.

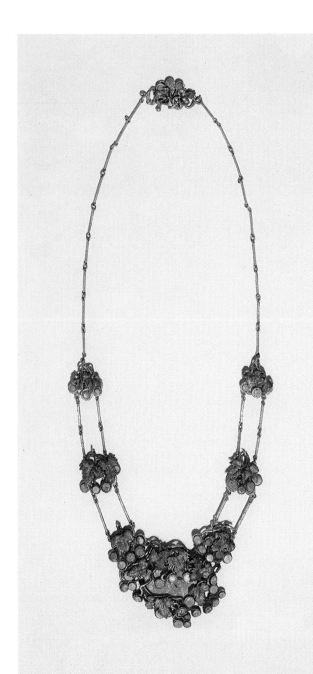

Studio Connection

How can you capture the beauty of the natural world around you? Scenes of nature can be close-up views or faraway vistas. For a close-up view, create a still-life arrangement of natural forms from your area. Let one or more main shapes fill your paper. Focus on the shapes, lines, and subtle changes in color, light, and shadow that you see. Make a sketch first. As you plan your composition, think carefully about your choice of media. Try creating a resist by combining crayon or oil pastel with watercolor. Notice how you can achieve rich textural effects using this technique.

5.1 Art History

Check Your Understanding

1. Give examples of how artists in the last forty years of the nineteenth century helped North American communities connect with the beauty of nature.

2. How did American Impressionist painters create landscapes? Describe their style of painting.

3. What natural elements appear in decorative items of the Art Nouveau style?

4. What designer is particularly known for his Art Nouveau designs?

Fig. 5–15 Tiffany created a pattern of grapes and vines in the design of this necklace. How has he simplified the forms of the grapes? Louis Comfort Tiffany, *Necklace with grape and vine motifs,* 1914–15. Opals, gold and enamel, length (open) 18" (45.7 cm). The Metropolitan Museum of Art, Gift of Sarah E. Hanley, 1946 (46.168.1) Photograph © 1988 The Metropolitan Museum of Art.

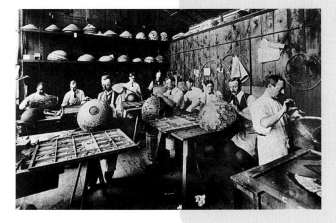

Fig. 5–16 All of the men in this photograph are crafting Tiffany lampshades. How might this studio have been different from a present-day lampshade factory? Tiffany Studio, Madison Avenue and 45th Street, ca. 1902. J. and F. Van Brink collection.

Responding to Nature

Graphic Design

What Is It?

In **graphic design,** designers create packages, labels, and logos for products and businesses. The messages expressed in graphic designs can help people decide whether to buy a product or service. Graphic designs can provide information. They can persuade people to support other people, groups, and ideas. And they can identify places and services in the community. These messages are conveyed on posters, billboards, and in newspaper and magazine advertisements. Other examples of graphic design include wallpaper, fabrics, greeting cards, and books.

Fig. 5–18 What ideas does this image convey? How does color contribute to the message? What might be a good commercial use for an image like this? Jim Frazier, *Hands Wrapped Around Globe,* 1995. Mixed media, paint and paper, 8" x 8" (20.3 x 20.3 cm). Courtesy Stock Illustration Source, Inc.

Fig. 5–17 Why can the side of this bus be considered an example of graphic design? What form of graphic design is it similar to? American Museum of Natural History, *Mobile Museum,* 2000. Courtesy American Museum of Natural History.

Effective Graphic Design

For a graphic design to work, the designer must consider the following questions:
1. What is the message?
2. Who is the audience?
3. What is the best way to get the message to the audience?

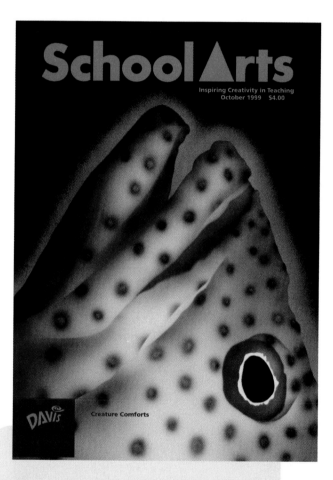

Fig. 5–19 Why might the image of a fish have been a good choice for the cover of an art education magazine? What ideas about art does it suggest? *School Arts* cover, October 1999. Courtesy *School Arts*.

Messages are most easily expressed by combining images and words. The next time you're at a supermarket, take a look at several different brands of bottled spring water. How does each label suggest the idea that spring water is natural, clean, clear, and good for your health? Look carefully at the images, colors, and lettering. The images might show clear, fresh water. The colors can suggest healthful moods and feelings. The choice of lettering might suggest how clean and natural the water is. All of these elements work together to send the message.

Studio Connection

Sometimes, the shapes of letters used in a word can help illustrate the meaning of the word. For example, the word ice might have letters that look like chunks of carved ice. The word flower could have letters that resemble flowers. Choose a word that represents something in nature. Create an illustrated version of your word. Plan the shape of each letter and the spacing between them. What colors can you use? Make several sketches. Choose your best design and create a finished drawing.

5.2 Forms and Media

Check Your Understanding
1. What can graphic designs provide to people in communities?
2. Why are images, colors, and lettering important to graphic design?

Finding Beauty in Northern Light: Scandinavian Art

Scandinavia

Global Glance

Scandinavia includes the countries of Norway, Sweden, and Denmark, although many experts also include Finland and Iceland in the list. Norway and Sweden make up the Scandinavian peninsula.

The Scandinavian countries share the seafaring Viking culture. Germany had some influence in the area during the Middle Ages. France influenced Scandinavia in the centuries that followed. However, there has always been a strong feeling of individualism in Scandinavia. "Every person's right" is an expression of freedom in Norway, Sweden, and Finland.

Fig. 5–20 **Can you tell what time of night is shown in this painting? Notice the wispy, impressionistic quality of the brushstrokes. How would you describe the artist's use of light in this picture?** Anders Zorn, *A Midsummerdance*, 1897.
Oil on canvas, 55 1/8" x 38 5/8" (140 x 98 cm). Courtesy Nationalmuseum, Sweden.

Nature in Isolation

If you look at a map of Europe, you can see how the countries on the Scandinavian peninsula are somewhat isolated. The people who live there understand the forces of nature and how those forces can affect their communities. Probably for this reason, they developed a style of art that is deeply rooted in nature and community life.

This relationship between people and nature is the focus of the art and cultural life of Scandinavia. Annual festivals and traditions follow the cycles of nature. Myths and folk tales take place in deep, dense forests full of elves, trolls, or nymphs.

Scandinavia has vast amounts of unspoiled land. Although winters are long and dark, in midsummer nights the sun does not set. Scandinavian artists in the late nineteenth century focused their art on nature and its cycles. *A Midsummerdance* by artist Anders Zorn (Fig. 5–20) shows us a Scandinavian celebration of the unique northern midsummer night.

While studying in Paris, many Scandinavian artists discovered the decorative and expressive possibilities of their own country's light and landscape. French *plein-air* painting, or painting in the open air, inspired the artists to paint the beauty of their own homeland. They created images of the countryside, particularly at dawn and dusk. In their artwork, they captured the many changing moods of nature. Artist Edvard Munch was a master at showing the light of the northern summer night in landscapes. In *White Night* (Fig. 5–21), he uses soft light to create a calm mood.

Fig. 5–21 Munch's flowing brushstrokes add a dreamlike, fluid quality to this image. How do his brushstrokes also suggest the closeness of the girls to their surroundings? Edvard Munch, *White Night*, 1904–07.
Oil on canvas, 31 1/2" x 27 1/4" (80 x 69 cm). Pushkin Museum of Fine Arts, Moscow, Russia. Scala/Art Resource, NY © 2000 The Munch Museum / The Munch-Ellingsen Group / Artist Rights Society (ARS), New York.

A Sense of Community

Scandinavian art and design reflect the Scandinavian sense of community. In the late nineteenth century, most people in Scandinavia lived in the countryside. Handcrafted textiles, furniture, and other household items were made at home or in small community groups. Scandinavians believed that decoration in community design and home furnishings was important. Each villa, or house, within a community shared common design elements. Notice the decorative details on the villa in Fig. 5–22. Imagine a community in which all the houses are decorated in a similar way.

Nature was the great source of ideas for the artists and designers of the period. Painted furniture, such as the cabinet in Fig. 5–23, was decorated with *stylized*, or simplified, flower motifs. For many designers, images of flowers were a way of expressing national identity. For others, beauty was found in the natural grain of unpainted wood furniture.

Fig. 5–22 **In the late nineteenth century, people in Scandinavia were interested in creating a national style in architecture and household goods. The style of this villa was inspired by the storehouses on Norwegian farms. How would you describe the decorations on this villa?** *Professor Carl Curman's Villa in Lysekil,* 1875 and replaced due to fire in 1878.
Photograph by M. Jacobson, date unknown. Nordiska Museum, Stockholm, Sweden. (8169)

Fig. 5–23 **Many of the flower forms in Scandinavian art are stylized. Would you consider these flowers to be stylized? Why or why not?** *Cabinet in Carl and Karin Larson's home,* Sondborn, Sweden, early 20th century.
Photograph courtesy Nisse Peterson.

A Scandinavian Style

In the late nineteenth century, the artworks made in Sweden, Denmark, Norway, Iceland, and Finland shared certain similarities. The *Arts and Crafts Movement*, which reacted against the industrialization of crafts design, influenced Scandinavian artists. People involved in the movement were interested in the individuality of handmade items. In Scandinavia, people wanted to make affordable household goods that were both practical and beautiful.

Various community arts and crafts groups and home-industry organizations were committed to preserving the Scandinavian design style. There was a blending of old and new ideas, and of painted and natural wood. Designs included simple plant motifs and clean, sharp lines. Handcrafted products were known for their beauty and simplicity. These ideals in Scandinavian design are still seen today.

Studio Connection

Make a monoprint of objects from nature. A monoprint starts as an image that is created with paint or ink. Then, while the image is still wet, it's transferred to another surface. Collect leaves, blades of grass, feathers, flower petals, and other flat objects from your yard or neighborhood. Paint or ink the surface of a square of smooth plastic or glass. Lay your objects on the ink or paint and then place a sheet of paper on top. Rub evenly, but gently, over the entire paper. When you remove the paper, the shapes of your objects will be white. Using a different color, paint or ink another surface. Position the objects differently, and lay the same sheet down to make a second impression. What happens when the colors overlap?

5.3 Global View

Check Your Understanding

1. What role did nature play in the art of Scandinavian countries?
2. What characteristic of midsummer is unique to the Scandinavian region?
3. What is a common characteristic of the art of Scandinavian countries?
4. What was the basic idea behind the Arts and Crafts Movement in Scandinavian countries?

Fig. 5–24 Notice the delicate design of this embroidered door curtain. How does this plant motif compare to the one on the cabinet doors in Fig. 5–23?
Gunnar Gunnarson Vennerberg, *Embroidered Door Curtain*, 1899.
Made by The Association of Friends of Textile Art (Handarbetets Vanner). Photography Nordiska Museum. Nordiska Museum, Stockholm, Sweden.

A Relief Sculpture

The Nature of Clay

Studio Introduction

Did you know that clay is a fine-grained material that comes from the earth? When some people see clay, they think of mud. But some artists look at clay and imagine making a beautiful pot or vase with it. They know that moistened clay can keep its form when it's shaped by hand. And they know that *firing* clay, or baking it

at a high temperature, can change it to a rocklike material.

Some artists use clay to create a **relief** sculpture—a sculpture with parts that are raised from a background. **In this studio experience, you will create a relief sculpture that shows a natural environment.** Pages 192 and 193 will tell you how to do it. What natural environment is in your area? A forest, an ocean, or a prairie? A mountain or a desert? A river, a flat plain, gentle hills? Think about the plants and animals that live there. How can you show a natural environment in a relief sculpture?

Studio Background

Ceramic Tiles

Ceramic, or clay, tiles have been used as flooring in homes for centuries. Your kitchen or bathroom may have ceramic tile on the walls, floors, or countertops. During the Arts and Crafts Movement of the late nineteenth century, decorative ceramic tiles for homes became popular. Tiles from this period show scenes from nature and other designs impressed into their surfaces. They were used on floors and fireplaces, and served as decorative elements in kitchens and bathrooms.

Craftspeople create art tiles by pressing layers of clay into a mold. The mold usually has a relief design in the bottom. This design forms an impression in the clay. After the tile dries, colored slip is poured into the impression and allowed to dry slowly. Then the tile is fired.

Fig. 5–25 This tile comes from a series of tiles that shows woodland scenes. It was made by an American company in the late 1800s. How would you describe the lines and shapes in this scene? Grueby Faience Co., *Woodland Scene,* ca. 1895. Tile, 13" (33 cm). Courtesy National Museum of American History, Smithsonian Institution, Washington, DC.

Fig. 5–27 "I got the idea from a photograph in *National Geographic*. I thought about where my colors would go and where each of my leaves were to be placed." Jacqueline Driscoll, *Volcano View,* 2000.
Clay with glaze, 6 1/2" x 6 1/2" (16.5 x 16.5 cm). Wescott Junior High School, Westbrook, Maine.

Fig. 5–28 "I wanted to glorify the beauty of the land through texture, color, and shape. Painting and choosing colors was easy and the most fun. Forming the detailed trees into shapes was the most difficult. I like the finished product, where all of my ideas came together." Madison Echols, *Majestic Mountainside,* 2000.
Clay with glaze, 6 1/2" x 6 1/2" (16.5 x 16.5 cm). Wescott Junior High School, Westbrook, Maine.

Fig. 5–26 As you can see in this example, not all tiles are square. They are made in many different shapes and sizes. What kind of natural environment does this tile show? How has the artist added humor to the image? American Encaustic Tiling Co., Ltd., Zanesville, OH, *Frog Plaque,* prob. 19th century.
Ceramic, 6" x 18 1/6" (15.4 x 45.9 cm). Cincinnati Art Museum, Gift of Theodore A. Langstroth, 1970.515

Creating Your Relief Sculpture

You Will Need

- sketch paper
- pencil and eraser
- clay
- two flat sticks
- rolling pin
- plastic knife
- dowel
- clay modeling tools
- sheet of plastic

Try This

1. Choose a natural environment to show in your relief sculpture. What features of the land can you show? What plant and animal forms can you include? Sketch your ideas.

2. Place a ball of clay between two flat sticks. Roll out a slab of clay with a rolling pin. Place the slab on a moveable surface, such as a piece of cardboard covered with plastic. Cut the slab into the shape that will best represent your environment. Will it be an oval? A rectangle? A square? Another shape?

3. With a pencil, lightly draw the important features of your environment into the clay surface. Create a foreground, middle ground, and background. Use the pencil eraser or a dowel to carve along the guidelines. Foreground areas should be raised higher than the middle ground and background areas.

4. Add textures to your sculpture. Press objects into the clay to make patterns. Draw textures into the clay with a pencil or dowel. Shape the clay with your fingers or press small shapes of clay, such as tiny balls or coils, onto the surface.

5. When you are finished, cover your sculpture with plastic and allow it to dry slowly.

Check Your Work

Did you create a variety of textures? Is there a clear distinction between foreground, middle ground, and background areas? Do the features of your sculpture show a particular natural environment?

Sketchbook Connection

Find a small natural form with an interesting texture. Draw it so the textural qualities stand out. You might create a series of drawings showing different combinations of overlapping shapes and textures. What patterns do you see? Think about a decorative design you might create based on this form from nature.

Fig. 5–30 The student who made this artwork was thinking about swimming. What do you think is most effective about the colors he chose? Alexander Cuddy, *Ocean Life*, 2000. Clay with glaze, 6 1/2" x 6 1/2" (16.5 x 16.5 cm). Wescott Junior High School, Westbrook, Maine.

Fig. 5–29 Having made this tile during January in Maine, the artist comments, "I like the bright colors and the jungle-like bird. I think winter can be drab, so I like to brighten things up." Jenna Frank, *Jungle*, 2000. Clay with glaze, 6 1/2" x 6 1/2" (16.5 x 16.5 cm). Wescott Junior High School, Westbrook, Maine.

Studio Collaboration

Work with classmates to create a ceramic tile mural based on impressions of nature. As a class, collect interesting leaves, shells, flowers, seedpods, nuts, twigs, and other natural forms. Make one size of square tiles, about 3/8" thick. Press the objects into the clay. Score the back of the tiles to prevent warping. Glaze and fire the tiles, then glue them to a large piece of plywood. Display the mural in your school.

Computer Option

Use a paint program to create a simple graphic design based on nature imagery in the style of the tiles in Figs. 5–25 and 5–26. Search the Web for sites that show examples of tiles. Apply a bas-relief effect to the design.

Connect to...

Other Subjects

Social Studies

Have you ever witnessed a **Japanese tea ceremony**? The tea ceremony, which developed under the influence of Zen Buddhism, symbolizes simplicity and the basic Zen principles of harmony, respect, purity, and tranquility. The ceremony varies with the seasons: appropriate tea bowls, types of tea, flowers, and scrolls are chosen for each time of year. Participants follow certain rules and procedures that communicate the highest ideals of the tea ceremony. Are there any similar ceremonies in other cultures? How could you find out?

Language Arts

Why, do you think, have so many people from different times and cultures written poetry about the **beauty in nature**? Why are we so attracted to the natural world? Choose one artwork from this text that you believe is the best depiction of natural beauty. What are the reasons for your choice? How would you persuade another person to agree with you?

Mathematics

In 1202, the Italian mathematician Fibonacci (Leonardo of Pisa) developed a sequence of numbers in which each term after the first two terms, which are both 1, is the sum of the two preceding terms. Do you see this pattern in 1, 1, 2, 3, 5, 8, . . .? What, do you think, is the next number in the sequence? Fibonacci made this and other significant contributions to the history

Fig. 5–31 **The Japanese word for tea is** *cha* **and the tea ceremony is called** *Chaji.* **Along with tea, guests are usually served a small meal.** *Tea Room in a Japanese Inn,* 1989. ©Bob Krist/CORBIS.

of mathematics. The **Fibonacci sequence** appears in growth patterns in natural objects such as shells and has fascinated mathematicians and artists for centuries.

Science

You may recall the story of an apple falling on Sir Isaac Newton's head, but do you remember the reason this event was so important? In 1687, Newton— possibly inspired by seeing an apple fall from a tree—proposed the **law of universal gravitation**. With this law he could account for the motion of the falling apple, the motion of the moon around the earth, the motion of the planets around the sun, and the paths of comets. Today, many of us take his theories for granted; but, in Newton's day, they dramatically transformed people's ideas about the natural world. How, do you think, does Newton's law of universal gravitation represent ideas of beauty in the organization of the universe?

Internet Connection
For more activities related to this chapter, go to the Davis website at **www.davis-art.com.**

What kind of artist would be most likely to use natural materials for media? What do you think were the very first art materials? Since prehistoric times, **ceramists** (also called potters or clayworkers) worldwide have produced objects from clay. At first, pottery was made for practical purposes—for cooking food, storing grains, or use in ceremonies. Today's ceramists still produce functional items, but they also create work that is more aesthetic than practical. These artists may be production potters, who make large quantities of standardized pieces; or they may be fine artists, who create original, individual pieces. To work with clays and glazes, potters need some knowledge of chemistry. No matter how they practice their art—building pieces by hand or "throwing" them on a potter's wheel—ceramists are drawn to the hands-on pleasures of working with the physical and natural qualities of clay.

Are you always in a hurry, or do you take the time to notice what happens around you in the natural world? In our fast-paced society, we often forget to slow down and really see the **world around us**. How can we develop a greater aesthetic awareness of the world's natural beauty? How can we learn to look more closely and appreciate the simplicity of a flower, the curve of a seashell, or a reflection in a raindrop?

Fig. 5–32 **Nature is full of interesting shapes, colors, and designs. What color scheme does this leaf have? What type of balance do you see?** Photo © Karen Durlach.

Music

Musicians, like artists, have often been **inspired by nature**. For instance, Navajo musician R. Carlos Nakai plays a Native-American flute, an instrument made from natural materials, and he produces music that seeks to represent the connection that the Navajo feel with nature. Vivaldi also was inspired by the natural world: he produced the piece of classical music known as *The Four Seasons*. Paul Winter, a contemporary musician, took his interest in nature a step further: he performed and recorded his album *Canyon* in the Grand Canyon. The sounds of the natural environment and the acoustical characteristics of that huge outdoor space have given Winter's music a uniquely appealing sound.

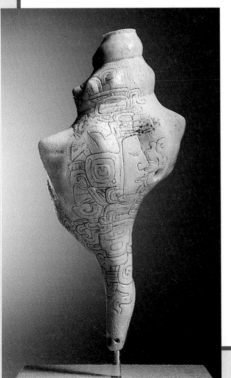

Fig. 5–33 **This Mesoamerican artist combined art, music, and nature by transforming a shell into a decorated trumpet. Why do you think people have used natural objects as musical instruments?** Pre-Columbian, Maya (Guatemala), *Incised Conch Shell,* 250–400 AD.
Shell with cinnabar tracings, height: 11 9/16" (28.6 cm). Courtesy Kimbell Art Museum, Fort Worth, Texas.

Portfolio

"I got the idea of painting it when we were working on Georgia O'Keeffe paintings. My favorite part is when the colors run." **Michael Santa Maria**

Fig. 5–34 Michael Santa Maria, *Watercolor Flower,* 1999. Watercolor, 18" x 24" (46 x 61 cm). Desert Sands School, Phoenix, Arizona.

"I have always loved animals, so this seemed like a perfect project for me. My ideas just seemed to spring onto my paper as I began to think of what animal shapes to draw." **Heidi McEvoy**

Fig. 5–35 Heidi McEvoy, *Animal,* 1999. Acrylic paint, 8 1/2" x 23 1/2" (21.5 x 59.5 cm). Fairhaven Middle School, Bellingham, Washington.

"The moon and sky are inspiring to me. I wanted my monoprint to be bright with the colors of nature and the sunset." **Vicki Rokhlin**

CD-ROM Connection
To see more student art, check out the Community Connection Student Gallery.

Fig. 5–36 Vicki Rokhlin, *Funky Universe,* 1999. Monoprint, 14" x 17" (35.5 x 43 cm). Atlanta International School, Atlanta, Georgia.

Chapter 5 Review

Recall

How do artworks from the past show the awesome power of nature?

Understand

Explain how artists help people investigate nature.

Apply

Find examples of artworks in your home, school, or community that show our admiration for the beauty of nature.

Analyze

Select an artwork from this chapter and tell how the artist used the principles of design to show the power and beauty of nature. Make sure to explain how the artist used design principles to attract and hold the attention of a viewer.

Synthesize

Create an exhibition of items designed by graphic designers who were inspired by natural forms. Organize the exhibition according to categories. Your categories might indicate, for example, how graphic designers show the awesome power of nature, the beauty of nature, and the need to care for our natural environment.

Evaluate

Imagine that you are a member of a group of people who will select a winning design for a set of postage stamps about nature (*see example below*). Write a brief statement of the rules for entering the contest, indicating the kinds of subject matter that might be submitted, and the standards that will be used to select the winning design.

For Your Portfolio

Develop an artwork for your portfolio based on the theme of nature. Exchange your artwork with a peer and write a critique of each other's work. Describe important details and make connections between what you see and the artwork's message about nature. Comment on strengths and offer suggestions for improvement. Respond to the peer review. Include all of this in your portfolio.

Page 178

For Your Sketchbook

Select one thing from nature and draw it in many different ways, from different points of view. Use different color combinations and explore different media and technical effects.

Changing

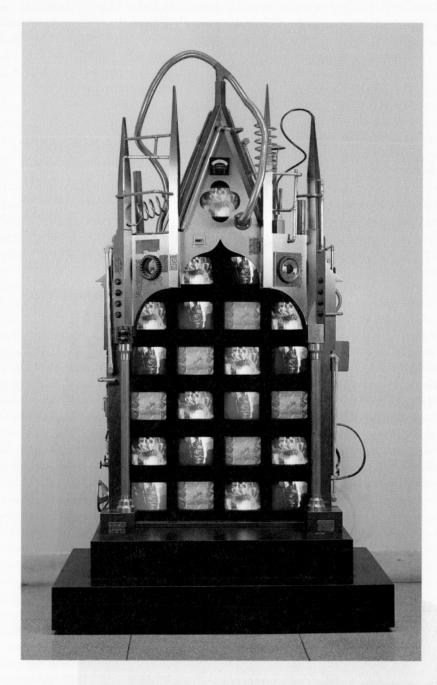

Fig. 6–1 **What message does this artwork send about television? What do you think it says about technology? Why do you think so?**
Nam June Paik, *Technology*, 1991.
25 video monitors, 3 laser disc players with unique 3 discs in cabinet. National Museum of American Art, Smithsonian Institution, Washington, DC./Art Resource, NY.

- How do we adapt to changes in our lives?
- How does art reflect and inspire change?

As you've grown up, what kinds of changes have taken place that make your daily life easier or more pleasant? Perhaps your school library has become computerized. Or perhaps your family's newest car has a CD player in it.

Changes sometimes happen because of a new technology. **Technology** can help make life easier or more enjoyable. It can offer ways for people to meet their needs more quickly than they could before. New technology has also changed people's ability to communicate with each other. Can you remember when people didn't have cell phones, pagers, fax machines, or the Internet?

As technology changes, so do the materials and tools used to create art. New technology and its influence on communities often inspire artists to create art that reflects these changes. For example, the invention of the television in the early twentieth century changed the way people spent their free time. Now, the television is sometimes used as an art material. In the early 1960s, Nam June Paik began to experiment with television sets in his art (Fig. 6–1). He continues to use television sets as a sculptural medium. The television image is also important in Paik's artworks. He alters the shape, color, motion, and sound of each image to give the viewer a constantly changing experience.

What's Ahead

- **Core Lesson** Discover how art reflects and inspires changes.
- **6.1 Art History Lesson** Learn how art in the early twentieth century reflected changes in art and community life.
- **6.2 Forms and Media Lesson** Learn how change influences painting traditions.
- **6.3 Global View Lesson** Explore how Russian artists changed the direction of art in Eastern Europe in the early twentieth century.
- **6.4 Studio Lesson** Create a painting that celebrates or promotes change in your community.

Words to Know

technology	avant-garde
Post-Modern	kinetic sculpture
cityscape	pointillism
pigments	Abstract

Art and Change

Changes in Technology

Look at the buildings around you. What materials were used to build them? You might see materials from nature, such as stone and wood. Or you might see human-made materials, such as glass, steel, and concrete.

From the earliest of times, artists have used technology to create art and architecture. In ancient Rome, the invention of the arch, vault, and dome led architects to design huge buildings with no visible supports. Centuries later, architects designed suspension bridges, factories, and warehouses.

As cities grew, more and more people needed places to live and work. So, architects created high-rise buildings called *skyscrapers*. Before skyscrapers, most city buildings were low and spread out. Skyscrapers, such as the Woolworth Building in New York City (Fig. 6–2), provided space in a new and inventive way: from the basement to the "sky." See Studio Background (pages 204 and 205) to learn more about skyscrapers.

Changes in People's Lives

In the late 1800s and early 1900s, many factories were built in North American cities. People from other countries and farm communities moved to the cities to find jobs. Workers and their families crowded into apartments. They had to adapt to many changes as they began their new life in the city.

During this time, artists made artworks to show both the good and the bad parts of living in urban areas. George Bellows was one of several American painters who tried

Fig. 6–2 **As more and more people moved into the city, skyscrapers became a necessity. The Woolworth Building is nestled in the center of this group of skyscrapers. Notice its decorative elements. How does it compare to the surrounding buildings?** Cass Gilbert, *Woolworth Building, New York, NY,* 1911–13.

Fig. 6–3 **The term "cliff dwellers" was used to describe groups of people who built their homes in cliff walls or rocky ledges. Why might this artist have used the same term as a title for this painting?** George Bellows, *Cliff Dwellers*, 1913.
Oil on canvas, 40 ³/₁₆" x 42 ¹/₁₆" (104.6 x 106.8 cm). Los Angeles County Museum of Art, Los Angeles County Fund © 1998 Museum Associates, Los Angeles County Museum of Art. All Rights Reserved.

to capture the changes that were taking place in urban life. What does his painting titled *Cliff Dwellers* (Fig. 6–3) say about city life during this time?

Changes in Ideas

At the beginning of the twentieth century, people all over the world were adapting to changes. After many years of hardship in Russia, a new form of government began there. The form of government was called *communism*. The main idea of communism was to create communities in which people worked together. They shared food and other necessary goods and services equally. Russian artists created artworks that pro-

Fig. 6–4 **How do the poses of the figures in this sculpture help express the idea of equality?** Vera Mukhina, *Industrial Worker and Collective Farm Girl*, 1937.
Stainless steel, h. 79' (24 m), weight 75 tons, base h. 131 ¹/₂" (334 cm). Courtesy SovFoto/EastFoto. © Estate of Vera Mukhina/ Licensed by VAGA, New York, NY.

moted this change in people's daily lives. The sculpture by Russian artist Vera Mukhina (Fig. 6–4) shows a factory worker and a farm worker posed together and striving toward a common goal.

The Art of Persuasion

What are some ways in which you receive messages? Your answer might include letters, phone calls, newspapers, magazines, books, or conversations. You can also receive messages from art.

From the time of the earliest cave paintings, art has influenced, and even changed, people's views and opinions. For example, political posters have persuaded people to change the way they think about issues such as equality and democracy. Artworks can call attention to environmental concerns, such as erosion, endangered species, or poverty. Through their art, artists can inspire changes within their own communities.

With the invention of photography, artists were quick to use the new medium. First, they used it to make photographs that looked like paintings. They could also document what was happening in the world. Now viewers could see real people and real-life situations. When artists realized the possibilities, they explored photography as its own art form.

Artworks that Change Minds

The three artworks shown here try to influence people's views in different ways. Jaune Quick-to-See Smith's painting, *The Spotted Owl* (Fig. 6–5), makes a strong statement against the timber industry. The artist hoped that this artwork would encourage people to think about our endangered environment. In *Little Girl in Carolina Cotton Mill* (Fig. 6–6), Lewis Hine tried to draw attention to a need for change in a community. When this photograph was taken in 1908, children were sent to work long hours in dirty, dangerous factories. Since then, child labor laws have stopped this practice in the United States. The poster from Russia (Fig. 6–7) is another example of art for political change. In 1705, Peter the Great passed a law that angered the people. Part of the law stated that all but certain groups of men had to shave off their beards. The act went against ancient custom and the rules of the church. In this image, the bearded gentleman shows his resistance.

Fig. 6–5 In this artwork, the artist reminds viewers about the need to care for the delicate balance of nature. The timber industry is endangering the spotted owl by cutting old growth forest in the Northwest. What elements of the artwork symbolize the danger? Jaune Quick-to-See-Smith, *The Spotted Owl*, 1990. Oil, beeswax on canvas, 2 axes, wood panel, 80" x 116" (203.2 x 294.6 cm) triptych. Courtesy Bernice Steinbaum Gallery, Miami.

Fig. 6–6 **Imagine having to work in a factory instead of going to school or playing on the soccer team. If you were to see a photograph like this in the newspaper, how would it make you feel about your own life?** Lewis Hine, *Little Girl in Carolina Cotton Mill,* 1908.
Silver gelatin print. ©Corbis-Bettmann.

Fig. 6–7 **While most of us can't read the Russian words on this poster, we can guess that they might show the dialogue between the two men. How does poster art influence people to think about artists' messages?** Russia, *The Barber Wants to Cut the Old Believer's Whiskers,* ca. 1770.
Woodcut, 38" x 30" (96.5 x 76.1 cm).
Courtesy Scott Archive.

Making a Skyscraper

The next time you're in a city, look closely at the buildings around you. You will probably see vast differences in their forms, decorations, and colors. You will probably also recognize the different materials, such as stone, glass, or steel that were used to build them.

The buildings in most cities were designed at different times over many decades. Clearly, the styles of buildings have changed over time. Skyscrapers reflect some of the biggest changes in architecture of the twentieth century. **In this studio experience, you will build a model of a Post-Modern skyscraper.** To learn more about Post-Modern architecture, read the Studio Background.

You Will Need

- sketch paper
- pencil and eraser
- cardboard or foam board
- scissors
- glue or tape
- tempera or acrylic paint
- colored pencils or markers

Try This

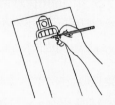

1. Sketch your ideas for a skyscraper. Determine the main shapes of your building. What materials might be used to build it? How big will it be?

2. Cut the main shapes from cardboard or foam board. Glue or tape them together to construct a model of your design.

3. Add windows and doors to your model with drawing materials or cut paper.

Studio Background

The Rise of Skyscrapers

At the turn of the century, two changes in technology allowed architects to develop the skyscraper. The first change was the use of steel as a building material. With steel, architects could create building frames that were taller and stronger than the frames of buildings from the past. The second change was the invention of elevators. As elevators were designed to

Fig. 6–8 This Post-Modern skyscraper borrows elements from Gothic architecture seen in Europe. What similarities and differences do you see between this skyscraper and the Seagram Building (Fig. 6–10)? John Burgee Architects with Philip Johnson, *PPG Place,* 1984. Pittsburgh. Courtesy Richard Payne.

4. Use paint or drawing materials to create colors and surface textures. Add other details as desired.

Check Your Work

Display your completed model and statement with those of your classmates. What features of Post-Modern architecture do you see in each model?

Fig. 6–9 **This student pictures his skyscraper in Chicago. He imagines it as an office building and a place for people to come sightseeing.** Dan Quinn, *Quinn Towers,* 2000. Cardboard, glue, paint, 62 ½" x 14" x 8" (159 x 35.5 x 20 cm). Thomas Prince School, Princeton, Massachusetts.

Sketchbook Connection
Walk through your town or city and notice the different materials that were used to create its buildings. What colors and textures do you see? Sketch a variety of the buildings' textures and note their colors. Refer to your sketches when you build your model.

Core Lesson 6

Check Your Understanding

1. What are some ways that art reflects change in community life?
2. Cite examples from this chapter that show how art inspires change in communities.
3. What do changes in architecture say about communities?
4. The invention of elevators allowed for the development of skyscrapers. How might the use of moving sidewalks influence architectural design in years to come?

rise faster and farther, buildings could be made taller. These early skyscrapers had clean, simple lines. They clearly showed the structure of the buildings and the materials used to create them.

In the 1960s and 1970s, architects felt that the simple lines of this *Modern* style of architecture were too rigid and tiresome. They began looking to buildings from the past for ideas. Soon they were adding decorative forms and details to the simple lines that characterized Modern architecture. This new **Post-Modern** style of architecture combined line, color, and decoration. Post-Modern architects used new materials to build their skyscrapers, and combined the materials in unexpected ways.

Fig. 6–10 **This Modern-style skyscraper is made of amber glass and bronze. Notice the simple lines of its design. Almost every city has an imitation of this building. Why might cities find this skyscraper design so appealing?** Ludwig Mies van der Rohe, *Seagram Building, New York, NY.* Photograph by Ezra Stoller © Esto. All rights reserved.

Changing

Confidence and Change: 1900–1920

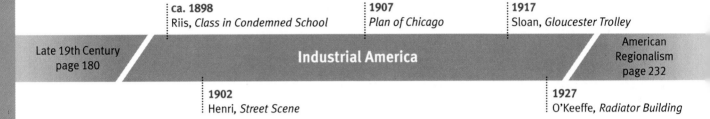

ca. 1898
Riis, *Class in Condemned School*

1907
Plan of Chicago

1917
Sloan, *Gloucester Trolley*

Late 19th Century
page 180

Industrial America

American Regionalism
page 232

1902
Henri, *Street Scene*

1927
O'Keeffe, *Radiator Building*

History in a Nutshell

During the first decade of the twentieth century and the years before World War I, industry grew rapidly in the United States. The thousands of immigrants who arrived on American soil added to the growth of cities. For the nation's communities, this was a period of expansion and hope for the future.

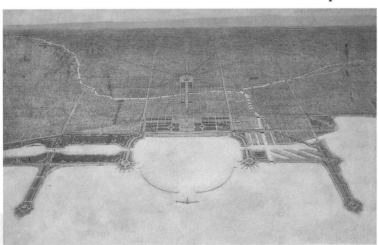

Fig. 6–11 As cities developed, there was a need to design parks and places where people could gather. This plan of Chicago was created in 1907. It shows a proposed civic center, a park, and the waterfront. Why might newcomers at the time have found this plan exciting? Jules Gherin, (Daniel H. Burnham and Edward H. Bennett, Chicago, Illinois partnership 1903–12), *Chicago: View Looking West over the City Showing the Proposed Civic Center, the Grand Access, Grant Park and the Harbor; Plan of Chicago, 1909,* plate 87, 1907.
Watercolor and graphite on paper, 57 1/8" x 91 3/4" (145.5 x 233 cm). Gift of Patrick Shaw, 1991.1381. Photograph courtesy The Art Institute of Chicago.

Art for Change, Changes for Art

During these years of industrial and economic strength in the United States, American artists turned their attention to cities. The subjects of their artwork were places where people gathered: streets, parks, beaches, restaurants, theaters, and nightclubs. Look at the **cityscapes** —artworks that show a view of a city—of New York and Chicago. *Radiator Building–Night, New York* (Fig. 6–13) by Georgia O'Keeffe shows an inviting nighttime scene. It reflects people's feelings at this time about cities as good places to live. The view of Chicago (Fig. 6–11) is shown from above, as though the artist were looking down on it from an airplane.

At first, artists of this time were mainly interested in how the change in cities gave them new subject matter for their art. They could shift the focus of their art from landscapes to cityscapes. After a while, however, artists and photographers wanted to use their art to influence new changes in communities. Their artworks called attention to social and economic problems, such as injus-

tice, poverty, and overcrowding in American cities. Artists began to express their feelings about these problems. The photograph by artist Jacob Riis (Fig. 6–12) shows students in a city classroom. Look closely at the photograph. Imagine what city schools were like in the early twentieth century.

In 1913, a major art exhibition in New York City greatly influenced change in the art of the United States. The show was called the "International Exhibition of Modern Art" (later called "the Armory Show"). After viewing this exhibition, people in the United States thought that American art was behind the times compared to the new art by European artists. In the years following the Armory Show, artists shifted their attention away from the public community. Instead, they began using their art as a way to express their personal feelings.

Changing

207

Fig. 6–14 **What colors help make this painting cheerful? How do they compare to the colors in** *Street Scene with Snow* **(Fig. 6–15)?** John Sloan, *Gloucester Trolley*, 1917.
Oil on canvas, 25" x 30 1/2" (63.5 x 76.8 cm). Courtesy Canajoharie Library and Art Gallery.

Art in the City

One group of artists from the early twentieth century became known as "The Eight." Artists Robert Henri and John Sloan led the group, which included George Luks, William Glackens, Everett Shinn, Maurice Prendergast, Arthur B. Davies, and Ernest Lawson. These eight artists also were called the *Ash Can School* because they liked to show real scenes of city life in their artworks. They painted images from both the upper class and poorer neighborhoods of New York City. They did not create their artworks to express feelings about the differences between these neighborhoods. These artists thought this subject matter made

their art interesting and lively. They showed the streets and people of city communities as they really looked. Some people didn't like this realistic look at city life.

Artists of the Ash Can School dared to show the dirt and grime of real life. Their artwork reflected how the changes of the twentieth century affected people's daily lives. John Sloan's *Gloucester Trolley* (Fig. 6–14) shows neighborhood people rushing to catch the trolley. While the neighborhood might be poor, Sloan creates a cheerful feeling in his painting. Robert Henri captures a more somber mood in *Street Scene with Snow* (Fig. 6–15).

Studio Connection

Create a cityscape. How can you show a real life scene from your community or a community you know? What statement can you make about life there? Think about the media you might use. Be imaginative about your subject matter. Will you include a waterfront or an industrial area? An old factory or building that stands empty? Is there a beautiful view that you like? Think about the colors of shop displays, houses, and buildings. What do the people on the street look like? Try to capture something about the community that could not be seen anywhere else.

Check Your Understanding

1. Why did artists turn their attention to cities as a source of subject matter?
2. How did art in the first decades of the twentieth century reflect changes in art and community life?
3. What major art exhibition in New York influenced the future of art in the United States?
4. What was the main subject matter of Ash Can School artists?

Fig. 6–15 Do you think that the city street shown here actually looked like this? Why or why not? How did the artist create the mood of a city neighborhood in this painting? Robert Henri, *Street Scene with Snow, East 57th Street, New York,* 1902.
Oil on canvas, 26" x 32" (66 x 81.3 cm). Yale University Art Gallery, Mable Brady Garvan Collection.

Changing

209

Painting

Painting is one of the oldest and most colorful forms of art. Paintings hang in people's homes and offices and in libraries, hospitals, and museums. How many different styles of painting, such as realistic, abstract, or fantasy, have you seen? Subjects, themes, and styles of painting can reflect the culture, artistic traditions, and time period in which the artist lives. As communities change, so do painting traditions. Since the Renaissance period, most artists in Western culture have tried to develop their own individual styles and methods of painting.

Painters must make decisions about subject matter, materials, and techniques. Local traditions and changes in communities can influence these decisions. Painters' choices of subjects or themes may reflect the history and traditions found in the places where they live. An artist's decisions about tools and materials may depend on what is available at the time.

Most paints are made from powdered **pigments**—coloring materials made from earth, crushed minerals, plants, or chemicals. Pigments are held together with glue, egg, wax, or oil. Paint is applied to a surface such as paper, canvas, wood, or plaster. It is usually applied with a paintbrush. Paintbrushes come in all sizes and shapes. A painter might also use a palette knife—a dull-edged tool for spreading and mixing paint.

Artists experiment with paints and painting techniques. Some recent artists have used house paints and paints mixed with sand or other materials. They have applied paint with rollers, sponges, and their hands. Some pour, drip, or spray paint onto a surface, or squeeze it directly from the tube.

Compare the paintings in this lesson. In what ways are their styles different? What techniques did the artists use to create their images?

Fig. 6–16 When artists plan a painting, they choose a color scheme that will help express their ideas. This artist has created a *monochromatic*—one color—color scheme with shades of blue-green. What kind of mood does his color create? Mark Tansey, *Action Painting no. 2*, 1984.
Diachrome, 76" x 100" (193 x 254 cm). Collection du Musée des beaux-arts de Montreal/The Montreal Museum of Fine Arts' Collection. Photograph: Brian Merrett, MMFA.

Fig. 6–17 **This style of painting is called Action Painting or Abstract Expressionism. Notice how the brushstrokes look like they were placed anywhere and everywhere. Do you feel a sense of energy when you look at this artwork?** Joan Mitchell, *Mountain*, 1989.
Oil on canvas, 110 1/4" x 157 1/2" (280 x 400 cm). Photograph courtesy Robert Miller Gallery, New York (RGM# MITC-0228) © The Estate of Joan Mitchell.

Studio Connection

Make a painting to convey an idea about the theme of "change." What kinds of change do you see around you? How could you use paint to express an idea about such changes?

Make decisions about the idea you wish to express and the kind of materials you will need to express the idea. How big will your completed work be? What painting techniques will best convey your idea? Look at many examples of painting in your book and elsewhere to help plan your work.

6.2 Forms and Media

Check Your Understanding

1. What decisions must painters make about their work?
2. How do changes in communities influence painters' decisions?

Changing

211

Changing Perspectives in Russian Art

Global Glance

For many centuries, Russia looked west of its borders for cultural inspiration. One of Russia's best-known traditional art forms is religious icons. These are based on the Byzantine traditions. During the nineteenth century, Russian artists continued to rely on western European styles such as Realism, Impressionism, and Art Nouveau for ideas. In the early twentieth century, however, Russian communities and their art changed. Revolutionary movements in Russia now interested western European artists. They began looking to Moscow for new and revolutionary ideas.

Russia

The First Avant-Gardes

The first two decades of the twentieth century were marked by a rapid series of new artistic styles in Russia. Russian artists wanted to do things differently than they had in the past. Those artists who took the lead in these changes became known as **avant-garde.**

In the military, the term *avant-garde* means an advance force. In the world of art, it refers to a group or style that is at the front of artistic change. It generally describes art that is very different or experimental. Russian avant-garde artists wanted to modernize Russian art. Early avant-garde artists, such as Natalia Goncharova, drew ideas

Fig. 6–18 Look carefully at this painting. What qualities of abstract art do you see? Can you find the lady that's referred to in the title? Natalia Goncharova, *Lady with Hat*, 1913.
Oil on canvas, 35 ¹/₂" x 26" (90 x 66 cm). Musee National d'Art Moderne, Paris. Photo Philippe Migeat © Centre Georges Pompidou. © 2000 Artist Rights Society (ARS), New York/ADAGP, Paris.

from medieval icon painting and the Russian folk art traditions (Fig. 6–18). They experimented with color and line, and created art that was not realistic in style.

New Ways of Seeing

Avant-garde artists wanted people to abandon their usual way of seeing things. The group continued to investigate new ideas, particularly the use of abstraction. (See page 12 of Foundation 1 to learn more about Abstract art.) Some artists based their ideas on scientific theories of light. Others, such as Kasimir Malevich, based their work on geometric shapes and forms (Fig. 6–20).

The artists of these movements did not think art should have any practical purpose. They thought art should exist only to be looked at as beautiful forms. Some artists used a variety of materials to construct abstract, freestanding, or suspended sculptural works. Others created **kinetic sculptures,** which have moving parts (Fig. 6–19). Where have you seen mobiles and other sculptures that move?

Fig. 6–19 Take a close look at the shape and form of this kinetic sculpture. What might the physical movement of it be? Alexander Rodchenko, *Oval Hanging Construction Number 12,* ca. 1920.
Plywood, open construction partially painted with aluminum paint, and wire, 24" x 33" x 18 1/2" (61 x 83.8 x 47 cm). The Museum of Modern Art, New York. Acquisition made possible through the extraordinary efforts of George and Zinaida Costakis, and through the Nate B. and Frances Spingold, Matthew H. and Erna Futter and Enid A. Haupt Funds. Photograph © 2000 The Museum of Modern Art, New York. © Estate of Alexander Rodchenko/Licensed by VAGA, New York, NY.

Fig. 6–20 In 1913, Kasimir Malevich started the suprematist movement in art. He and other suprematists were interested in arranging simple geometric shapes to show pure colors and nonobjective forms. Do you think this painting is beautiful? Why or why not? Kasimir Malevich, *Suprematist Painting,* 1915.
Oil on canvas, 40" x 24 1/2" (101.5 x 62 cm). Stedelijk Museum, Amsterdam.

Revolutionary Ideas

Another avant-garde community of artists were called *Productivists*. These artists wanted to be actively involved in reshaping society. They felt that the combined forces of art, craftsmanship, and industry could help build a better world. This group believed that art is useful to society. Artists played important roles in cultural activity and teaching. They were expected to concentrate on architecture, the design of household objects, and printing. Artists rejected any creativity that did not have a purpose. *Monument to the Third International* (Fig. 6–22) is a model for a building that was never built. The artist who designed the model was trying to create a structure unlike any other. Have you ever seen a building that looks like this monument?

Fig. 6–21 **This poster illustrates the change from tsarist Russia to communist Russia. The image through the window represents the future. The details inside the room represent the past. How might the meaning of the worker and peasant, standing on each side of the window, be similar to that of the figures in** *Industrial Worker and Collective Farm Girl* **(Fig. 6–4, page 201)?** Alexander Apsit, *A Year of the Proletarian Dictatorship, October 1917–1918*, 1918. Poster. Courtesy David King Collection.

214

In these and other ways, the success of the Russian Revolution in 1917 brought many Russian artists together. This group shared an interest in promoting the revolution's ideals of change. Alexander Aspit's poster (Fig. 6–21) uses strong images to teach people about political change. Later, some Russian artists who took part in these changes moved to Paris. They became part of western European movements.

Fig. 6–22 **This artist believed that art should be composed of simple shapes and forms. Inside this tower are four forms that seem to float in space. What do you think the artist wanted this building to say about art and Russia?** Vladimir Tatlin, *Monument to the Third International,* 1919 (reconstructed in 1979). Sculpture, wood and metal, h. 16 1/4" (500 cm), diam. 9' 8" (300 cm). Musee National d'Art Moderne, Paris. © Centre Georges Pompidou. © Estate of Vladimir Tatlin/Licensed by VAGA, New York, NY.

Studio Connection

A kinetic sculpture has moving, changing parts. Today, there are many different types of kinetic sculpture. A *mobile* hangs from a supporting structure so that air currents can move it freely in space. Some kinetic sculptures have motor-driven parts. Others use solar power or the energy of moving water. Electricity and computers can also be used in kinetic sculptures. How can you create a kinetic sculpture around the theme of change? You can show change by planning the relationships between sizes, colors, and other visual elements in your sculpture. Will you use only flat shapes or three-dimensional forms? Will your shapes and forms be geometric or organic? You can suspend or connect moving parts with string, wire, or wooden dowels.

6.3 Global View

Check Your Understanding

1. What is one of Russia's best-known traditional art forms?
2. What is meant by avant-garde art?
3. How did Productivist thinking change the direction of art in Russia?
4. Many Russian artists developed new styles simply because they wanted to do things differently. Is this a good reason to change something? Why or why not? When might change not be appropriate or good? Why?

Painting in the Studio
Exploring Styles

Paintings for Change

Studio Introduction

As you have grown up, what changes have taken place in your town or city? Perhaps your community has built a new school or begun a strong recycling program. Perhaps it has improved its recreation facilities or opened a health food store. You might have your own ideas about changes you'd like to see in your community. Is there an unused lot where you'd like to see a park or a playground? Is there a leash law or other pet restriction that you'd like to see changed? Maybe you'd like new school lockers or more time between classes.

In this studio experience, you will create a painting that celebrates or promotes change in your community. Page 218 will tell you how to do it. As you know, many artists create paintings that celebrate or promote change in their community. They choose the style of painting that will best express their ideas. These styles might include abstract, realistic, impressionist, expressionist, or the artists' personal style. (To learn more about art styles, see Studio Background and Foundation 1, pages 10–13.) Create your painting in the style of your choice. When you are finished with the painting, write a short paragraph expressing your feelings or ideas about the change you show.

Studio Background

New Ways of Looking

During times of change, painters and other artists often experiment with the media and techniques they use to create art. The Impressionist artists of the late nineteenth century wanted to capture the change of color and light at exact moments in time. They used feathery brushstrokes and painted quickly. Other artists of the time used a technique called **pointillism.** They created tiny dots of color with the tip of their paintbrush. They placed the

Fig. 6–23 **John Henry Twachtman was an American Impressionist painter. Look carefully at this painting. How would you describe the brushstrokes?** John Henry Twachtman, *The Rainbow's Source,* ca. 1890–1900. Oil on canvas, 34 1/8" x 24 1/2" (86.7 x 62.2 cm). The St. Louis Art Museum (Modern Art), Purchase 124:1921. [ISN 3470]

Fig. 6–24 "My picture has to do with my feelings about homeless people. My teddy bear represents love and warmth for people. If I could change one thing in the world, I would make sure that homeless people had homes and there would be no more violence and crime." Tammy M. Dagen, *A Bear and His Bike,* 2000. Tempera paint, 18" x 12" (48 x 30.5 cm). Plymouth Middle School, Minnesota.

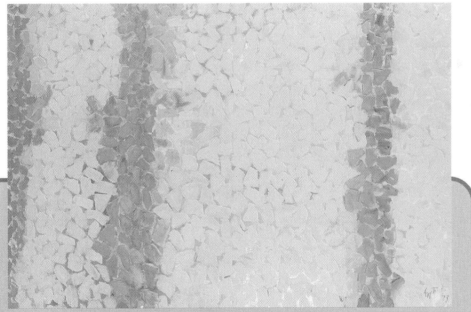

dots next to each other. When viewers stand back from pointillist paintings, their eyes blend the dots together and see shapes.

Abstract artists found yet another way to look at subject matter. They discovered that by drawing and painting simple shapes, they could suggest a realistic subject without details. Sometimes their artworks have no recognizeable subject at all. Abstract artists use color and shape to express their ideas.

Fig. 6–25 Alma Thomas was an abstract artist who often chose nature as her subject matter. Crepe myrtle has very colorful masses of flowers that hang down and blow in the wind. A concerto is a musical composition for one or more solo instruments and orchestra. Why do you think Thomas titled this painting as she did? Alma Woodsey Thomas, *Wind and Crepe Myrtle Concerto,* 1973. Acrylic on canvas, 35" x 52" (88.9 x 132.1 cm). National Museum of American Art, Smithsonian Institution, Washington, DC /Art Resource, NY

Painting in the Studio
Creating Your Painting

You Will Need

- drawing paper
- paintbrushes
- paint
- water
- paper towels
- pastels (optional)

Try This

1. As a class, discuss changes that have taken place in your community as you have grown up. Then discuss changes that you would like see happen in your community.

2. Decide which change you would like to show in a painting. Will you choose a change that has already taken place or one that you would promote? How can you show the change, as it's happening, in a painting? For example, if you want to show your new school, you might show how the school looked when it was under construction. If you want to promote the idea of a new park, you might show it being constructed in the location where you imagine one.

3. Experiment with different styles of painting. Try creating lines and shapes in different styles. For example, how might the lines and shapes in an abstract painting look different from the lines and shapes in a realistic painting? How might the colors be different?

4. When you have chosen a subject and the style in which you will create your painting, sketch your composition. Are there any changes you would like to make?

5. Create your finished painting.

Check Your Work

Display your artwork with those of your classmates. Discuss the different art styles and subject matter that you see. Why do you feel the style of art you chose suits the community change you show? How did you use line, shape, and color to express your feelings about the change?

Computer Connection

With a paint or multimedia program, create a background scene that includes buildings or other structures. Create cars and other objects to place in the scene, or use software that allows for the creation of 3-D models. Use animation to move the objects or models through the scene.

Sketchbook Connection

Make quick sketches of the changes you see happening in your community. You might see a building under construction, a new billboard, or a road being built. Some changes are not as obvious, such as feelings or opinions about things that are happening in your community. Try sketching these kinds of changes, too. Use lines, shapes, and colors to suggest mood and emphasis.

Studio Collaboration

Join with other students in your class who have chosen to work in the same style as you. Discuss the painting techniques used in this style. Talk about how you can work together to create a series of paintings about change in your community. Give your group a name. Working in the same style, you might each paint different subject matter. All of your paintings together should reflect changes you see in your community.

Fig. 6–26 **"We brought in objects that reflect how we live today compared to when baby boomers were kids. Although they had a lot of bikes back then, kids today are getting more into extreme sports like bike jumping. The hardest part was mixing colors to the right shade using only black, white, red, blue, and yellow paints."** Joonas Woullet, *Rocket Sprocket,* 2000. Tempera paint, 18" x 12" (46 x 30 cm). Plymouth Middle School, Plymouth, Minnesota.

Connect to...

Careers

Have you ever played with Lego blocks? The Lego block was named "Toy of the Decade" by a business magazine in 1999, evidence that the simplest toys remain some of the best. (The Lego company began in 1932.) Despite the continuing success of classic toys that require no batteries or microchips, **toy designers** now incorporate advances in technology in all kinds of toys. However, these designers not only research and design new toys, but they also consider factors such as safety, child psychology, manufacturing procedures, packaging, and promotion. They may specialize in designing hard toys, soft toys (such as stuffed animals and dolls), or board or electronic games. What were your favorite toys

Fig. 6–27 **Toy designer Sean Lee enjoys every aspect of his job: from working with other designers on new toy ideas to meeting with engineers to decide on how a toy will actually work.** Photo reproduced with permission of Sean Lee.

when you were young? How are they different from the toys that your siblings or young relatives play with now? If you could design a new toy, what would it be?

Other Arts

Theater

Technological changes have affected not only the visual arts, but also the art of theater. The most profound impact on theater was the **invention of the motion picture**, in the early twentieth century.

Theater had been a popular form of entertainment for people of all classes. However, with the first public showing of movies, theaters began to lose their audiences. Movies could be duplicated cheaply and played in many locations simultaneously, so more people could view a film than any particular theater production, and they could do so less expensively. Also, films realistically depicted places unfamiliar to viewers, documented real events, and used fascinating special effects. To compete with all this, theater artists had to identify and promote the unique characteristics of theater: that theater is a live event is perhaps the most important.

What are the similarities and differences between attending a live event, such as theater, and a recorded event, such as film? Which type of event do you prefer? Why? What is the effect of the audience on actors in theater? On actors in a film? How would you use film to tell the story of Jack and the beanstalk? How would you use theater? How would you show the beanstalk growing? How would you show the difference in size between the giant and Jack?

Internet Connection
For more activities related to this chapter, go to the Davis website at **www.davis-art.com.**

Other Subjects

Fig. 6–28 **Angel Island has a long history. It was once a favorite hunting and fishing place of the Native-American tribe the Miwok. Today it is a California state park with many trails and paths.** *Angel Island, Ayalla Cove.*
Courtesy California State Parks, 2000.

Social Studies

What do you know about Ellis Island? Have you ever heard of its counterpart, Angel Island? **Angel Island**, near San Francisco, was the western point of entry, mostly for Chinese immigrants, to the United States in the early 1900s. At Angel Island, prospective immigrants were met by harsh procedures for processing. Subjected to humiliating medical exams and lengthy interrogations, many Chinese were held on the island for up to twenty-four months in intolerable conditions. Where could you look to compare immigration processing today with that at Ellis and Angel islands?

Fig. 6–29 **A caterpillar hatches from an egg and is the larva stage of a butterfly or moth. Is this an example of simple or complete metamorphosis?**
Photo ©Karen Durlach.

Language Arts

When have you tried to change a friend's opinion? How did you go about it? Verbally? In writing? Many writers—especially critics—use **persuasive writing**, in which they present and discuss arguments or reasons to change or influence the reader's opinion. Most articles written by art critics are persuasive pieces. Try to find real-life examples of persuasive writing in the arts section of your local Sunday paper. Which articles represent persuasive writing? Are any of these articles about art? Where else could you look for examples of persuasive writing about art?

Science

What represents change in the area of natural science? Consider **metamorphosis**—a change, or transformation, through distinct stages in the life cycle. For instance, an insect hatches from an egg; as it grows, it molts (sheds) its exoskeleton (skin). Changes in form may occur with each molt. In simple metamorphosis, an insect develops from egg to larva to adult, but the larva resembles the adult. In complete metamorphosis, development moves from egg to larva to pupa to adult. How could you depict in a drawing or painting each stage of the complete metamorphosis of a toad or another creature?

Daily Life

By what ways do you communicate with your friends? Have these ways changed since you were a child? Since your parents were teenagers? Especially rapid changes in **personal communications** have resulted from recent technological advances. E-mail, cell phones, and pagers allow nearly instant contact, but their use may affect other, more traditional avenues for interpersonal communication. For instance, when did you last write and mail a personal letter? Do you think e-mail will replace regular, or "snail," mail? Will handwriting a letter become a lost art? What might be the consequences of such a loss?

Portfolio

"I liked this scene because of the peaceful mood of the pond in contrast to the rowdy soccer players. I like how this scene looks out into the forest. You can see a picture of the playground against the forest. Boys at my school like to play soccer." **Marysa Leya**

Fig. 6–30 Marysa Leya, *Autumn at Avery Coonley*, 1999.
Colored pencil and marker, 9" x 12" (23 x 30.5 cm). Avery Coonley School, Downers Grove, Illinois.

Fig. 6–31 Meg Weeks, *Twilight Trek to Freedom*, 1999.
Construction paper collage, 18" x 24" (46 x 61 cm). Winsor School, Boston, Massachusetts.

"I made a dolphin diving into water, but as it dives it eventually turns into a drop of water. I did this piece because I love animals and the sea." **Cami Rosboschil**

This collage was inspired by stories of the Underground Railroad for runaway slaves during the Civil War, a time of great change in our country. The artist says, "Despite the fact that this piece is set at night, the colors of the people and their surroundings are not bleak, thus the piece still has some light and cheer—to express the hopeful emotions of the people."
Meg Weeks

CD-ROM Connection
To see more student art, check out the Community Connection Student Gallery.

Fig. 6–32 Cami Rosboschil, *Dolphin Mobile*, 1999.
Foam, acrylic, 23" high (58.5 cm). Hayfield Secondary School, Alexandria, Virginia.

Chapter 6 Review

Recall

How does the art of Nam June Paik (*see below*) refer to changes in technology?

Understand

Use examples to explain how art reflects and inspires changes in communities.

Apply

Styles in music have undergone many changes over the years. What might account for changes in music over time?

Analyze

Select an artwork in this chapter and tell how the art elements are arranged to reflect or inspire change.

Synthesize

Speculate about how art might look in twenty years. Give reasons for your predictions.

Evaluate

Select an artwork from this chapter that you believe is a good example of how artworks can inspire change in communities. Give reasons for your judgment.

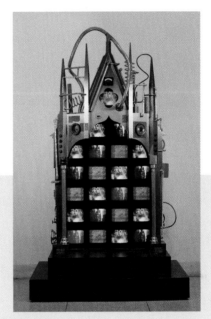

Page 198

For Your Portfolio

Look at the global view lessons for each of the chapters in this book to see art from another place in the world. Select one work that interests you. Find out as much as you can about the place where this artwork was made. Prepare a written report including a map, a description of geography, climate, natural resources, beliefs of the people, etc. Speculate about how the characteristics of the place are reflected in the artwork you have selected.

For Your Sketchbook

Look through the pages in your sketchbook and make a list of the characteristics or qualities that are consistent throughout your sketchbook. Do you see color preferences, for example? Also identify ways that your entries have changed. Summarize your findings on continuity and change on a blank page in your sketchbook.

Celebrating

Above: Fig. 7–1 **This full-size operating carousel celebrates Tennessee history and culture. If you were to create a carousel to celebrate the heritage of your own community, what people or events would you include?** Red Grooms, *Tennessee Fox Trot Carousel,* Riverfront Park, Nashville, TN.
Fiberglass over an aluminum frame, 35' x diam. 46' (88.9 x 116.8 cm). Illustrations © 1998 Red Grooms. Photo courtesy of Tennessee Fox Trot Carousel Operating Company. © 2000 Red Grooms / Artist Rights Society (ARS), New York.

Right: **Adelicia Acklen is one of many Nashville figures featured on this carousel. Why might an artist create an artwork that celebrates a specific person or group of people?** Red Grooms, *Tennessee Fox Trot Carousel* (detail).

- What do people celebrate?
- How is art a part of celebrations?

Does your town or city celebrate, or honor, things that have special meaning to the community? Some cities and towns have annual festivals, such as a dogwood festival or a potato festival, to celebrate a plant or food that is an important part of their environment. Other places **celebrate** the anniversary of the founding of their town or city. This kind of celebration might happen only once or twice in the life of the community and honors its history.

There are countless kinds of community celebrations and countless ways to show these celebrations in artworks. Sometimes an artwork can be a kind of celebration in itself. For example, imagine learning about the history of your hometown by riding a colorful carousel such as this one in Nashville, Tennessee (Fig. 7–1). The carousel is a way for Nashville to celebrate its heritage and community spirit. It focuses on the history of the city, the people who live there, and what they have accomplished.

Many artists have helped communities celebrate their heritage by creating artworks about the local people and their way of life. Often, artworks that reflect community spirit are made to be seen and used in public. What kinds of public art have you seen that honors a community or its heritage? Are there any such artworks in your town or city?

What's Ahead

- **Core Lesson** Discover ways that art helps people celebrate and express pride in their communities.
- **7.1 Art History Lesson**
  Explore how American artists celebrated regional and national spirits in their art from the 1920s through the 1950s.
- **7.2 Forms and Media Lesson**
  Learn how artists capture celebrations in photographs.
- **7.3 Global View Lesson**
  Investigate the art and celebrations of communities in the Caribbean.
- **7.4 Studio Lesson**
  Create a three-dimensional photomontage that celebrates community spirit.

Words to Know

celebrate	montage
traditions	Dada
Regionalist	Surrealist
Harlem Renaissance	

Pride in Community

Local Customs

When we meet people from other places, we are sometimes surprised to learn their different words for the simple things we use and do every day. For instance, people refer to soft drinks as "soda" or "tonic" or "pop," depending on where they live or grew up. The words people use are just a small part of what makes the spirit of a community special. A community's spirit comes from the pride its members have in their heritage. Language, clothing, mannerisms, and local customs can all add to the spirit of a community.

To celebrate the spirit of a community is to celebrate its people and their way of life. Stories about other times are passed down through generations. Local customs can also be traced back in time. It can be fun to learn about the differences in the way people live in other regions. Artists can help us learn by creating artworks that show people going about their lives in local ways.

Local Heroes

Another source of community spirit is the pride people have in the accomplishments of local heroes and celebrities. The *Watts Tower* (Fig. 7–3) is an example of such pride. Artist Simon Rodia built this tower with millions of found objects: broken jewelry, toys, pieces of plastic and glass, and so on. When local officials tried to tear it down, people in the community fought to keep it. It is now a symbol of pride and spirit in the Watts district of south-central Los Angeles. Even though the artist left the area after working on it for thirty-four years, he is still considered a local hero.

Fig. 7–2 **Most communities in the United States celebrate the Fourth of July. Here, a little boy dresses like Uncle Sam. How does your town or city celebrate the Fourth?** Russell Lee, *Boy on Float in Fourth of July Parade*, 1941.
Silver gelatin print. Courtesy of the Library of Congress (LC-USF33-013103-M1)

As you travel into cities and towns, you may see welcome signs that tell you about the famous people who were born or lived there. Motels, restaurants, and parks are often named after favorite citizens. Communities sometimes ask artists to help them create artworks that show the accomplishments of their citizens. For example, many cities and towns have a mural that an artist might have made with the help of local volunteers. The people of Atchison, Kansas—hometown of aviator Amelia Earhart—asked Kansas artist Stan Herd to help them commemorate Earhart's 100th birthday. Many townspeople volunteered to help the artist create her portrait (Fig. 7–4) using native stone, grasses, and other ground covers. Like most of Herd's artworks, the portrait of Amelia Earhart is best seen from the air!

Fig. 7–3 **This tower is made of thousands of found materials put together by one man. Why might he still be considered a local hero after leaving the area?** Simon Rodia, *Watts Tower,* Los Angeles, California, 1921–55.
© Rene Burri / Magnum Photos.

Fig. 7–4 **Stan Herd is known for his "crop art." He uses plants to make images. Is there an artwork in your area that people worked on together?** Stan Herd, *Portrait of Amelia Earhart,* Atchison, Kansas, 1997.
Native stone with perennial grasses and other ground covers. Photograph © by Jon Blumb, 1997.

Celebrating

227

Community Festivals

When you look at a tour book for any region in North America, you can usually find a list of many local festivals. These celebrations provide an opportunity for people in a city or town to take part in local cultural events, seasonal customs, religious beliefs, and community traditions. Seasonal festivals highlight special activities associated with each time of the year. Snow sculptures are common activities at winter festivals in colder regions (Fig. 7–5). Festivals are also held to honor religious figures and events. Regional festivals often celebrate local foods—such as chili, bratwurst, tomatoes, or pumpkins—or local crafts and music. Some communities hold festivals to honor local celebrities, such as astronauts, war heroes, or poets.

Common Festival Traditions

While community celebrations differ in many ways, there are some **traditions**—customs or beliefs that are passed down from earlier generations—that festivals have in common. Parades and fireworks, for instance, have long been part of community celebrations. Banners, flags, costumes, and music are often part of parades. Some communities parade their animals and vehicles, too. In some places, parades are even held on water with decorated boats. Public dance, theater, and concert performances add to the festivities. Many communities celebrate with puppet shows that tell religious or other familiar stories. In Indonesia, puppeteers perform all-night shows with shadow puppets (Fig. 7–7).

Fig. 7–5 **The largest winter festival in Canada, called the Festival du Voyageur, is a celebration of Manitoba's French-Canadian history. It is internationally famous for its snow sculpture competition. Would you guess that this snow sculpture was designed by an artist from China? Why or why not?** Hong Kong's entry in the International Snow Sculpture Symposium, 1993.
Courtesy Festival du Voyageur.

People with a common interest sometimes come from all over the world to attend festivals. For several years, Houston, Texas, has been the destination for people interested in art cars—vehicles transformed into spectacular moving sculptures (Fig. 7–6). Although people bring their art cars from many different places, the community of Houston has adopted the festival as its own.

Fig. 7–7 Shadow puppet shows are featured in festivals throughout Indonesia. Traditionally, they tell stories from Hindu mythology. The shows start late and last all night. Have you seen puppet shows at festivals? How were they related to the festival's theme? Indonesia, Central Java, *Shadow Puppets*.
© Luca Tettoni / Viesti Associates Inc.

A Festival in Pastel

Community celebration is a popular theme for drawings and paintings. Artists who create these works make choices about subject matter, media, and techniques. Some choose to draw festivals from up close; others work from far away. Artists can create the excitement of festivals by using bright colors and lively lines and shapes in their artworks.

In this studio experience, you will create a pastel drawing of a community celebration. Will the point of view of your scene be from up close or far away? Will you show the event or the people? How will you use color, line, and shape to create a particular mood or feeling?

You Will Need

- sketch paper
- pencil
- pastels
- scrap paper
- facial tissues
- cotton swabs
- drawing paper

Try This

1. Choose a community celebration to show. Then choose a format and point of view for your drawing. Will it be horizontal or vertical? Will you show a daytime or nighttime scene? Sketch your ideas.

2. Experiment with pastels on scrap paper. Try making different kinds of marks. Blend colors with a tissue or cotton swab. Decide which colors and pastel techniques will best express your ideas.

3. Create your final drawing. Draw large shapes first. Then fill in colors and details.

Fig. 7–8 **This artist created a series of paintings that capture the 100th birthday celebration of the Brooklyn Bridge, in New York. Do you think her painting shows what it's like to watch a fireworks display?** Colleen Browning, *Fireworks III,* 1983–84. Oil on canvas, 19" x 27" (48.3 x 68.6 cm). Courtesy Hamon-Meek Gallery, Naples, Florida.

Studio Background

Festive Crowd Pleasers

Parades and fireworks displays are by far the most popular expressions of celebration. Most people love parades for their music, floats, clowns, balloons, confetti, and general excitement. People often work together to create different kinds of art for parades, such as banners, sculptures for floats, and costumes. Many artists then go on to record these events in paintings and drawings.

Fireworks are more mysterious than parades. People are entranced by their delicate and instantaneous beauty. Artists have been actively

Display your completed artwork with your classmates' artworks. Separate them according to subject matter and point of view. Use descriptive words to indicate the moods or feelings of the artworks. Determine how the use of color, line, and shape contributes to the moods and feelings conveyed.

Fig. 7–9 "I used chalk pastels to make a drawing of northern lights and a fireworks show. It takes place on New Year's eve." Cathy Mae Searles, *An Alaskan Light Show,* 2000.
Pastel, 12" x 18" (30.5 x 46 cm). Colony Middle School, Palmer, Alaska.

Check Your Understanding

1. Use examples to explain how artists help communities remember and celebrate their local heroes and celebrities.
2. How might an artist show the spirit of a community?
3. Identify two traditions that community festivals have in common.
4. Why, do you think, do people use fireworks in community celebrations?

Sketchbook Connection
Take your sketchbook to a festive event. Focus on just one kind of object or action—people's faces, the movements of people's bodies, food, banners, or toys, for example. Keep sketching until you feel comfortable with your subject matter.

involved in the design of fireworks displays. Famous artists Michelangelo, Leonardo da Vinci, Rubens, and Bernini all helped design fireworks displays. People rely on artists to create images that will help them remember the momentary fireworks experience.

Fig. 7–10 Jacob Lawrence used bright colors and simple shapes to draw viewers into this scene. The close-up view helps viewers feel like part of the celebration. How did Lawrence use color and shape to create the rhythm and excitement of a parade? Jacob Lawrence, *Parade,* 1960.
Tempera with pencil underdrawing on fiberboard, 23 7/8" x 30 1/8" (60.6 x 76.5 cm). Hirshhorn Museum and Sculpture Garden, Smithsonian Institution, Gift of Joseph H. Hirshhorn, 1966. Photographed by Lee Stalsworth.

Celebrating

Art and Pride: 1920–1950

1930
Benton, *Changing West*

1936
Dike, *Copper*

Industrial
America
page 206

American Regionalism

American Social
Causes
page 258

1932
Jones, *The Ascent of Ethiopia*

1937
Magafan, *Wheat Threshing*

History in a Nutshell

Major international wars took place between the 1910s and the 1950s. In 1918, the United States was emerging from World War I, which was fought in Europe. Americans were tired of European political and economic affairs. They wanted to focus on the quality of life in the United States. Then, in 1929, the American stock market crashed, triggering the Great Depression of the 1930s. During this time many people in the United States lost everything they owned as well as their means of earning a living. Economic recovery programs, such as the Works Progress Administration (WPA), helped the United States recover from these losses. So did World War II. World War II dominated the first half of the 1940s, and was followed by the Korean War, in the early 1950s.

Fig. 7–11 In this painting, the artist created a variety of snapshots of the American West. Why might people consider this artwork an expression of the national spirit of the time? Thomas Hart Benton, *The Changing West* from *America Today*, 1930.
Distemper and egg tempera on gessoed linen with oil glaze, 92" x 117" (233.7 x 297.2 cm). Collection, AXA Financial. © AXA Financial. © T.H. Benton and R.P. Benton Testamentary Trusts / Licensed by VAGA, New York, NY.

Fig. 7–12 **Communities receiving government-funded murals had to approve the artworks first. The murals often showed the things in which a community took pride. What do you think the people in this community valued?** Ethel Magafan, *Wheat Threshing*, 1937.
Egg tempera on gessoed masonite panel, 17 1/2" x 34 1/8" (44.5 x 88.6 cm). Museum Purchase, Art Purchase Fund, Friends of the Wichita Art Museum, Wichita Art Museum, Wichita, Kansas. (1981.19)

Fig. 7–13 **Would you consider this painting the work of an Urban Regionalist or a Rural Regionalist? Why?** Philip Latimer Dike, *Copper*, 1936.
Oil on canvas, 38 3/16" x 46 1/4" (96.5 x 117.5 cm). Phoenix Art Museum, Museum purchase with funds provided by Western Art Associates. (78.10)

Community and National Spirit

In the years following World War I, many artists focused their attention on specific regions or sections of the country. They became known as **Regionalists.** Some of these artists used the city as subject matter for their art. *Urban Regionalists*, as they came to be called, celebrated the spirit of the community. Their artworks showed scenes crowded with people, new architecture, and changing styles of clothing. People began to think about where their ancestors came from. Groups of people gathered together to celebrate their common heritages.

Outside of cities, artists searched for ways to celebrate a national spirit. Artists such as Grant Wood and Thomas Hart Benton became known as the *Rural Regionalists*. Their works captured American pride, traditions, and morals. They recorded the roots of America, often looking back to American folk art for inspiration. Figures 7–11 and 7–13 celebrate the spirit of the American West.

During the Great Depression, the United States started one of the most extraordinary programs of support for the arts ever imagined. Inspired by the Mexican mural movement, the government paid artists minimum wages to create public works of art. These works included murals that focused on regional and community spirit. Many of these murals are landmarks in North American art history. How does the mural by Ethel Magafan (Fig. 7–12) show community spirit?

Harlem Renaissance

In the 1920s, a group of artists, writers, photographers, and entertainers gathered in Harlem, a section of New York City, to express their heritage as African Americans. Their celebration is known as the **Harlem Renaissance.** *Renaissance* means a rebirth of culture. In Harlem, artists helped the African-American community explore its background and express pride in its culture. Some artists, such as photographer James VanDerZee, captured scenes of important figures and events of the Harlem Renaissance in their artwork (Fig. 7–15). Others, such as

Meta Warrick Fuller, used their art to teach and remind people of African-American history (Fig. 7–16).

The Harlem Renaissance ended with the stock market crash in 1929. Artists such as Lois Mailou Jones (Fig. 7–14) continued to create important works in the decades that followed. These artists spread cultural pride to other African-American communities throughout the country. Although less publicized, creative activities were taking place in African-American communities in many other cities, such as Philadelphia, Chicago, Boston, Baltimore, and San Francisco.

Fig. 7–14 **How does this painting celebrate the heritage of African-American people?** Lois Mailou Jones, *The Ascent of Ethiopia,* 1932.
Oil on canvas, 23 1/2" x 17 1/2" (59.7 x 43.8 cm). Milwaukee Art Museum, Purchase, African-American Acquisition Fund, matching funds from Suzanne and Richard Pieper, with additional support from Arthur and Dorothy Nelle Sanders. Photo credit: Larry Sanders.

Fig. 7–15 **James VanDerZee was the most successful of Harlem's commercial photographers during the Harlem Renaissance. He used his camera to record the life and glamour of urban Black America. This photograph shows Marcus Garvey, an important community leader of the time.** James VanDerZee, *Marcus Garvey in Regalia*, 1924. Silver gelatin print, 5 5/16" x 10" (15.2 x 25.6 cm). © Donna Mussenden VanDerZee

Fig. 7–16 **Meta Warrick Fuller created this sculpture before the Harlem Renaissance. Notice the Egyptian headdress and bandages of mummification, which the woman is unwrapping. These are believed to represent the greatness of the African people. Why might African Americans be interested in this sculpture?** Meta Warrick Fuller, *Ethiopia Awakening*, ca. 1907–10. Plaster (bronze cast), 67" x 16" x 20" (170 x 40.6 x 50.8 cm). Art and Artifacts Division, Schomburg Center for Research in Black Culture, The New York Public Library, Astor, Lenox and Tilden Foundations. Photo by Namu Sassoonian.

7.1 Art History

Check Your Understanding

1. Explain the basic differences between the art of the Urban Regionalists and the Rural Regionalists.

2. How did the Mexican mural movement have an impact on the United States during the Great Depression?

3. What is meant by the term *Harlem Renaissance*?

4. What role did artists have in the Harlem Renaissance?

Studio Connection

Crowds of people are among the many subjects artists painted to capture the spirit of community life in the twentieth century. You can create a mixed-media painting of people. Experiment with ways to combine different media, such as collage techniques with painting. Use magazine or newspaper cutouts of figures for your crowd scene. Then combine these with your own drawings and a painted background. Use a variety of thick and thin lines. Use light colors for highlights and dark colors for shadows.

Photography

You probably have at least one photograph of yourself with your family or friends during a holiday celebration. When cameras became relatively inexpensive, people all over the world began using them to record memorable times. After photography was invented, in 1826, artists slowly began to realize the possibilities for creative expression. Using a camera, they could look around and "frame" pictures. Some artists have taken photographs as guides for later paintings. Others value photographs for their unique characteristics. For over 175 years, artists have been using photography to explore their world and create unforgettable images.

Some of these unforgettable images document important celebrations in our communities, such as a bicentennial parade or a moment during the Olympics. Many photographers focus on people in the artworks they create. Photographs like these remind us that we all share basic human emotions and do very similar kinds of activities. Some photographers are not interested in showing the world as it actually exists. They create images by posing actors or objects and then photographing them. They often create eerie scenes for us to contemplate.

Photography as Art and Science

The art of photography starts with the person who uses the camera. A professional photographer needs to know the elements and principles of design when preparing to take a picture. (See Foundation 3 to learn more about the elements and principles of design.) Good photography also comes from a scientific knowledge of camera tech-

Fig. 7–17 **This photograph represents one city's perspective of a once-in-a-lifetime world celebration: the ringing in of the new millenium. Notice how the photographer has used the design principles of balance and emphasis to create his image. Besides the blazing 2000, what other element in this photograph will never be seen again?** Fireworks in Washington, New Year's, 2000, Celebration.
© Reuters Newmedia Inc. / CORBIS

236

niques, films, light sources, and printing processes. In the darkroom, an artist can change images to hide or reveal details caught on film. Photographic technology has changed over the years. Today, many photographers are experimenting with computer technology and digital cameras to create and manipulate pictures.

7.2 Forms and Media

Check Your Understanding
1. What do photographers do?
2. What does a photographer need to know to create a good picture?

Studio Connection
Cinematography is the art of making moving, or motion, pictures. The illusion of motion is created by rapidly showing a series of photographs called frames. The picture in each frame is slightly different from the preceding one. Flip books are a way to create motion pictures without using a camera. Try making a flip book that shows something from a community celebration, such as fireworks or a festival dance. Make a series of drawings by hand or on a computer. Each drawing should be slightly different from the one before it. Staple the drawings together at one end. When you are finished, rapidly flip the pages to show the action.

Fig. 7–18 **This photograph shows a different kind of celebration. Communities in many parts of the world celebrated the surrender of German forces at the end of World War II. Here we see a neighborhood in New York City. What makes this a powerful photograph?** Large group of people celebrating V-E Day. Silver gelatin print. © Corbis / Bettmann-UPI

Caribbean Art

Caribbean

Fig. 7–19 In the Caribbean, small woodcarvings such as this are used for religious rituals performed in the home. Most are sculptures of saints. Anonymous, Caban family member, *La Mano Poderosa*, Camuy area, Puerto Rico, 19th century.
Wood, 10" (25.5 cm). Private Collection, San Juan, Puerto Rico. Courtesy Galeria Botello, Hato Rey, P.R.

Global Glance

The Caribbean is a chain of many large and small islands from Cuba and the Bahamas in the north to Trinidad and Barbados in the south. The communities of these islands do not all share the same culture and language. The four main language groups of the Caribbean are Spanish, French, English, and Dutch. West African and Asian languages are also spoken on the islands. All the island communities of the Caribbean, however, have two things in common: religious icons and carnival or festival traditions. These traditions are important to the art of the Caribbean.

A New Beginning

Before the seventeenth century, the Caribbean was not known for its artwork. No large-scale monuments or stone architecture stopped explorers on their way through the region, and most early Caribbean art has been lost or destroyed. The artworks of this early period that remain, such as funerary figures and pottery, are religious, utilitarian, or related to ritual.

By the end of the seventeenth century, the Caribbean was a mixture of European cultures, African slave groups, and an emerging Creole society. The first important Caribbean-born artists became known in the second half of the eighteenth century. The European influence on their artworks is easy to see. During this time, religious artworks and portraits were in great demand by the upper classes. Religious and ritual art remained popular through the nineteenth century.

A Celebration of Culture

In the early twentieth century, Caribbean artists turned their attention to cultural symbols, the daily work of islanders, and the gaiety of life and leisure. Their artworks were filled with the bright colors and excitement of festivals, such as carnival.

Even as Caribbean art celebrated its island cultures, artists looked to communities around the world for inspiration. Caribbean artists of Spanish descent began to create images of local island conditions, such as poverty, in much the same way as the Mexican muralists of the time. The connection between African-American communities and the Caribbean became strong. Several Caribbean artists were key figures in the Harlem Renaissance.

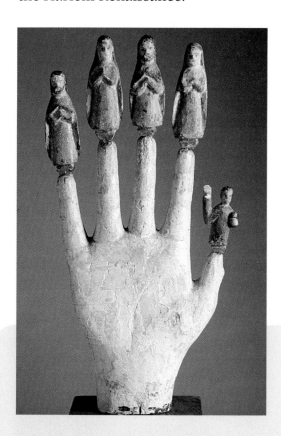

Fig. 7–20 **Edna Manley created some of her works at the time of the Harlem Renaissance. Notice the upturned face and the strong arms of this sculpture. How might these features suggest the Renaissance idea of rebirth or reawakening?** Edna Manley, *Negro Aroused,* 1935.
Mahogany, height: 51" (129.5 cm). National Gallery of Jamaica, Kingston. Photograph © 2000, Denis Valentine.

Fig. 7–21 **Notice the tall and narrow format of this painting. Why might the artist have chosen this format for this festive scene?** Andre Normil, *The Greased Pole,* 1966.
Oil on masonite, 49 1/2" x 17 1/2" (125.7 x 44.5 cm). Milwaukee Art Museum, Gift of Richard and Erna Flagg. Photo by Larry Sanders (M1991.136)

Carnival as Art

At carnival, there are no rules except one: to have fun. People wear bright and funny costumes, parade through the streets, throw candy and trinkets to the crowds, eat and drink traditional fare, dance and sing all in a colorful jumble of noise, movement, and music. It's a party on a massive scale. It's a celebration of what it means to live in a community where carnival is one of the most important festivals of the year.

Carnival celebrates life. Latin communities around the world hold this traditional festival in the spring of each year. Traditionally, carnival comes from ancient celebrations of many civilizations: European, African, Asian, and Middle Eastern. European traditions seek new and creative ideas for ways to celebrate. From Africa, traditions of masquerade combine music, dance, costume, sculpture, and drama in a single performance. The influence of East Indian Islamic cultures contributes abstract, geometric, colorful patterns to costumes, parade floats, and other artworks.

Some might say that a Caribbean carnival is performance art at its best. As an art of celebration, carnival is an opportunity to be part of the energy and spirit of a community of people. It allows individuals to be a part of something larger than themselves. For some individuals, it satisfies a need to stand out in a crowd. For others, it provides a means of expressing community pride.

Fig. 7–22 The artist created this elaborate costume from strips of cloth. Would you believe that the theme of the costume is life and death? Which features represent life? Which features represent death? Peter Minshall, *The Merry Monarch,* Caribbean Festival of Arts, 1987.
Courtesy John W. Nunley.

Fig. 7–23 **This costume featured a macaw on one side and a scarlet ibis on the other. Compare this costume to *The Merry Monarch* (Fig. 7–22). What characteristics do the two costumes have in common?** Wayne Berkeley, *Diana, Goddess of the Hunt,* Caribbean Festival of Arts, 1987. Courtesy John W. Nunley.

7.3 Global View

Check Your Understanding

1. What are the basic similarities among the art of Caribbean cultures?
2. Name some influences on Caribbean art.
3. How might Caribbean festivals or carnivals be considered an art form?
4. What traditions are associated with carnival?

Studio Connection

Festival or carnival art includes sculptural forms that are made from assembled parts. An *assemblage* is a sculpture made by combining discarded objects such as boxes, pieces of wood, parts of old toys, and so on. To explore assemblage, create a relief sculpture in a shallow box. Try creating a freestanding sculpture of a festive figure or a small environment. Collect some discarded objects or fabricate some interesting shapes and forms from clay, wood, paper, or wire. From your collection, choose things that express the theme of celebration. Think about the symbolism of the materials—what they mean to you or to other people. Consider the principles of design in arranging the items. Work with layers of texture, color, and collage-like forms.

Celebrating

241

3-D Montage

The Spirit of Celebration

Studio Introduction

Have you ever been disappointed with a photograph you've taken to remember an event? You might have been disappointed because the photograph showed only one split second of the event, and not the whole story. Do you wonder how you can capture the whole story next time? Here's one way: You can create a **montage**—a collage that is created mainly from photographs.

In this studio experience, you will create a three-dimensional (3-D) montage that celebrates the spirit of your community. Page 244 will tell you how to do it. The community you celebrate might be your family, neighborhood, school, team, or the like. What kinds of photographs will help capture the spirit of your community? Focus on the people, places, or objects that will remind viewers of the community you choose.

Studio Background

The Story of Montage

Artists have been combining photographic images for almost as long as photography has been around. In the early twentieth century, a group of European artists created artworks by combining parts of photographs. These artists from the **Dada** movement—a movement that was known for rejecting traditional art styles and materials—named this process montage. They arranged photographic images in nonsensical ways. **Surrealists**—artists who created artworks based on dreams and fantasy—and other artists later found that the art of montage can convey new or unintended meaning.

Although a montage is made up mostly of photographic images, it might

Fig. 7–24 To celebrate the history of Colorado, artist Barbara Jo Revelle created this ceramic tile mural. She used photographs of people who took part in shaping the character and spirit of the state. What other public artwork in this book could be considered photomontage? Barbara Jo Revelle, *Colorado Panorama: A People's History of Colorado.*
Courtesy the artist.

also include drawing or painting. Artists who create photomontages use parts of magazine and newspaper images, as well as snapshots and other single photographs. They use photographs in many ways to help them tell the complete story of their subject.

Fig. 7–26 Paul Nagano uses entire photographs to create his artworks, and he does not overlap them. He invented the word *photofusion* to describe his process of assembling photos into panoramic views. How is Nagano's "story" different from Revelle's (Fig. 7–24)? Paul Nagano, *Balinese Offerings,* 2000.
Photofusion, 22" x 32" (55.9 x 81.3 cm). Courtesy of the artist.

Making Your 3-D Photomontage

You Will Need

- magazines
- newspapers
- stiff cardboard
- ruler
- scissors
- X-acto knife
- tape
- glue

Safety Note
Use knives and other sharp tools with extreme care to avoid cuts and other accidents.

Try This

1. Collect photographs from magazines, newspapers, or your own home. Which photographs will best show your community's spirit? Will you use photographs of people, objects, or places? Remember that you can use all or part of an image.

2. Create a cardboard form. (Your photos will be glued to the form.) Cut, score, and fold flat pieces of cardboard. Or use slotting techniques and tape to join cardboard pieces. How can the form you create help express your message?

3. Try arranging your images in different ways on your cardboard base. Which images work well together? What surprising combinations can you come up with? As you work, you may need to find additional photographs.

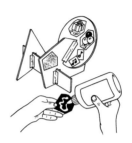

4. When you are satisfied with your arrangements, glue the photographs in place.

Check Your Work

Share your artwork with a classmate. Talk about the decisions you made and how you think the photographic images show the spirit of your community. Write a short paragraph about your artwork that will help others better understand its meaning. Display the statement and your artwork with those of your classmates. Take time to look at the work and read the accompanying statements.

Sketchbook Connection

Use your sketchbook to help plan your artwork. Sketch various shapes and forms that might help show the spirit of your community. Try drawing several recognizable forms, such as buildings or trees, related to your community. Then sketch some geometric or organic forms. Decide which shapes and forms might best convey your ideas about the community.

Computer Option

Collect images around a theme by scanning photos or taking photos with a digital camera. Use a paint or digital-imaging program to arrange selections from the various photos. Make some selections appear to float (by adding cast shadows) and seem unrealistic or surrealist (by placing unrelated items next to each other).

Fig. 7–27 **"This photo project was a lot of fun! Using color in the background helped to make all the photos flow together."** Stephanie Bacino, *I'm All About Life*, 1999.
Photographs, mat board, colored pencil, 6" x 8" x 5 ¹/₂" (15 x 20 x 14 cm). Plum Grove Junior High School, Rolling Meadows, Illinois.

Connect to...

Careers

What were your favorite picture books when you were a child? Did you realize that artists created the images in the books? The artists who provide images for picture books, juvenile nonfiction and novels, and textbooks are **children's-book illustrators**. They may write and illustrate their own books or create illustrations to accompany another author's text. A children's-book illustrator, usually a freelance artist, may develop a distinctive style and technique by which he or she is known. One such artist is Carmen Lomas Garza, who illustrates and writes the text for captivating, bilingual storybooks that celebrate her childhood memories, especially those that involved her family and community. Through her books, she honors images that are recognized and appreciated by Mexican Americans, and that serve to inform those who are unfamiliar with the culture.

Fig. 7–28 **Some communities use music and dance to honor group members, either living or dead. The Yoruba of Nigeria hold egungun festivals in honor of their ancestors.** Nigeria, Africa, Yoruba peoples, *Egungun dancers.*
Courtesy Davis Art Slides.

Internet Connection
For more activities related to this chapter, go to the Davis website at **www.davis-art.com.**

Other Arts

Music

Musicians, like artists, celebrate their community. Duke Ellington, a famous jazz composer and performer, wrote the symphony *Harlem* to celebrate this community. Ellington wrote: "We would like now to take you on a tour of this place called Harlem … It is Sunday morning. We are strolling from 110th Street up Seventh Avenue … Everybody is nicely dressed, and on their way to or from church. Everybody is in a friendly mood . . . You may hear a parade go by …"

In *Opelousas Hop*, Clifton Chenier celebrates his Louisiana home, where Cajun music developed from a blending of European and African-American traditions. Here, Chenier's "squeeze box" (accordion) sounds celebrate one French contribution to Cajun music. Listen to the two pieces of music. Can you hear ways that the composers celebrated their communities?

Social Studies

Artists often depict **traditional foods** of individual cultures. In his work, Mexican artist Diego Rivera celebrates maize (corn), an important food plant in the Americas. Corn provides basic nutrition in the daily diet of many areas of North and Central America. The Maya and other Mesoamerican civilizations were founded on the cultivation of corn, the basis of their diet. Corn-based foods are still prepared for special celebrations: tamales, made from corn and cooked in cornhusks, are traditionally served in Latino families on Christmas Eve; cornbread dressing is an essential part of many Thanksgiving dinners. What particular foods does your family enjoy on special occasions?

Language Arts

What sort of people are the subjects of biographies? Are they ordinary people, or accomplished individuals? **Biographies** usually tell about people celebrated for their achievements, discoveries, or heroism. Can you think of something in art that is like biography? A portrait is a visual image of a particular person, and it often provides insight into the subject's personality or accomplishments. Do you think portraits, like biographies, mostly depict celebrated people?

Fig. 7–30 **This sculpture shows the Aztec corn goddess, Chicomecoatl (*che-co-ME-co-ah-tul*). Are the features of the sculpture stylized or naturalistic?** Mexico Aztec (1325-1519/21), *Chicomecoatl (Corn Goddess)*.
Stone, height: 13 1/2" (34.3 cm). The Metropolitan Museum of Art, Purchase, 1900 (00.5.51). Photograph ©1981 The Metropolitan Museum of Art.

Fig. 7–29 **Festivals and other celebrations are common in communities throughout the world. Why do you think people enjoy getting together for such events?** Ghana, Africa, Bono peoples, *Festival*.
Courtesy Davis Art Slides.

Daily Life

Has your neighborhood ever celebrated by holding a street fair, a block party, or a backyard barbecue? Do your neighbors ever gather just for fun? Have you ever experienced a community parade for a sports victory, a returning hero or celebrity, or a holiday, such as the Fourth of July? Such celebrations allow neighbors to meet and get to know one another. What other benefits might these celebrations have?

Portfolio

Fig. 7–31 **Turning cartwheels is a classic way for young people to celebrate the spirit of fun.** Stephen Torosian, *Caught in the Act*, 1997. Clay. Remington Middle School, Franklin, Massachusetts.

"I did this work to become more familiar with my hometown. What better way to come closer to something than to draw it? I think the Elissa Ship was the easiest because I practiced it many times before I drew it on the main paper."
Dennis McClanahan

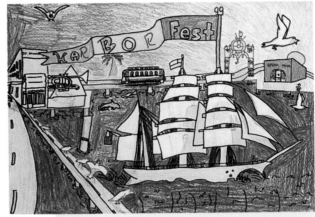

Fig. 7–32 **Every year Galveston has a celebration called Harborfest, the inspiration for this poster.** Dennis McClanahan, *Favorite Places*, 1999. Colored pencil, 12" x 18" (30 x 46 cm). Central Middle School, Galveston, Texas.

CD-ROM Connection
To see more student art, check out the Community Connection Student Gallery.

Fig. 7–33 **Four students worked together to create a lively scene large enough to cover a classroom door. One artist says, "I have basketball almost every night of the week and it's a big part of my life." Another says, "With every work of art I do, a part of me goes into it and I can become more and more expressive and skilled in creating."** Jayme Kimball, Cecelia Ortega, Elissa Teasdale, Kay Thibealt, *Fastforward: Girls' Basketball*, 2000. Acrylic, 5' x 3' (1.5 x 1 m). Merrimack Valley Middle School, Penacook, New Hampshire.

Chapter 7 Review

Recall

Identify an artist from this chapter whose artworks are best seen from the air. Identify an artist whose artworks are best considered up close.

Understand

Use examples to explain how art plays a role in community festivals and celebrations.

Apply

If you were asked to help your own family or group of friends celebrate their heritage and spirit, how might you suggest using art to do this?

Page 234

Analyze

Select one artwork from this chapter (*see example below*) and discuss how the arrangement of art elements contributes to its message about community heritage and spirit.

Synthesize

Imagine that a major manufacturer of cameras has asked you to suggest ways that photography might be used to celebrate a community's special heritage, traditions, and community spirit. What suggestions would you offer? Be as specific as possible.

Evaluate

Select an artwork from the chapter that you believe is an excellent example of how art can play a significant role in celebrating community spirit. Give reasons for your selection, considering such things as subject matter, materials and techniques, moods, feelings and ideas, and the organization of art elements.

For Your Portfolio

Develop an artwork especially for your portfolio based on the theme of celebration. Exchange your artwork with a peer and write a critique of each other's work. Be sure to tell what you see in the work, describing details. Interpret the meaning, making connections between what you see and what the work is about. What is its message about celebration? Comment on how the artwork is successful. Offer suggestions for improvement, with reasons or questions. Make a written response to the peer review.

For Your Sketchbook

Design a series of four postage stamps to commemorate your community. Focus on the theme of celebration and feature your community in connection with four different holiday celebrations.

8 Making a Difference

Fig. 8–1 Elijah Pierce's barbershop was a place where people could view his art and learn lessons about how to live a good life. What story could you tell in an artwork? How might it make a difference in someone's life? Elijah Pierce, *Monday Morning Gossip,* 1934. Carved and painted wood relief with glitter, mounted on painted panel, 33 1/2" x 24" (85.1 x 61.0 cm). Collection of Michael D. Hall. Courtesy the Columbus Museum of Art.

- How do people work to improve their communities?
- How does art make a difference in community life?

When friends or family members are sick or feeling sad, you try to cheer them up. You might tell a joke, give a gift, or simply be there to listen. Whatever you do, you try to make a difference in the way a person you care about feels. Many groups and individuals want to help the people around them. For example, artists often use their talents to make a difference in their communities.

The artwork shown in Fig. 8–1 was made by Elijah Pierce. For most of his life, Pierce was a barber in Columbus, Ohio. While waiting for his customers, Pierce whittled wood. He sometimes carved small sculptures of animals and people. Most of the time, however, he made relief carvings that illustrated stories that teach lessons about life.

Pierce didn't think of himself as an artist. He was a very religious man who wanted to share his faith with others and help them lead good lives. He used his whittling talent as a way of making a difference. For a long time, he shared his artworks only with customers. After another local artist told others about the carvings, Pierce's artworks were exhibited for the city of Columbus.

It doesn't always take a lot of people to make a difference in the lives of those around them. Elijah Pierce, working alone, made a difference in the lives of his customers and, eventually, in the lives of people around the world.

What's Ahead

- **Core Lesson** Learn how other artists have used their talents to make a difference in their communities.
- **8.1 Art History Lesson** Explore how artists in the second half of the twentieth century addressed social issues with their art.
- **8.2 Forms and Media Lesson** Learn about printmaking and how artists use it to send a message to many people.
- **8.3 Global View Lesson** Discover how twentieth-century African artists have made a difference in the way we think about African art.
- **8.4 Studio Lesson** Create a relief print that shows an endangered natural environment in a positive way.

Words to Know

collaborate	lithographic print
cause	serigraph
mural movement	traditional art
relief print	tourist art
intaglio print	linoleum cut

Artists Can Make a Difference

Throughout history, artists have used artwork to address the problems that communities face. Through their artworks, artists can express points of view about problems and try to influence the way people feel. For example, an artist might create a painting that shows how war or poverty can affect people. Some people who see the painting might then actively seek a way to help prevent war or diminish poverty. Other viewers might become more aware of the effects of war or poverty on all people. Through their work, artists can make a difference.

Protesting War

You have probably heard of the great twentieth-century artist Pablo Picasso. Picasso is famous for his development of *Cubism*, an abstract style of art, and for other ways of making art. He made one of his most powerful artworks after a village in Spain was bombed. The terrible bombing killed hundreds of innocent people. Picasso hoped *Guernica* (Fig. 8–2), named for the village that was bombed, would show the anguish and confusion people felt. Although *Guernica* is about a single event, its message is about all wars. *Guernica* has been seen by millions of people. Picasso is one artist who used his talents to make a difference in our attitudes about the horrors of war.

Fig. 8–2 In his own way, Picasso shows the horrors of war. What details are most expressive to you? How does this artwork make you feel about war?
Pablo Picasso, *Guernica,* 1937.
Oil on canvas, 137 3/4" x 307 9/10" (350 x 782 cm). Museo del Prado, Madrid, Spain. Giraudon/Art Resource, New York. © 2000 Estate of Pablo Picasso / Artist Rights Society (ARS), New York.

Fig. 8–3 When you look at this painting, you might first see the gentlemen reading the paper. How does the retitling of the work change the way you look at it? Ernst George Fischer, *Country Life,* ca. 1850.
Oil on canvas. Courtesy Maryland Historical Society, Baltimore, Maryland.

Fig. 8–4 In many of her artworks, Miriam Schapiro focuses on the beautiful items that women have created over the years. What details in this artwork celebrate the creative work of women? Miriam Schapiro, *Wonderland,* 1983.
Collage: acrylic, fabric and plastic beads on canvas, 35 1/2" x 56 3/4" (90 x 144 cm). National Museum of American Art, Washington, DC / Art Resource, NY.

Celebrating Differences

The 1960s Civil Rights movement in the United States led to laws that prohibited discrimination. However, people in many communities continue to struggle against prejudice and stereotyping based on race, ethnic background, and gender. Many women artists, such as Miriam Schapiro (Fig. 8–4), create artworks with strong messages. They try to make a difference in the way people think about the contributions and abilities of women.

Through his art, African-American artist Fred Wilson challenges people to see history in a different way. Sometimes he makes objects, but often he creates new exhibits by changing existing gallery or museum displays. For example, he was invited to work with the collection of the Maryland Historical Society in Baltimore. He changed the title of a painting that showed a wealthy white family enjoying a picnic. By changing the title from *Country Life* to *Frederick Serving Fruit* (Fig. 8–3), he drew attention to the young male slave who was serving the family. The title change made a difference in the way viewers saw the subject matter of the painting.

Collaborating to Make Art

Sometimes artists **collaborate**, or work together, with communities to create artworks. Collaborative artworks are made for many reasons. They can address the concerns of the community. Some of them celebrate the diversity of our nation's culture and people. Others express powerful feelings that we share as human beings.

Collaborations can involve any number of people—from two people to thousands. By working with communities to create artworks, artists try to help people see how their attitudes and behavior affect others.

Collaborating to Make a Difference

There are many examples of people working together to make a difference through art. One example is the *AIDS Memorial Quilt* (Fig. 8–6). As thousands of Americans faced the loss of loved ones to the AIDS disease, they were invited to create a quilt square in memory of those people. The AIDS quilt was displayed at a public space in Washington,

Fig. 8–5 Each panel on this quilt square is a personal expression of loss. This is a close-up of a single square from the quilt at left. In what ways do you think the quilt makes a difference? *AIDS Memorial Quilt* (detail) 1985–present.
Fabric and mixed media, each panel measures 36" x 72" (91.4 x 182.9 cm). Photo by Paul Margolies. Courtesy the NAMES Project Foundation.

Fig. 8–6 Caring for others sometimes means helping them accept the death of a loved one. Why might a collaboration like this be comforting for the people involved? How might the experience have been different if each person created his or her own artwork independently? Cleve Jones, Founder, *AIDS Memorial Quilt,* 1985–present.
Fabric and mixed media, each panel measures 36" x 72" (91.4 x 182.9 cm) (over 43,000 panels as of 1999). Photo by Mark Theissen. Courtesy the NAMES Project Foundation.

DC, and in other places around the country. This enormous quilt was a collaborative artistic effort. It provided a solemn comfort for those who contributed to it. It also brought public attention to the need for medical research to find a cure for AIDS.

Revival Field (Fig. 8–7) is another example of a collaboration. *Revival Field* is the name given to a series of "growing" sculptures. Artist Mel Chin thought of the project when he read an article about certain plants that absorb heavy metals from the soil in which they grow. He contacted scientist Rufus Chaney to see if he would help him create test plantings as an art project.

Chaney, a plant and soil expert, agreed enthusiastically. Between 1990 and 1993, Chin and others planted these special plants in a landfill in Saint Paul, Minnesota. The plants are meant to transform the ecology of a site from dead or dangerous to living. After three years and annual soil testing, scientists noted that the plan was working. The plants were "cleaning" the toxic soil in which they grew. Another *Revival Field* was established in Pennsylvania. The artist hopes that his work on these projects will make a difference in the future, as communities seek ways to restore the environment.

Fig. 8–7 The artist who worked on this collaboration was concerned about the environment. Does this work challenge your idea of what art is? How? Why do you think it is considered a sculpture? Mel Chin, *Revival Field*, 1990–93.
Plants and industrial fencing on a hazardous-waste landfill, approximately 60' x 60'x 9' (18.3 x 18.3 x 2.7 m). Pig's Eye Landfill, Saint Paul. Photo: David Schneider, 1993.

Making a Collaborative Sculpture

When people work together on an artwork, they choose the subject matter, plan the artwork, and create it as a group. **In this studio experience, you will work with classmates to create a sculpture that will change the way people think about an issue or problem.** You and your group will choose the issue or problem together. Then you will sketch a plan for the sculpture and choose the materials that will best express your ideas.

Fig. 8–8 **Artist Lynne Hull was concerned that hawks and eagles were being electrocuted when they roosted on telephone poles. So, she created structures for them. In what ways is this sculpture different from others you have seen?** Lynne Hull, *Raptor Roost L-1 with Swainson's Hawk: a safe roosting sculpture for hawks and eagles,* 1988.
Wood, found metals, stone from site, height: 16' (4.9 m). Photo by Bertrand de Peyer. Courtesy of the artist.

You Will Need

- sketch paper
- pencil
- variety of sculptural materials
- related sculpture tools

Try This

1. Work with your group to create a plan for your sculpture. How can your sculpture make a difference in the way people think about the issue or problem you chose as a theme? What materials will help send your message? Sketch your ideas.

2. Decide who will be responsible for each section or phase of the project. For example, one person might collect the materials, another might arrange them, and another might assemble them into the sculpture.

3. As you work together, discuss any changes or ideas you might have. Offer helpful suggestions to classmates working on a particular phase of the project.

Studio Background

Sculptures That Make a Difference

Many late-twentieth-century artists have created artworks that force us to change our ideas about sculpture. Artists such as Lynne Hull (Fig. 8–8) and Krzysztof Wodiczko (Fig. 8–9) often choose a social or environmental problem as the theme of their artwork. They discuss their ideas with experts on the problem. They decide what art materials to use. Then, the artists create a sculpture they think can change the way people feel about the problem.

Check Your Work

Display your completed artwork with class-mates' artworks. Each group should present its work to the class. Identify the issue you have addressed, and explain how your art-work will make a difference in the way people think about the issue.

Sketchbook Connection
Use your sketchbook to plan your work. Take notes during discussions with your class-mates. Investigate the issue or problem you wish to address by reading about it and talking to others. Sketch ideas that come to mind during your research.

Core Lesson 8

Check Your Understanding
1. How have artists used their art to address the problems that people face in communities?
2. Why might the painting *Guernica* help make a difference in the way people think about war?
3. Provide examples to explain how artists sometimes collaborate with others to make a difference with their art.
4. Do you think it is a good idea for artists to collaborate with others as they make their art? Why or why not?

Fig. 8–10 **Working together, students created maquettes of hot air balloons. They also met with a local balloonist to learn more about the technology, materials, and safety issues involved in full-sized hot air balloons. How does a balloon make a difference? It's art for everyone to enjoy as it drifts across the sky.** Students of Logan Fontenelle Middle School, *Transformation Transportation,* 1999. Tissue paper, white glue, wire. 8' x 6' (2.4 x 1.8 m). Bellevue, Nebraska.

Fig. 8–9 **This artist worked with a team of homeless people and designers to create a vehicle for the home-less. The vehicle is made to carry belongings and to store recyclable trash. It has an insulated sleeping space, washing basin, toilet, and storage space. How do you think viewers respond to this artwork when they see it?** Krzysztof Wodiczko, *Homeless Vehicle, Version 3,* 1988. Aluminum, lexan, plywood, plastic, fabric, steel, 72" x 92" x 40" (182.9 x 233.7 x 101.6 cm). Courtesy of the artist and Galerie Lelong, New York.

To some viewers, the main purpose of the sculptures you see here might be the messages they send. Some people might not even consider these to be art-works, because they look very different from sculp-tures that most people are used to seeing. Yet, these sculptures *are* works of art. The artists came up with a plan. They thought about how to use color, line, shape, form, space, balance, and unity. And they expressed their ideas and feelings in the artwork. These artists, however, tried to make a difference.

Making a Difference

257

Making a Difference: 1950–1980

1962
Rosenquist, *A Lot to Like*

1970
Rauschenberg, *Signs*

1974–75
Chicago Mural Group, *History of Mexican American Worker*

American Regionalism
page 232

American Social Causes

American Art
Since 1980
page 284

1962
Marisol, *The Family*

1973
Chicago Mural Group,
Wall of Self-Awareness

History in a Nutshell

The second half of the twentieth century was a time of great unrest and turmoil. People lived with the threat of war and atomic weapons. Communities worldwide debated over different forms of government: capitalism versus communism, democracy versus fascism. Cities expanded into large suburbs. In America, some community groups formed in opposition to each other, expressing hatred that came from prejudice and fear. Groups struggled with a variety of social, environmental, and political issues.

Art and Social Causes

You've probably heard the expression "that's a good cause" or "that cause is worth supporting." A **cause**, or movement that focuses on an issue, happens when a group of people shares a belief that something needs changing. Following World War II, groups began to focus on social causes such as civil rights, women's issues, and the environment. This was also a time of antiwar protests. Many twentieth-century artists addressed these issues through artworks such as community murals. Robert Rauschenberg (Fig. 8–11) believed that art can make a difference in social and political causes.

Artists working in different styles shared the belief that art has a social and political purpose. The social commentaries of *Pop Art* were based on the products and images of popular culture. Other artists used the environment itself as the material for *Earth Art*. Earth Art draws people's attention to environmental issues. Some sculptures focused on social issues in all kinds of communities, from family groups to national and international concerns.

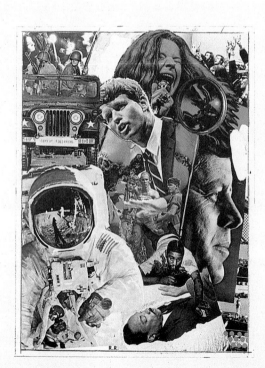

Fig. 8–11 Each image in this silkscreen print is a powerful expression of the political and social turmoil America faced in the late 1960s and early 1970s. Robert Rauschenberg, *Signs*, 1970. Silkscreen print, 43" x 43" (109 x 109 cm). Edition: 250. Published by Castelli Graphics. © Untitled Press, Inc. / Licensed by VAGA, New York, NY.

Art and Art Issues

Not all of the art during this period, however, was about social causes. Some artists chose not to use their art for making a difference in society. Their subject matter and images did not represent environmental conditions or social needs. For these artists, making a difference in the way art is made and viewed seemed most important. These artists explored the qualities and effects of lines, shapes, colors, and surfaces. Artists such as James Rosenquist (Fig. 8–12) invited other artists to create art in new ways.

Fig. 8–12 **Does this painting remind you of a collage? How does it compare to** *Signs* **(Fig. 8–11)? What do you think this painting means?** James Rosenquist, *A Lot to Like,* 1962. Oil on canvas, 93" x 204" (236 x 518.2 cm) (triptych). The Museum of Contemporary Art, Los Angeles. The Panza Collection. © James Rosenquist / Licensed by VAGA, New York, NY.

Fig. 8–13 **When you look at this family portrait, you might wonder where the father is. What might this artist be saying about the American family in this artwork? How might she be trying to make a difference?** Marisol Escobar, *The Family,* 1962. Painted wood and other materials in three sections, overall, 6' 10 5/8" x 65 1/2" x 15 1/2" (209.8 x 166.3 x 39.3 cm). The Museum of Modern Art, New York. Advisory Committee Fund. Photograph © 2000 The Museum of Modern Art, New York. © Marisol / Licensed by VAGA, New York, NY.

Art and Community Involvement

Does your community have a mural? Do you know how or when it was made? What message does it send? In the early 1970s, artists began a **mural movement** in many cities throughout the United States. The mural movement helped add beauty to city neighborhoods and gave people an opportunity to express pride in where they live.

The first murals appeared in Chicago. The Chicago Mural Group included about a dozen artists, both men and women, of different races and backgrounds. The group has created more than fifty outdoor murals and twenty-four indoor murals (Figs. 8–14 and 8–15). Money to pay for supplies and artists' time comes from national nonprofit sources, such as the National Endowment for the Arts (NEA), and from local support.

The success of the Chicago Mural Group inspired artists to create murals on walls in neighborhoods from Boston to Los Angeles. Often, the residents of the neighborhoods helped. Through these murals, artists have helped people in communities make a difference in their lives.

Fig. 8–14 Look carefully at this mural. What issues does the artist address? Why might the people who live in the neighborhood where the mural is located be proud of the work? Chicago Mural Group, Chicago, *Wall of Self-Awareness,* 1973, by Mitchell Caton (1249 East 63rd Street).
Courtesy Chicago Public Art Group.

Fig. 8–15 City neighborhoods can be very different from one another in terms of the people who live there and the issues they're concerned about. How are the ideas expressed in this mural different from those in Fig. 8–14? Chicago Mural Group, Chicago, *History of Mexican American Worker* (detail), 1974–75. (13337 South Western).
Courtesy Chicago Public Art Group.

8.1 Art History

Check Your Understanding

1. For what purposes did artists use artwork in the period following World War II?
2. Name some of the different styles of art in the second half of the twentieth century.
3. How did artists make a difference in the second half of the twentieth century?
4. What was the mural movement and how did it affect community life?

Studio Connection

Create a *monoprint* based on the theme of making a difference. A monoprint is made by transferring one image from a painted or inked surface onto a sheet of paper. Cover a piece of glass or other smooth, nonabsorbent surface with printing ink. Draw into the ink with cotton swabs, a comb, a brush, or the eraser end of a pencil. Try laying paper shapes on the ink. When you are satisfied with your image, place a sheet of drawing paper over the prepared surface. Rub the paper carefully until you see a faint image of your work through the back of the paper. Carefully lift the print. The drawn lines and shapes will remain white on the paper. Note that you must work quickly. Try not to let the ink dry before you finish the print.

Printmaking

In the simplest terms, printmaking is a process of transferring an image or words from one surface to another. For instance, when you use a rubber stamp, you make a print of the image or words that are on the stamp. When you create a poster using letter stencils, you make a print of those letters. Artists use printmaking techniques to tell stories, express ideas, and create beautiful designs. As with other art forms, ideas for printmaking can come from observation, imagination, or personal feelings.

Printmaking allows artists to make multiple copies of an image. This makes it an especially good way to send a message to many people.

Types of Prints

There are three basic steps for making any print. Create an image on a printing plate. Ink the plate. Transfer the image by pressing the inked plate against paper or cloth. By varying the three basic steps, artists make different kinds of prints.

Relief Prints To make a relief print, artists carve into a wood or linoleum block with a sharp tool. When the block is inked and pressed on paper, the raised part of the block prints. The carved out areas remain the color of the paper.

Intaglio Prints In this process, artists scratch lines into a smooth metal plate. After the plate is inked, they use a printing press to apply even pressure between the plate and the paper. Most intaglio prints have very fine, thin lines or soft, velvety shadows. Their look is usually more delicate than relief prints.

Lithographic Prints To make a lithographic print, artists draw an image on a flat slab of stone (or a special

Fig. 8–16 The lines and shapes in this intaglio print are bolder than you might expect to see in an intaglio print. How might the artist's message be different if she had used fine lines and soft shadows to create the image? Sue Coe, *The New World Order,* 1991.
Photo-etching, 13 3/8" x 10 5/8" (34 x 27 cm). Copyright © 1991 Sue Coe. Courtesy Galerie St. Etienne, New York.

metal plate) with a greasy crayon. Then they coat the blank areas of the stone with a special chemical. The ink sticks to the drawn areas, but will not stick to the chemical. The print is made using a printing press.

Serigraphs or Silkscreen Prints In the serigraph printing process, artists use stencils to overlap colors. First they place a stenciled image on a fine screen mounted on a frame. Then they place paper under the screen. When they pull ink across the screen with a squeegee, the image is transferred to the paper. They can use several stencils to apply different colors through the same screen.

Fig. 8–17 **This artist combined lithography with collage techniques to express his personal concern for the environment. What message does this image send?** Tom Nakashima, *Turtle*, 1994. Lithograph on paper, hand-colored newsprint collage, 51 ³/₄" x 38 ⁵/₈" (131.5 x 98.2 cm). Photo by Noel Allum, NY, Courtesy Bernice Steinbaum Gallery, Miami.

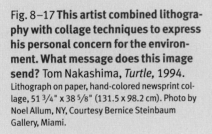

8.2 Forms and Media

Check Your Understanding

1. For what reasons do artists use printmaking techniques?

2. What are the three basic steps of printmaking?

Studio Connection

Create a relief print that will make a difference in the way people think or feel about your school community. You can create the print from almost any raised surface that can be inked. You might try using shells, leaves, bottle caps, or wood scraps. Or try cutting designs into the flat surfaces of a potato. Create an image with glue or string. Allow it to dry before inking and printing. Tear or cut cardboard, foam, or other flat materials. Glue the pieces down and, when dry, ink and print. Plan your design. Use what you know about the principles of design to create a unified composition.

Making a Difference

263

African Art in a Modern World

Global Glance

During the last half of the twentieth century, communities in Africa have experienced great changes in their political, economic, social, and religious ideas. These community changes have caused changes in art as well. From these modern African communities, four types of art have made a difference in the way we think about African art today: traditional art, Christian art, tourist art, and new African art.

Africa

Traditional Art

Africa is a vast continent with two major regions of culture and geography. In the north, around the Mediterranean Sea, there are many records of the artwork of ancient Egypt, near the Nile River. This art influenced the Greek and Roman civilizations and the development of Western art throughout Europe and much of Russia. In the region south of the Sahara, African kingdoms also have a long artistic heritage. People of this region created **traditional art** such as textiles, masks, ritual power figures, sculptured heads, wall decorations, and ceremonial and everyday objects. The painted house in Fig. 8–18 is an example of traditional African art.

In all parts of Africa, traditional art is similar in one way. Most

African traditional art forms have been created as expressions of religious or social needs in the community. The traditional art forms, styles, and processes of working with wood, fibers, metal, and clay have survived throughout Africa's history. Changes in Africa's politics created changes in the communities that make African art.

Fig. 8–18 **The technique of house painting is similar to that of fresco painting. The paint or pigments are applied to a wall when the plaster is fresh. The designs usually have some symbolic meaning. Where do you see geometric designs? Where do you see organic designs?** Africa, Nigeria, Giwa, Hausa People, *Painted house,* 20th century. Facade, left side. © Maude Wahlman

Other Traditions in Art

Traditional art fills the everyday and ceremonial needs of the African people. Other kinds of art serve different purposes. *Christian art* began in the fifteenth century and continues today. Sculptures and paintings decorate the walls, altars, and doorways of mission churches such as the one in Fig. 8–19. The artworks are made by craftspeople or Christian artists.

Probably the most widely recognized form of African art is souvenir, or **tourist, art.** Travelers buy tourist art to help them remember places they visited in Africa. It is also popular with people not able to visit Africa. Much tourist art realistically depicts the animals of Africa or shows scenes of village life. It is sold in art stalls at African markets such as the one in Fig. 8–20. As a business, it has been very successful and a source of income to the African economy.

Fig. 8–19 **You might be familiar with the scenes shown on these doors. What lessons do you think the images teach?** Lamidi O. Fakeye, *Doors for St. Mary's Roman Catholic Church,* Oke-Padi, Ibadan, 1956.
Iroko wood. Photographed by David H. Curl.

Fig. 8–20 **In a traditional market, like the one you see here, all kinds of objects are bought and sold. Notice the examples of traditional art, such as the decorated pots and the patterned fabrics of the women's clothing.** Africa, Nigeria, Nupe People, *Market Scene: Selling Bide-Pottery,* 1974.
© Maude Wahlman

Making a Difference

265

New African Art

Since the mid-twentieth century, a new African art has caught the attention of art museums and collectors around the world. The majority of these artists have been trained in art schools such as Makerere School of Fine Arts in Uganda. These artists are aware of both historic and modern art traditions in Africa and other parts of the world. They are aware of political and social events occurring in modern Africa. They use their art to comment on these events.

The style of new African art is similar to modern art movements around the world, but the subject matter and themes are distinctly African. These artworks show African subjects in African settings, and deal with African political and social issues. The new African art shows the artists' views of scenes from their world (Figs. 8–21 and 8–22). In the last half of the twentieth century, African artists have continued to make a difference as they use their talent, training, and ideas to describe the exciting and unique experience of life in African communities.

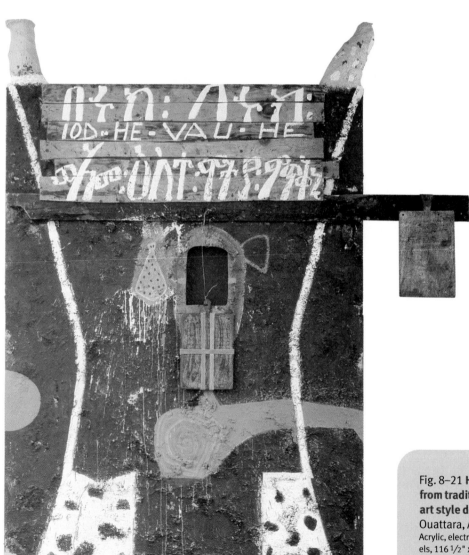

Fig. 8–21 **How is this artwork different from traditional African art? What modern art style does it make you think of?**
Ouattara, *Masada*, 1993.
Acrylic, electric cord, and mixed media on 2 wood panels, 116 1/2" x 101 1/2" x 7 1/2" (296 x 257.8 x 19 cm). Signed and dated on the reverse. Courtesy Cavaliero Fine Arts, New York.

Fig. 8–22 **What qualities of Expressionist art does this painting show? (See page 10 to learn about Expressionist art.) How is this artwork different from the traditional artworks on pages 264 and 265?** Elimo Njau, *Milking,* undated.
Oil on canvas, 20 1/8" x 15 3/4" (51 x 40 cm).
Museum fuer Volkerkunde, Frankfurt am Main.
Photo: Maria Obermaier.

Fig. 8–23 **This is a picture of Ethiopian artist Afework Tekle's studio. Notice the unfinished portrait of a West African leader. What do you see in the studio that suggests the artist's African heritage?**
Photo courtesy Eldon Katter

Studio Connection

Create a sculpture of a person or animal using wire or papier-mâché. Many sculptures are made over a wire *armature*. An armature is like a skeleton. For small sculptures, an armature is usually made of twisted wire. After the basic skeleton has been attached to a base, you can decorate it with details or cover it with papier-mâché. Plan your work before you begin. Think about how you can use your sculpture to make a difference in the way people think about the world. What subject matter might catch people's attention? How can you inspire viewers to think about your subject matter differently?

8.3 Global View

Check Your Understanding

1. What are the four areas of art production that have made a difference in the way we think about African art?
2. What are some traditional forms of African art?
3. Why do people buy tourist art?
4. How does the art of the new African artists differ from other art-making communities in Africa's history?

Making a Difference

Making Relief Prints

Art That Makes a Difference

Studio Introduction

In this studio experience, you will make a relief print of a natural environment that is in danger of being destroyed. Create an image that will show the environment in a positive way. Pages 270 and 271 will tell you how to do it.

Look around you. There are natural environments everywhere. A seaside beach is an environment of crabs, seaweed, and barnacles. A garden is an environment of flowers, vegetables, animals, and insects. A marsh is an environment of grasses, cattails, and waterfowl. Some natural environments are in danger of being destroyed. How can you show an endangered environment in a positive way? You might think of a slogan that sums up what you want to say about this environment. Then try to illustrate your thought.

Fig. 8–24 **This artist created a woodcut, a relief print made from a block of wood. Notice how the areas of black (ink) and white (paper) create the main shapes. If you didn't know this was a woodcut, would you still be able to tell the image was cut from a block of wood? How?** Antonio Frasconi, *Feeding Time,* ca. 1960s.
Woodcut on cream wove paper, 6 9/16" x 4 3/4" (16.7 x 12.1 cm). Brooklyn Museum of Art. 1997.45 Gift of Judith Rappaport.

Studio Background

Introducing the Relief Print

Do you remember the first time you accidentally left a fingerprint of ink or paint on a sheet of paper? You may not have realized it at the time, but you had just made a relief print. The fine lines of the print were made by the ridges or raised areas of the fingertip itself. The recessed areas between the ridges were probably free of paint or ink and remained the color of the paper when printed.

When an artist makes a **linoleum cut,** a relief print made from a linoleum block, he or she uses cutting tools, such as gouges, veiners, and knives, to cut an image on the block. Gouges and veiners can be wide or narrow. Knives can range from X-acto knives and mat knives to sharp pocket knives.

Depending on the size of the cutting tool, an artist can make thick or thin lines, or remove entire areas of the block's surface. He or she might create a design with simple shapes and fine details or textures. The areas that are left uncut will be covered with a thin coat of ink. When the print is made, the areas of the block that are cut away will be the color of the paper.

Fig. 8–26 Some artists create relief prints to illustrate stories. Notice how this artist used several different colors. Do you think she used a wide or narrow cutting tool to create texture and detail? Why do you think so? Bonnie Mackain, Illustration from *One Hundred Hungry Ants* by Elinor J. Pinczes.

Making a Difference

Making Your Relief Print

You Will Need

- thin paper
- soft pencil
- carbon paper
- linoleum block
- cutting tools
- ink, inking slab, and brayer
- printing paper

Safety Note

Cutting tools must be handled with extreme caution. Always hold the block securely and point the cutting edge of the tool away from your hands, fingers, and body. Work slowly. Wear safety goggles.

Try This

1. Choose an endangered environment to show in a relief print. Think of ways to simplify the main shapes of the subject you choose. Sketch your image on thin paper that is the same size as your printing block. When you are finished, turn your sketch over and hold it up to a strong light. This will show you what your final print will look like.

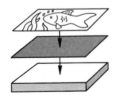

2. Use carbon paper to transfer your design onto the block. Place the carbon paper face down on your block. Lay your design face up over the carbon paper. Carefully trace over the design.

3. With your pencil, lightly fill in the areas on your block that you want to print in a color. Check your design when you are finished. Make changes as needed.

4. Carefully cut away the areas you do not want to print.

5. With a brayer, apply a thin even coat of ink to the raised areas of your design.

6. Carefully place the printing paper over the block. Gently rub the paper with your hand. When you can see your design faintly through the back of the sheet, slowly pull the print away from the block.

Check Your Work

What does your print say about the natural environment you've shown? How might it make a difference in the way viewers think about the environment? How did you create textures in your block?

Fig. 8–27 **"The idea came to me as I was looking through a book about my home country of Japan."** Atsushi Sato, *Travelling Through Nature,* 1999.
Linoleum block print, 5 1/4" x 7 1/2" (14 x 19 cm). Plum Grove Junior High School, Rolling Meadows, Illinois.

Computer Option

Create a high-contrast image that has the look and feel of a block print. Import a photo or art image of the natural world into a paint or digital-imaging program. Convert the image to grayscale or to 256 or fewer levels of gray. Choose the "posterize" option or two levels of black and white. Increase the contrast and sharpen the edges to separate the areas of the image into "black and white." Then use the resulting image as a pattern for a block print.

Sketchbook Connection

Use your sketchbook to experiment with different slogans or sayings that describe the natural environment you will show in your print. Observe and sketch images from this environment that relate to your slogan. Select images that you think will catch people's attention and best convey your message. Try combining images in different ways as you plan your print.

Connect to...

Careers

How might you use a camera to make a difference? You might choose a career in one of many areas of photography—for example, education, entertainment, or advertising. Or you might choose photojournalism. **Photojournalists** work for newspapers, TV stations, magazines, and news services. A series of photographs can tell a news story, and when they accompany written copy, they bring people a more complete understanding of the news. Photojournalists might be assigned to cover a particular story, usually with a reporter; or they might cover an event alone, working to create a photo-essay, a story in pictures. By capturing an image artfully and using the elements and principles of design to compose a shot, a photographer can make a powerful statement.

Other Arts

Theater

The tradition of **artists' working to serve their communities** is not unique to the field of visual art. During the first decade of the twentieth century, cities and towns across the United States began to establish community theaters to serve local interests and needs. Early on, many community theaters staged large pageants in which huge numbers of people could participate and learn about theater. However, such productions became too large, and community theaters began staging smaller productions that were to entertain as well as educate. Challenge students to name ways that the community might benefit from a local theater.

Daily Life

What can each of us do to **make our world a better place**? By combining our efforts with those of others, we *can* make a difference. For instance, you can volunteer in a hospital or a food bank, donate clothing to organizations such as the Salvation Army and Goodwill, and help prepare or deliver meals to the sick or a family in need. Can you think of any other charitable efforts you could make?

Fig. 8–28 Art can be used to inform people or to change their minds about particular topics. Keith Haring often used public spaces for his art—in this case a subway station. What message does this artwork seem to send? *Keith Haring photographed by Chantal Regnault in NYC subway, 1981.* ©The Estate of Keith Haring.

Fig. 8–29 **Does your school or local library have computers available for student use? Do you think it's important to know how to use a computer?**
Photo courtesy *SchoolArts*.

Language Arts

Do you consider yourself to be computer literate? Do you have access to computers at school or at home? Why, do you think, do some people believe that **computers** will have an impact on learning equal only to the separate inventions of the alphabet and movable type? Software for composing and publishing text and graphics has made a huge contribution to language arts; competition among ever-increasing numbers of Web sites promotes the development of meaningful content and exceptional graphic design. However, to be successful in our information age, students must develop both linguistic and visual literacy. What do you think will happen to students who do not have access to computers? How might such students get access?

Social Studies

Do you think it is possible to effect social or political change through the use of humor? The Guerilla Girls, an anonymous group of women artists, learned quickly that humor attracts people's interest and is an effective weapon against discrimination: they have been practicing peaceful activism for over ten years, in an effort to make the art world and the public aware that most influential galleries and museums exhibit very few women artists. The members of the group hide their identities under gorilla masks and "identify" themselves by the names of dead women artists and writers so as to reinforce their place in history. The anonymity also directs the focus to the issues rather than their personalities or artwork. The Guerilla Girls stage peaceful demonstrations and express—on billboards, posters, and buses—their opinions about sexism and racism in our culture. Why, do you think, do they call themselves the "Guerilla Girls, Conscience of the Art World"?

Science

Have you heard of the Human Genome Project? It is an international research effort begun in 1990 to determine the sequence of all the approximately 100,000 genes of the human genome, the complete instructions within our genes for making a human being. With such knowledge, **genetic-engineering techniques** could possibly manipulate the genetic material of DNA—deoxyribonucleic acid—to "reprogram" the genetic code. Scientists hope that discoveries that grow out of the project will aid in the treatment of diseases and the adjustment of harmful hereditary traits.

Fig. 8–30 **This is a model of the double-strand DNA molecule. The two strands twist around each other like a spiral staircase, a form called a double helix (***HE-lix***).** *Model of a DNA Molecule.*
©Digital Art/CORBIS.

What are some reasons that critics have raised ethical questions about the use of genetic engineering?

Internet Connection
For more activities related to this chapter, go to the Davis website at **www.davis-art.com.**

Portfolio

"When creating this piece of artwork, we wanted to show a friendly relationship between people of all races. We tried to demonstrate the evolution that Martin Luther King, Jr., and Rosa Parks evoked on our society."
Whitney Davis and Debbie Grossman

Fig. 8–32 Whitney Davis and Debbie Grossman, *I Have a Dream*, 1999.
Cut-paper collage, 18" x 24" (46 x 61 cm). Winsor School, Boston, Massachusetts.

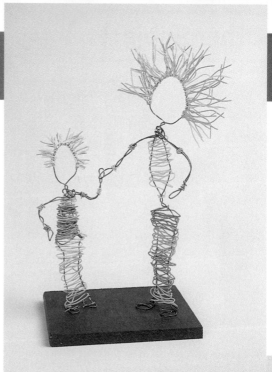

Fig. 8–31 Micale Mitchell, *Mother and Child*, 1999.
Wire, wood base, 11 1/2" (29 cm) high. Desert Sands School, Phoenix, Arizona.

"I wanted to somehow represent my mother in this sculpture. I constructed us holding hands to represent the closeness that I always want to have with her." **Micale Mitchell**

CD-ROM Connection
To see more student art, check out the Community Connection Student Gallery.

"My picture delivers an important message. We need to start treating our environment better because if we don't we won't be happy with our lives and the world we live in."
Thomas Reid

Fig. 8–33 Thomas Reid, *Time to Clean Up Our Act*, 1999.
Poster, 18" x 24" (46 x 61 cm). Jordan-Elbridge Middle School, Jordan, New York.

Chapter 8 Review

Recall

Why did Picasso create the painting *Guernica*?

Understand

Use examples to explain how art can be used to try to make a difference in the way people think about important issues.

Apply

How might you use printmaking to address a problem in your own school community? What problem would you address? What kind of print would you make?

Analyze

Find an artwork in this chapter that sends a positive message in an attempt to make a difference in the way people think or behave. Tell how the artist used subject matter, materials and techniques, and the elements of art to convey the positive message.

Synthesize

In what ways is artists' collaboration to make artworks a good thing? In what ways might it be difficult?

Evaluate

Consider the *Homeless Vehicle* (Figure 8-9, *shown below*). Do you think this vehicle is a good solution for helping the homeless? Why or why not? Do you think this is a good work of art? Why or why not? Select and rank three artworks from this chapter that you think should be in a twentieth-century art hall of fame. Justify your number one choice.

Page 257

For Your Portfolio

Keep your portfolio in good order. Once in a while, check the contents, and choose what to keep in your portfolio and what to remove. Check that each entry is well presented and identified with your name, date, and title of work. Protect each entry with newsprint or tissue paper.

For Your Sketchbook

Think about your portfolio artworks in terms of how they might make a difference. Do any express an opinion? What ideas do you explore most often? How might some of your works be changed to be more "opinionated"? Use a page for your sketchbook to describe your findings.

Looking
Beyond

Fig. 9–1 When we look at this image, it's easy to think that we're viewing someone's dream. Whose dream might it be? What might it mean? Sandy Skoglund, *Revenge of the Goldfish*, 1981.
Cibachrome color photograph, 30" x 40" (76.1 x 101.6 cm), ©1981, Sandy Skoglund.

- How do people look to the future and imagine possibilities?
- How can art help people imagine worlds beyond the present and familiar?

Let's face it. The image shown in Fig. 9–1 is strange. Parts of it are familiar: a bedroom, a person sleeping. But everything is blue-green except the people and those fish. What are they doing there? Is this scene underwater? Are the fish flying in the air? This is the sort of image that could take place only in a dream.

Artist Sandy Skoglund created this scene and others that are equally bizarre. She carves and paints objects and arranges them with people in environments that she also creates. Finally, she photographs the scene. Her artworks come in two forms. Usually, she sets up her scenes in a gallery or museum space. Viewers experience them in true-to-life scale. She also exhibits her large color photographs of the scenes. What makes Skoglund's artworks so unsettling is that they combine what we know with fantasy and imagination.

Since early times, artists have helped people imagine other worlds. Sometimes, these worlds remain fantasy. Other times, the dreams of artists and community members become reality in the future. Every invention begins as an idea of what someone imagines for the future.

What's Ahead

- **Core Lesson** Discover how artists help people imagine unfamiliar, fantasy, and future worlds.
- **9.1 Art History Lesson**
  Explore the new possibilities and challenges that artists face at the beginning of the twenty-first century.
- **9.2 Forms and Media Lesson**
  Learn how artists use traditional and nontraditional media and techniques to create new art forms.
- **9.3 Global View Lesson**
  Investigate how artists around the world preserve traditions while exploring new directions in art.
- **9.4 Studio Lesson**
  Create a videotape that explains an idea.

Words to Know

installations	multimedia
activism	global community
performance art	global style
computer art	storyboard
video art	

Beyond the Present

New Ideas

Have you ever wished for a machine that could do your homework, walk your dog, or make your lunch? Artists help whole communities imagine what might be possible. They design futuristic objects and environments for us to contemplate. Leonardo da Vinci, for example, created drawings of flying machines. For him and others who lived in the late fifteenth and early sixteenth centuries, such machines could exist only on paper or in dreams. We know, of course, that what once seemed beyond the possible is now reality. Airplanes take us to all points around the globe. We can fly to the moon and, possibly, even beyond.

People in communities dream about how they can make their environment better. They ask architects and other artists to help in their planning. In some cases, teams of people who represent various groups in a community will help imagine these new

places. What would you tell such a team if the goal was to create a totally new school? Students, parents, and other community members all worked together to create the plan of the school in Fig. 9–4. The students wanted the school to have separate buildings and to be like a farm.

New Kinds of Art

As artists explore new ways of making art, they help us look beyond what we think of as artwork. Contemporary artists around the world experiment with new materials and technology to create new kinds of art forms. Like Sandy Skoglund, many contemporary artists create environments, or **installations**—temporary arrangements of objects in galleries, museums, and outdoors. Installations give viewers an art experience that is different from viewing a painting or sculpture. Some artists include sound and video or computer technology in an installation, such as the work by Jenny Holzer

Fig. 9–2 **The backs that this artist created are life-size. Imagine seeing eighty of them at one time. If you could see this artwork in real life, how might it make you feel?** Magdalena Abakanowicz, *Backs* (group of 80 figures), 1976–80.
Burlap and resin, 3 different sizes: 24" x 19 5/8" x 21 5/8", 27 1/4" x 22" x 26", 28 1/4" x 23 1/4" x 27 1/4" (61 x 50 x 55 cm; 69 x 56 x 66 cm; 71.8 x 59 x 69.2 cm). © Magdalena Abakanowicz, courtesy Marlborough Gallery, New York.

(Fig. 9–3). Occasionally, an artist will become part of the artwork, engaging in a kind of performance.

Some artists use traditional materials in nontraditional ways. Magdalena Abakanowicz, for example, works in fiber and often builds her structures on a loom. But those are the only traditional aspects of her work. To make the artwork shown in Fig. 9–2, she molded burlap and glue to create forms that look like the backs of seated humans. She has installed them at different sites, including a room and a hillside. The forms suggest a different mood, depending on where and how they are positioned.

Fig. 9–3 **How might the experience of seeing this installation be different from the experience of seeing a painting? How does this work change your ideas about what art is?** Jenny Holzer, *Untitled* (Selections from Truisms, Inflammatory Essays, The Living Series, The Survival Series, Under a Rock, Laments, and Child Text), 1989.
Extended helical tricolor L.E.D. electronic-display signboard, dimensions subject to change with installation. Solomon R. Guggenheim Museum, NY. Partial gift of the artist, 1989. Photo by David Heald © The Solomon R. Guggenheim Foundation, NY. (FN89.3626)

Fig. 9–4 **Which parts of this school resemble a farm?** Stephen Bingler, *Lincoln High School Environmental Resource Center*, 1996.
Digital graphic illustration. Courtesy Concordia Architects.

Beyond the Familiar

Think about the legends and stories you know. Remember *Paul Bunyan, The Wizard of Oz, Alice in Wonderland,* and *Peter Pan?* Humans like to imagine fantasy worlds and creatures. Throughout history, artists have illustrated the stories and legends of their communities. In cultures around the world, stories passed down through generations have inspired artists to create imaginary monsters and other creatures. They appear as decorations for buildings, on everyday objects, and in paintings and sculptures.

The sculpture in Fig. 9–6 is of an imaginary fire-breathing monster with three heads: a lion's and a goat's, with a snake's head as its tail.

Artists also create their own fantasy worlds for others to consider. Artist Paul Klee created worlds in which creatures, plants, and people floated as if in a dream. Klee explained that many of his images resulted from allowing himself to draw freely with line. In one of his writings, he encourages others to "take a walk" with line and see where it leads. His imaginary worlds show that he not only drew with line but

Fig. 9–5 **Paul Klee was very interested in the drawings he made as a child. He also studied those made by his son, Felix. How is this image like those made by children you know?** Paul Klee, *Fish Magic,* 1925.
Oil on canvas, mounted on board, 30 3/8" x 38 1/2" (77.3 x 97.8 cm). Philadelphia Museum of Art, The Louise and Walter Arensberg Collection. Photo by Graydon Wood, 1994. Acc. # '50-134-112 © 2000 Artists Rights Society (ARS), New York / VG Bild-Kunst, Bonn.

also scratched lines into painted surfaces, revealing the colors underneath (Fig. 9–5).

Just as in dreams, where people, objects, and events are mixed in unlikely ways, some artists create artworks by placing things together as if by chance. In *Nostalgia* (Fig. 9–7), for example, the artist placed a chunk of watermelon in a bare landscape. The watermelon does not seem to have much to do with what's happening in the scene. Yet it is in the foreground of the picture.

Fig. 9–6 Chimera was a Greek mythical creature. What creatures from mythology are you familiar with? How might they be shown in an artwork? Etruscan, *Chimera of Arezzo*, 6th century BC.
Bronze. Museo Archeologico, Florence, Italy. Scala/Art Resource, New York.

Fig. 9–7 How would you describe the landscape inhabited by these people and other objects or creatures? Does the title help you understand the meaning of this artwork? How? Arturo Elizondo, *Nostalgia*, 1995.
Oil on canvas, 78" x 103 1/4" (198 x 262 cm). Courtesy Galeria OMR, Mexico City.

Art That Looks Beyond

In this studio experience, you will use collage techniques to create a world of your dreams. What kind of fantasy world for the future can you create?

Think about a theme or main idea for your imaginary world. What images will you include? How will you combine similar and different images to create an unreal scene? How can you show realistic and unrealistic elements? What will be in the background, middle ground, and foreground areas of your collage?

You Will Need

- lightweight card-board
- scissors
- glue
- a variety of papers
- magazine or other photographs

1. Plan your collage. Collect magazine, newspaper, or photocopied images that will help show your ideas. Cut or tear other shapes from construction paper, colored tissue, foil, or patterned papers.

2. Carefully arrange your shapes and photos. Create unity in your artwork by repeat- ing shapes, colors, or images. Try different arrangements before choosing the one you like best.

3. Carefully glue the images to the cardboard background.

Fig. 9–8 How is this image like a collage? Which part or parts might the artist have drawn himself? Francois Colos, Illustration from *The Student Who Became King in Spite of Himself,* 1974.
© 1974 by Francois Colos. Reprinted by permission of Henry Holt and Company, LLC.

Studio Background

Imaginary Worlds in Art

Artists sometimes put objects or images that we don't expect to see together side by side. Sometimes the objects or images are in different sizes than we expect. These artworks might show parts of a world that seem real and other parts that don't seem normal to us. This style of art is called *Surrealism*. Surrealist artists create artworks that look beyond what is real. They show fantasy or imaginary worlds where realistic objects are combined in unusual ways or with unfamiliar scenes.

Figures 9–8 and 9–9 have elements that seem perfectly normal, yet something makes them look odd. Figure 9–8 is a children's book illustration by the graphic artist Francois Colos. What makes this illustration look real and unreal? In Magritte's paint-

Check Your Work

Display your completed collage with each of your classmates'. Discuss the different worlds you've created. Note the elements in the collages that are part of what we see in daily life. Note how each collage suggests a world that is beyond what we normally experience.

Check Your Understanding

1. Identify two ways that artists help communities imagine what might be possible.
2. Explain the role of fantasy worlds and creatures in community traditions.
3. What challenges would a community face if all its members got together to plan a new school?
4. How could you use what you know about Surrealism to explain Sandy Skoglund's work in Fig. 9–1 to someone who did not understand it?

Fig. 9–10 **"I started the project by finding things I liked, for instance clothes, cologne, etc. Then I changed my whole idea and was a little discouraged. Then I thought of a mirror-imaging idea, and that is what I came up with. It was rather challenging to make, but I used a little perseverance and got it done."** Craig Delaney, *The Sky,* 1999. Magazine cutouts and paper collage, 14" x 16" (35.5 x 40.5 cm). Isleboro School, Isleboro, Maine.

ing, the apple is shown realistically, just as we might expect to see it in our own home. However, by making it unusually large, the artist creates a dreamlike world of an ordinary object.

Fig. 9–9 Rene Magritte has exaggerated the scale, or size, of the apple in this painting. Do you think the painting would be as interesting if the apple was a normal size? Why or why not? Rene Magritte, *La chambre d'écoute* (The Listening Chamber), 1952. Oil on canvas, 17 5/8" x 21 5/8" (45 x 55 cm.) The Menil Collection, Houston. Gift of Philippa Friedrich. Photographed by Paul Hester, Houston. © Charly Herscovici, Brussels / Artist Rights Society (ARS), New York.

New Directions in Art: 1980–?

History in a Nutshell

In the closing decades of the twentieth century, many people became caught up in the pace of contemporary life. In this Information Age, people had multiple and instant ways of communicating with others in their communities and beyond. Cell phones, portable computers, e-mail, and the Internet made it possible for people to be in constant touch with families, friends, business connections, and worldwide news and events. Suddenly, a person's community extended beyond his or her local geographic area to encompass the world.

New Approaches

You've probably said to yourself many times, after a thrilling roller-coaster ride or other exciting adventure, "Where do we go from here?" Well, that's probably what many artists in the United States were thinking at the end of the twentieth century.

In the last decades of the twentieth century, artists all over the world challenged many traditional ideas about art and explored new possibilities. They tried many new technologies as tools and materials for making art.

Fig. 9–11 Celebration is a common theme in art. This artist shows it in a new way. How does this painting compare to Jacob Lawrence's painting of the same title (Fig. 7–9, page 231)? Mark Innerst, *Parade*, 1999.
Acrylic on board, 45 3/8" x 23 3/8" (115 x 59.4 cm). Courtesy Paul Kasmin Gallery.

Fig. 9–12 **Look carefully at each panel that makes up this artwork. Do you see styles and techniques in each that remind you of other artists you have studied?**
Pat Steir, *The Brueghel Series* (A Vanitas of Styles), 1997.
Oil on Canvas, 64 panels, each panel 28 1/2" x 22 1/2" (72.4 x 57.2 cm).
Courtesy the artist.

They displayed and exhibited their work in new settings and situations. They even recycled the art of the past. At the turn of this century, the world of art includes revivals of traditional styles, humorous copies of classical works, and new looks at familiar images. Pat Steir, for example, created her own interpretation of the artwork of Dutch master Jan Brueghel (Fig. 9–12).

Working Without Boundaries

Since 1980, artists have created work that spans a wide range of styles, materials, and techniques. From realistic to abstract, technical perfection to wild abandon, serious, humorous, soothing, and shocking, the world of art became a world with no boundaries. Some of the artwork from this time was large-scale outdoor art created with industrial equipment. Other art was handcrafted work with many tiny details. The artworks of Liza Lou, for example, are made entirely of beads (Fig. 9–13). Notice the message in the art. What do you think it means?

Fig. 9–13 **Each of the objects in this life-sized room is made of tiny beads. The artist also created a yard from beads. What words can you think of to describe this work?.** Liza Lou, *Kitchen*, 1991–95 (detail).
Mixed media with glass beads, 168 sq. ft. (51.3 m).
Courtesy the artist.

Community Involvement

At the end of the twentieth century, artists continued to challenge the idea that art should be made by individual artists working alone. Through collaboration, activism, and performance art, artists found ways to involve communities, groups, and the general public in the creation of artworks. **Activism** is the practice of working to change attitudes or beliefs related to politics or other issues within a community. **Performance art** combines any of the creative forms of expression, such as poetry, theater, music, architecture, painting, film, slides, and the like. Through such interaction, artists can emphasize the importance of art in community life. Looking at and creating art adds joy to many people's lives, whether they are artists or not.

Does your community hang banners along busy streets to celebrate events or holidays? Who creates these banners? What makes them unique to your community? Banner projects are one example of community involvement in the creation of art. Across the country, more and more communities participate in the design and production of banners about their neighborhoods or business districts. Such banners are usually two or three silkscreen designs that are produced in great numbers and hung to decorate public spaces. The banner in Fig. 9–14 was created as part of a banner project in the Kensington and Normal Heights neighborhoods of San Diego, California. Local artists created a total of 110 banners that celebrate the work of community members to clean up and rejuvenate the area.

The Future of Art

What's in store for the world of art? To help answer that, try to imagine the possibilities and challenges artists might have to meet. Imagine combining computer and video technologies with traditional art forms. Imagine developing artworks in which viewers experience new realities of time, space, and form.

Fig. 9–14 The banners that were created for this project show people who have made a difference in the community. Before the banners were made, the artists talked to the subjects about their histories, local politics, and the community in general. Pete Evaristo and Jodi Tucci, *On the Avenue, Brian,* from Adams Avenue, one of 110 unique street banners, 1998.
Mixed media on canvas, 27" x 48" (68.6 x 121.9 cm). Courtesy of the artists.

Fig. 9–15 **Artist Barnaby Evans uses water as his medium to create artworks. The mark he leaves is in viewers' memories of his work. Why might people consider this a work of art? What does it suggest about the kinds of art that might be produced in the future?** Barnaby Evans, *WaterFire Providence,* Water Place Park, Providence, Rhode Island, various dates, June 1996–present.

As exciting as these possibilities are, technology also challenges artists to preserve pride in craftsmanship and traditional skills. As new technologies make it easier for artists to produce a large variety of art forms, handmade objects may increase in value. And we hope that the value of individual skill and accomplishment will never be lost.

9.1 Art History

Check Your Understanding

1. What are some of the ways that artists challenged traditional ideas and explored new possibilities at the end of the twentieth century?
2. Name different kinds of art created at the end of the twentieth century.
3. How do artists involve communities in collaborative art projects?
4. What are some of the possibilities for art in the future?

Studio Connection

One way to explore new directions in art is to try imaginative drawing. In an imaginative drawing, you can combine unrelated ideas. These can be found by thinking of opposites. For example, you might combine parts of different kinds of animals (bird, fish, insect) into an imaginative creature. Suppose that people were small and insects were large. Imagine a world of soft, smooth surfaces and prickly or jagged vegetation. Select a drawing medium that will help you express an imaginative idea. Your work might be bold and startling or include lots of details. It might be filled with patterns or rhythms.

Looking Beyond

New Media

As you have learned, some artists use traditional media to create artworks in new ways. Other artists explore nontraditional media, such as computer and video technology, for making new kinds of artworks.

Computer Art

What do most people use a computer for? Your answer might include school, work, games, e-mail, or access to the Internet. Some artists use computers to create **computer art**. "Paint" and "draw" software allows artists to create original computer images. Artists can also scan other images into the computer. Or they can photograph objects with a digital camera, then import the photos into the computer. Once the images are on the computer, artists can edit them, change the colors, "draw" or "paint" on them, create a collage effect ... The possibilities seem endless!

Some computer art is intended for viewing on a monitor. Other works are printed as two-dimensional images.

Video Art

Video allows us to record and view images immediately. Many artists use video technology to create movies, documentaries, individual images, and other kinds of **video art**. Once they have collected their video images, artists can take out or rearrange parts, blur, or distort the images.

Some artists incorporate videotapes in their installations. Video artists have projected their artworks on the sides of buildings, large sheets of fabric hanging from a ceiling, the inside of aluminum buckets, or in the corners of a gallery. Some artists, such as Bill Viola (Fig. 9–16), combine video and sound in their work.

Fig. 9–16 This is one *frame*, or image, from a video and sound installation. Look at it carefully. What qualities does this image have that you probably wouldn't see in a painting or drawing? Bill Viola, *The Crossing,* 1996. Video / sound installation. Courtesy of the artist. Photo by Kira Perov.

Fig. 9–17 **The elements of this installation include 60,000 flowers, eleven shortwave radios, a ten-foot-high window, wool coats, and the artist herself. Do these seem like things you would normally see together? Why or why not? Can you guess what this installation means?** Ann Hamilton, *Mantle*, 1998.
Installation view, Miami Art Museum, April 2 – June 7, 1998. Courtesy Miami Art Museum. Photo by Thibault Jeanson.

Multimedia Art

Many artists can express their ideas best when they use **multimedia**, the tools and techniques of more than one medium. For instance, an artist might display videotapes on several monitors. In *Technology* (Fig. 6–1, page 198), artist Nam June Paik arranged monitors to create a sculpture. Many installations combine sculpture and architecture. Some computer software programs allow artists to create multimedia presentations. An artist can create a single computer document, or file, that includes still and moving images, words, and sound.

9.2 Forms and Media

Check Your Understanding
1. Identify three kinds of new media used by artists in the late twentieth century.
2. Describe ways that artists have used new media to create nontraditional art forms.

Studio Connection
Use a paint or draw program on a computer to design a community on Mars. How will that community be different from yours on Earth? What might you want or need to survive in a community on Mars? Experiment with the painting and drawing tools in the art program you are using. If you have access to a scanner, try scanning an image into your file and changing it to fit your design. Save your ideas in separate files. Decide which ones you like best, then cut and paste them into your final design. Print your design and share it with others in the class. Discuss the different features of your communities.

Meeting Global Challenges

In the **global community** (or worldwide community) of today, ideas cross cultural and geographic boundaries quickly. Advances in transportation and communication technologies, motion pictures, television, and satellites have challenged artists around the world to see and think differently about their own art and the artwork of others. Increasingly, artists are working in what might be called a **global style**. A global style cannot be linked to just one culture or tradition of art. It comes from the exchange of ideas among artists of many nations and cultures around the world.

Preserving Traditions

Remembering the past while anticipating the future is an important part of the human experience. Preserving cultural, ethnic, and religious heritage is just as important to artists as the challenge of breaking new ground. Within the history of art, countless artistic treasures and the techniques and processes used to create them have been lost. As cultures change, traditional art forms are often forgotten and then lost forever. If people and artists do not continue to use the traditional techniques and media of their communities, these art forms can disappear from our cultures.

In gallery and museum exhibitions of today's Native-American art, you can find artists who work in a variety of traditional styles. In some cases, artists continue to create art that is directly related to the artistic traditions and traditional beliefs of their cultures. In other instances, artwork might reflect only some of their artistic traditions, such as the use of traditional media, themes, or qualities of design. The Native-American artworks in Figs. 9–18 and 9–20 were made recently, but they preserve the techniques and images of ceremonial costumes and rituals within the artists' communities.

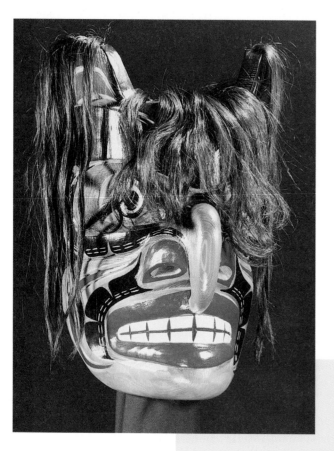

Fig. 9–18 The *Bookwus*, or Wildman of the Woods, is an exciting figure of Pacific Northwest Coast legend. The Bookwus lives deep in the woods but also hunts for food on deserted beaches. What features of this mask might be traditional? What features might be contemporary? Bill Henderson, Bookwus Mask: *Wildman of the Woods,* 1999. Painted red cedar with real hair, 13" x 9" (33 x 22.9 cm). Courtesy of the artist.

Fig. 9–19 Swentzell's sculptures capture gestures, poses, and facial expressions that seem to look different each time you look at them. The clown images recall traditional Native-American ceremonial costumes. Roxanne Swentzell, *The Emergence of the Clowns*, 1988.
Mixed media clay, 7" x 19" x 11" (17.8 x 48.3 x 27.9 cm). Shared Visions Collection, Heard Museum, Phoenix, Arizona.

Fig. 9–20 Herrera's combination of the dancer motifs with the nonobjective spattering technique brings a freshness and new vitality to this commonly portrayed subject. Joe Herrera, *Spring Ceremony for Owah*, 1983.
Watercolor on paper, 29" x 37" (73.7 x 94 cm). Courtesy Shared Visions Collection, Heard Museum, Phoenix, Arizona.

Breaking New Ground

Many Native-American artists today, like other artists around the world, are using art to express their ideas about issues such as identity, how they fit into the world, and how people relate to one another. These artists are working with new materials. They are meeting the challenge of new trends, and know that art will continue to change. Through their works, they invite us to examine the past and to question the present. They challenge us to envision better worlds for the future.

The contemporary Native-American art-works shown here combine traditional and nontraditional media and techniques. The artists make strong statements about their

Fig. 9–21 **The pueblo communities of the Southwest are popular places for people to visit. This sculpture is about the tourist tradition of shopping for Native-American artworks. What details of this sculpture suggest tourists?** Robert Haozous, *Portable Pueblo,* 1988.
Steel, 94" high (with cloud), 78" long (101" with handle extended), 33" deep (239 x 198 x 83.8 cm). Joselyn Art Museum, Omaha, NE.

Fig. 9–22 **In this installation, the artist challenged the stereotypical presentation of American-Indian cultures in museums. In what ways does this artwork reflect the past? What element makes the presentation highly unusual?** James Luna, *The Artifact Piece,* 1990.
Performance and mixed media, installation shot, dimensions variable.

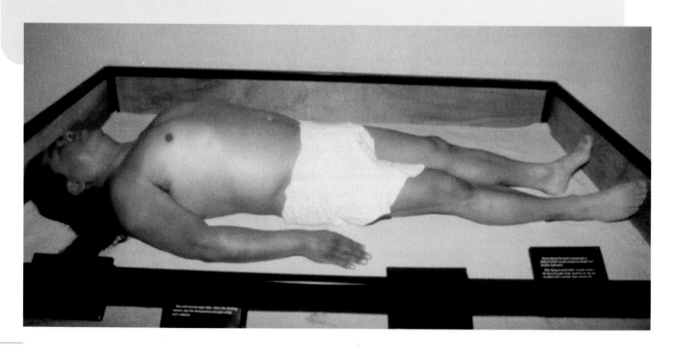

cultural traditions and the changes they see in their communities. Mary Adams's *Wedding Cake Basket* (Fig. 9–23) blends traditions of several cultures from different parts of the world. In Robert Haozous' *Portable Pueblo* (Fig. 9–21), the artist adorned an image of a traditional pueblo with symbols of twentieth-century transportation. In his performance installation, artist James Luna puts himself on display as an artifact (Fig 9–22). His work makes a statement about how Native-American art is presented in museums.

As in the past, the direction of art will depend on social, moral, and political changes within communities. New developments will come from new sets of ideas that are shared by using far-reaching technology. Certainly, artists will continue the tradition of observing and interpreting the world around them. The challenge of mastering skills and techniques, old and new, remains unchanged since the earliest times.

Fig. 9–23 This artist used traditional Mohawk and Iroquois basketweaving techniques to create the form of a traditional wedding cake. What might the artwork suggest about the relationship between Native-American and European cultures? Mary Adams (b. 1920s), *Wedding Cake Basket,* 1986. Woven sweet grass and ash splints, 25 1/2" x 15 3/4" (64.8 x 40 cm). Gift of Herbert Waide Hemphill, Jr., National Museum of American Art, Smithsonian Institution, Washington, DC. / Art Resource, NY.

Studio Connection

Make a small-scale sculpture in any medium that preserves or changes a tradition in your community. In planning your sculpture, think about the cultural, ethnic, religious, or shared interest traditions of a community you belong to. Research the heritage of these traditions by talking to others in your community. You might choose to continue the traditions of the past or to combine traditional and nontraditional materials and techniques in your sculpture. How can your sculpture show the importance of the traditions and heritage of your community? Think about ways you might change these traditions to reflect new ideas about your community.

9.3 Global View

Check Your Understanding

1. What is meant by a global style?
2. Why is it important for artists to continue to look to the past when creating their art?
3. How are Native-American artists using their art to meet the challenge of living in a global community?
4. What challenge for artists remains unchanged since the earliest times?

Looking Beyond

Film Arts in the Studio

Making a Videotape

Art That Looks Beyond

Studio Introduction
In this studio experience, you will work with classmates to create a videotape that tells a simple story or makes a presentation. Pages 296–297 will show you how to do it.

Become familiar with various types of television programs. These will be your models for your videotape. For instance, watch a news program. How does it begin?

How is each feature introduced? Note the setting and how it changes. Notice how the camera moves in for close-ups and out for long (distant) shots. Note how the camera *pans*, or follows, the action or view of a scene. Examine other types of television programs, such as situation comedies (sit-coms), cartoons, dramas, music videos, and commercials. Use one of the formats when you make your videotape.

Studio Background

The Filmmaking Process
Many people collaborate to make a film or movie. First, the screenwriter writes the script. Then, the director casts the film, or hires the actors. Meanwhile, a producer raises money to pay for the whole production. He or she rents or buys the cameras, lights, and other necessary equipment, and hires a film crew. The film crew operates the cameras and lighting and helps the actors with their costumes, makeup, and props.

Before filming can begin, film artists sketch **storyboards** that show each scene in the order it will appear. The storyboard in Fig. 9–25 was drawn for a movie about football, called *The Program.*

When the storyboard is finished, filming begins. Each day, everyone views the *dailies*, or the film shot the day before; then they shoot the footage for that day and prepare for the following day's filming. Shooting a film can last for months. After the film is shot, film editors perform the final step. They look at all the film footage along with the storyboard and find the best shots. Then they put these shots together so that they look seamless, as if the entire movie had been filmed without stopping.

Fig. 9–24 **This crew is discussing the plans for a film they are about to shoot. Why might it be important for the people in a film crew to work well together?**
Photo courtesy Linda Freeman, L&S Video.

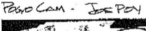
JOE AVOIDS SECOND TACKLE

POGO CAM · JOE POV

JOE DOUBLE BACKS AROUND

Fig. 9–25 **A storyboard is made up of hundreds of small, quick sketches like these.** Raymond C. Prado, *The Program.* Illustration storyboard. Courtesy of the artist.

Making Your Videotape

You Will Need

- pencil and paper
- costumes and props
- source of music or other sounds
- camcorder
- videotape
- tripod (optional)

Try This

1. As a group, choose a simple story or a presentation that you would like to videotape. Will your story have one, two, or three characters? Will you show and narrate a real-life event? What other ideas can you think of?

2. Plan your presentation. Decide on a sequence of events. List the images that come to mind as you discuss your ideas. Create an outline from your list of images.

3. Using your outline as a guide, create a storyboard. Base your storyboard on a television format. Indicate whether the camera should zoom in for a close-up, zoom out for a long shot, or pan the scene.

4. Write a script for your video. Will there be any dialogue? Or will you use a single narrator?

5. Select whatever actors, costumes, props, and music or other sounds you need.

6. Shoot the videotape scene by scene. When you are finished, view it with your group. Edit the video as needed. Then make the final tape.

Check Your Work

Plan a time for viewing your completed videotape along with each of your classmates'. Discuss how the videos tell a simple story or make a presentation that teaches viewers something. How does the selected television format add to or detract from each video?

Sketchbook Connection

Use your sketchbook to make visual notes as you examine different television formats. Try sketching a storyboard for a television program as you watch it or from your memory of it later. Do this for several different types of programs. This exercise may help you decide which type of programming you want to use for your video.

Computer Option

On the computer, input and edit a short video.

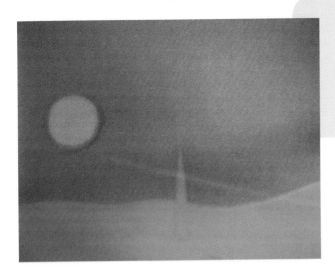

Fig. 9–27 **Students collaborated to show the life cycle of a plant as though it were equal to one single day (note the sun rising and setting).** Alison Oakes, Jamie Armstrong, Maggie Khouney, *Life of a Flower*, 1999. Videotape, Samford Middle School, Auburn, Alabama.

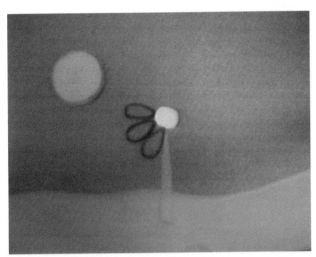

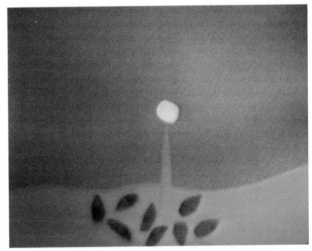

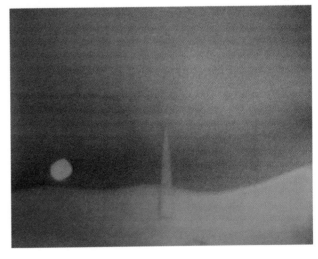

Connect to…

Daily Life

How do you think daily life will be different in 100 years? One intriguing prediction is that cars will essentially drive themselves: they will run on automatic pilot, guided by magnetic sensors to keep them in their lane, control their speed, and avoid obstacles. Another prediction is that cars will customize themselves for individual drivers, automatically adjusting the seat, steering column, and mirrors to each driver's preferences. In the case of an accident, the automobile's computers will call for the police and an ambulance. Future cars will likely be equipped with voice-operated computers that can receive e-mail and faxes, play videos, and access the Internet. How do you think the **cars of the future** will look in your lifetime?

Other Arts

Video and Performance Art

Theater, like art, can help people imagine the unfamiliar. In theater, the telling of a story can help people imagine what characters feel, what another time was like, or what the future may hold. **Performance artist** Anna Deavere Smith does just this— through the medium of video performance. In *Fires in the Mirror: Crown Heights, Brooklyn and Other Identities* (1992), Smith helps viewers gain an understanding of one community's conflicts. The work explores issues of race, ethnicity, and identity via role-playing by the people who actually experienced the events.

Careers

Have you ever drawn a picture of an astronaut, a spaceship, or an alien? If so, you may share the passion of **space artists**—artists who use astronomy and space exploration as inspiration and subject for their art. Space artists may be science, science-fiction, or fantasy illustrators, or even fine-art painters, but they all share a fascination about the possibilities of space exploration. NASA artist Robert T. McCall and astronaut Alan Bean paint "spacescapes" in response to ideas and images that have arisen from over forty years of space exploration. Television programs and movies, such as the *Star Wars* trilogy, have not only encouraged public interest in space but have also employed computer graphic artists, background painters, and modelmakers who are specialists in space art. What do you think might be a twenty-first-century discovery in space? Whatever is discovered, space artists will be ready to record it.

Fig. 9–28 **Astronaut Alan Bean has experienced firsthand the "spacescapes" he paints. Your imagination can lead you to create your own artworks based on the theme of space exploration.** *Alan Bean in His Studio.* Photograph by David Nance. ©The Greenwich Workshop, Inc. Courtesy Alan Bean.

Social Studies

Have you ever made a time capsule? The beginning of a millennium is when many groups prepare **time capsules** for future generations. But time capsules will be successful only with careful planning, record keeping, a durable capsule, and archival-quality documents. Not only is the time-worthiness of proposed items especially important, but so too is their media: newsprint paper deteriorates quickly; color photographs and slides tend to fade and discolor; computer disks, CD-ROMs, and videotapes, although they might seem like good items to include, may not be playable when the capsule is opened, because the machines needed to play them will be long gone. What items would you include in a time capsule that represented your community? How long would you want it to remain sealed?

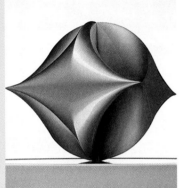

Fig. 9–29 **Each of this millennium capsule's four sections opens up for storage. Once objects are placed inside and it is sealed, it won't be opened again until the year 3000. If you could design a time capsule, what would it look like? What would you put inside?** Santiago Calatrava, *The* New York Times *Capsule* (model), 1999–2000.
Actual work: stainless steel, 5' x 5' x 5' (1.5 x 1.5 x 1.5 m). Stored at the American Museum of Natural History, NY. ©Santiago Calatrava. Photo courtesy Davies + Starr, New York.

Language Arts

Have you ever read a book online? That possibility is now available through **Project Gutenberg**. Named for Johannes Gutenberg, the developer of movable type and the printing press, the project is an online effort to make 10,000 of the most-read books available in electronic form by the end of 2001. Available at no cost, Project Gutenberg allows anyone who has

Fig. 9–30 **Johannes Gutenberg began using movable type—individual letters made from metal—in Europe around 1438. This new process revolutionized the printing of books.**

access to the Internet to read online books and other documents in the public domain. The project directors hope eventually to add art and music to the site. What books would you choose to make available through the site? What artworks?

Science

Can you imagine a computer no larger than a human cell? Such an invention is likely in your lifetime. One of the most anticipated scientific fields is **nanotechnology**, the science of miniaturized manufacturing by the use of nanoscale tools capable of manipulating one atom or molecule at a time. Technological advances in electronics, chemistry, and biology are fueling research in this field, encouraging scientists to discover ways to turn atoms and molecules into transistors, motors, pumps, and computer chips whose size is measured in billionths of a meter. If atoms can be manipulated individually, they could be placed exactly as needed to produce a desired structure. Medicine-bearing nanoparticles designed to interact only with diseased cells could eliminate most forms of disease or even slow the aging process. Can you think of any ethical issues that might be raised in response to nanotechnology?

Internet Connection
For more activities related to this chapter, go to the Davis website at **www.davis-art.com.**

Portfolio

Fig. 9–31 In this unique "digital quilt," portraits of students were taken using a digital camera, then downloaded into a computer. Each student manipulated his or her own portrait to create a high-contrast image, then enlarged it and carved it into a linoleum block. The finished 12" x 12" prints were assembled, like a quilt, on a school wall for display. Students of Summit Ridge Middle School, *Digital Quilt*, 1999. Littleton, Colorado.

"I was inspired to draw this picture by one of my old sketches of a bug. I thought it would be cool to make the picture look like a scene from an old horror movie. The area I was most concerned about was the color and having the bug catch your eye." **Ben Kwiatkowski**

Fig. 9–32 Ben Kwiatkowski, *Attack (Insects in City)*, 1998. Colored pencil, 12" x 18" (30 x 46 cm). Verona Area Middle School, Verona, Wisconsin.

"This piece shows the van in the Grand Canyon. The symbols on the side of the van add an ancient desert feeling to the picture, and the sandal on top represents the hot climate. The warm colors and antique appearance give the whole picture a sunset glow." **Leigh Jurevic**

CD-ROM Connection
To see more student art, check out the Community Connection Student Gallery.

Fig. 9–33 In a class project, an art teacher gave her students a digital image of her mini-van to manipulate in unusual ways. Leigh Jurevic, *Grand Canyon 4 Ever*, 1998. Computer art, 7" x 5 1/4" (18 x 13 cm). Riverdale School, Portland, Oregon.

Chapter 9 Review

Recall

Identify an artist from the past who envisioned flying machines long before the invention of air travel as we know it today.

Understand

Use examples to explain the main features of Surrealism.

Apply

You have studied how contemporary artists use new technology, how they create new art forms based on old traditions, and how they envision imaginary worlds in their artworks. Think about developments in your own world. In what other areas, besides art, are people using new technologies, changing traditions, and envisioning imaginary worlds? Provide examples to support your answers.

Analyze

Select an artwork from this chapter. Tell about its message and describe how the artist used the art elements to convey the main ideas.

Synthesize

In the 1850s, a group of people called Luddites (named after Ned Lud, an active member of the group) tried to prevent the introduction of new technology in factories, claiming that technology would destroy their community's way of life. Even today, there are people who oppose the introduction of technology. Write a dialogue between a modern-day Luddite and one of the artists featured in this chapter who uses new technology as an important part of his or her artworks. How would the Luddite feel about introducing technology into the world of art making? What would the Luddite want to preserve? How would your selected artist respond?

Evaluate

What do you think about installations as an art form? (*See example below.*) Is the installation a good way to express ideas? Is an installation a better form of communication than a painting, for instance? Why?

Page 279

For Your Portfolio

Your portfolio includes evidence of all you have learned through your study of art. Select four examples of artwork from the theme chapters in this book to demonstrate your ability to create artworks with meaningful themes. For each artwork, write a paragraph to explain how the piece is a good example of your skill and ability to focus on a theme.

For Your Sketchbook

Study the artworks in the global lessons in each chapter of this text. Design a page in your sketchbook on which you design a series of masks in the style of a particular culture or with some distinguishing characteristic associated with a cultural area.

Looking Beyond

301

Acknowledgments

We wish to thank the many people who were involved in the preparation of this book. First of all, we wish to acknowledge the many artists and their representatives who provided both permission and transparencies of their artworks. Particular thanks for extra effort go to Michael Slade at Art Resource, The Asian Art Museum, Roberto Prcela at The Cleveland Museum of Art, Anne Coe, Kenneth Haas, Charles McQuillen, Paul Nagano, Claes Oldenburg/Coosje Van Bruggen Studio, Bonnie Cullen at The Seattle Art Museum, and Bernice Steinbaum.

For her contributions to the Curriculum and Internet connections, we wish to thank Nancy Walkup. For contributing connections to the performing arts, we thank Ann Rowson, Kathy Blum, and Lee Harris of the Southeast Institute for Education in the Arts. A special thanks for the invaluable research assistance provided by Kutztown University students Amy Bloom, Karen Stanford, Kate Clewell, and Joel Frain and the staff at Kutztown University Library. Abby Remer's and Donna Pauler's writing and advice were greatly appreciated. Sharon Seim, Judy Drake, Kaye Passmore and Jaci Hanson were among the program's earliest reviewers, and offered invaluable suggestions. We also wish to acknowledge the thoughtful and dynamic contributions made to the Teacher's Edition by Kaye Passmore.

We owe an enormous debt to the editorial team at Davis Publications for their careful reading and suggestions for the text, their arduous work in photo and image research and acquisition, and their genuine spirit of goodwill throughout the entire process of producing this program. Specifically, we mention Colleen Strang, Jane Reed, Mary Ellen Wilson, Nancy Burnett, and Nancy Bedau. Carol Harley, our consistently upbeat "point person" on the project, provided thoughtful and substantive assistance and support.

Our editors, Claire Golding and Helen Ronan, carefully guided the creation of the program, faithfully attending to both its overall direction and the endless stream of details that emerged en route to its completion. We thank them for their trust and good faith in our work and for the spirit of teamwork they endorsed and consistently demonstrated.

For his trust in us, his vision and enthusiasm for the project, and for his willingness to move in new directions, we thank Wyatt Wade, President of Davis Publications.

Although neither of us has had the privilege of being her student in any formal setting, we owe our grounding in the theory and practice of art education to the scholarship of Laura Chapman. She has been both mentor and friend to each of us throughout the years and especially in this project. We thank her for her loyal support and for providing us the opportunity to continue her work in art curriculum development in this program for the middle school.

We offer sincere thanks to the hundreds of art teachers who have inspired us throughout the years with their good thinking and creative teaching. We also acknowledge our colleagues at Kutztown University, Penn State University, Ohio State University, and other institutions who have contributed to our understanding of teaching and learning.

Finally, we wish to thank our families, especially Adrienne Katter and Deborah Sieger, who have provided loving support and balance in our lives during the preparation of this book.

Eldon Katter
Marilyn Stewart

Educational Consultants

Numerous teachers and their students contributed artworks and writing to this book, often working within very tight timeframes. Davis Publications and the authors extend sincere thanks to:

Anita Cook, Thomas Prince School, Princeton, Massachusetts
Louisa Brown, Atlanta International School, Atlanta, Georgia
Monica Brown, Laurel Nokomis School, Nokomis, Florida
Will Caez, Logan Fontenelle Middle School, Bellevue, Nebraska
Kate Cross, Frank Borman Middle School, Phoenix, Arizona
Cappie Dobyns, Sweetwater Middle School, Sweetwater, Texas
Judith Durgin, Merrimack Valley Middle School, Penacook, New Hampshire
Suzanne Dyer, Bryant Middle School, Dearborn, Michigan
Elaine Gale, Sarasota Middle School, Sarasota, Florida
Catherine Gersich, Fairhaven Middle School, Bellingham, Washington
Rachel Grabek, Chocksett Middle School, Sterling, Massachusetts
Connie Heavey, Plum Grove Junior High School, Rolling Meadows, Illinois
Maryann Horton, Camels Hump Middle School, Richmond, Vermont
Anne Jacques, Hayfield Secondary School, Alexandria, Virginia
Alice S.W. Keppley, Penn View Christian School, Souderton, Pennsylvania
Bunki Kramer, Los Cerros Middle School, Danville, California
Karen Larson, Plum Grove Junior High School, Rolling Meadows, Illinois
Marguerite Lawler-Rohner, Fred C. Wescott Junior High School, Westbrook, Maine
Karen Lintner, Mount Nittany Middle School, State College, Pennsylvania

Publisher:
Wyatt Wade

Editorial Directors:
Claire Mowbray Golding, Helen Ronan

Editorial/Production Team:
Nancy Burnett, Carol Harley, Mary Ellen Wilson

Editorial Assistance:
Laura Alavosus, Frank Hubert, Victoria Hughes, David Payne, Lynn Simon

Illustration:
Susan Christy-Pallo, Stephen Schudlich

Betsy Logan, Samford Middle School, Auburn, Alabama

Sara Macaulay, Winsor School, Boston, Massachusetts

Patricia Mann, T.R. Smedberg Middle School, Sacramento, California

Shannon McBride, Riverdale Grade School, Portland, Oregon

Mary Ann McFarland, City View School, Worcester, Massachusetts

Phyllis Mowery-Racz, Desert Sands Middle School, Phoenix, Arizona

Debbie Myers, Colony Middle School, Palmer, Alaska

Kaye Passmore, Notre Dame Academy, Worcester, Massachusetts

Sandy Ray, Johnakin Middle School, Marion, South Carolina

Amy Richard, Daniel Boone Area Middle School, Birdsboro, Pennsylvania

Pat Rucker, Summit Ridge Middle School, Littleton, Colorado

Susan Rushin, Pocono Mountain Intermediate School South, Swiftwater, Pennsylvania

Roger Shule, Antioch Upper Grade School, Antioch, Illinois

Betsy Menson Sio, Jordan-Elbridge Middle School, Jordan, New York

Sharon Siswick, Islesboro School, Islesboro, Maine

Karen Skophammer, Manson Northwest Webster, Barnum, Iowa

Evelyn Sonnichsen, Plymouth Middle School, Plymouth, Minnesota

Ann Titus, Central Middle School, Galveston, Texas

Sindee Viano, Avery Coonley School, Downers Grove, Illinois

Karen Watson-Newlin, Verona Area Middle School, Verona, Wisconsin

Shirley Whitesides and Karen Hawkin, Asheville Middle School, Asheville, North Carolina

Photo Acquisitions:
Colleen Strang, Jane Reed, The Visual Connection, Mary Ellen Wilson, Rebecca Benjamin

Student Work Acquisitions:
Nancy Wood Bedau

Design:
Douglass Scott, Cara Joslin, WGBH Design

Manufacturing:
Georgiana Rock, April Dawley

Artist Guide

Abbott, Berenice (AB-bet, BER-a-nees) US, 1898–1991
Abakanowicz, Magdalena (ah-bah-kah-noe-vits, mahg-de-lay-nah) Poland, b. 1930
Adams, Mary US, b.1920s
Ahearn, John (A-hern) US, b. 1951
Al-fuzula, Miftah 15th century
Ali, M. 1500s
Amish (AH-mish) US
Anasazi (ah-nah-SAH-zee) Southwestern US
Ashevak, Kenojuak Canada, b. 1927
Apsit, Alexander Latvia, 1880–1844
Audubon, John James (AW-deh-bahn) US, 1785-1851
Aztec (AZ-tek) Mexico

Barthé, Richmond (BAR-tay) US, 1901-1989
Bearden, Romare (BEER-den, ro-mar-AY) US, 1912 or 1914–1988
Beg, Farrukh Kabul/Mughal Empire, 2nd half of 16th century-early 17th century
Bellows, George (BELL-lows) US, 1882–1925
Benin (beh-NEEN) Nigeria
Benton, Thomas Hart US, 1889–1975
Berkeley, Wayne Trinidad and Tobago, b. 1940
Bierstadt, Albert (BEER-stat) Germany, 1830–1902
Bingler, Steven US, b. 1948
Bishop, Isabel US, 1902–1988
Blank, Harrod US, 21st century
Brack, John Australia, b. 1920
Brown, Grafton Tyler US, 1841–1918
Browning, Colleen Ireland/US, b. 1929
Butterfield, Deborah US, b. 1949

Calder, Alexander Sterling US, 1898–1976
Callot, Jacques (kal-low, zhak) France, 1592–1635
Carter, Dennis Malone US, 1827–1881
Celtic (KELL-tik) Western and Central Europe
Chagall, Marc (sha-GAHL) Russia/France, 1887–1985
Chin, Mel US, b. 1951
Chola Dynasty (CHO-la) India
Coe, Sue British/American, b. 1951
Copley, John Singleton (KOPP-lee) US, 1738–1815
Cover, Sallie US, 1853–1936
Cuna (koon-ah) Panama

Das, Manohar India, 1500s–1600s
Davies, Arthur B. US, 1862–1928
Davis, Joseph H. US, active 1832–1837
De Maistre, Roy (de MEER-stra) Australia/England, 1894–1968
Delaunay, Robert (de-low-nay, roh-bair) France, 1885–1941
Delano, Pablo (de-LAN-o) Puerto Rico, b. 1954
Denes, Agnes Hungary, b. 1938
Dewing, Maria Oakey US, 1845–1927
Dike, Philip Latimer US, b. 1906
Duncanson, Robert Scott US, 1821–1872
Durand, Asher Brown US, 1796–1886

Edo (eh-DO) Nigeria
Elizondo, Arturo Mexico, 21st century
Escobar, Marisol Venezuela, b. 1930
Estes, Richard (ES-teez) US, b. 1932
Etruscan (eh-TRUSS-ken) ancient Etruria
Evans, Barnaby US, b. 1953
Evaristo, Pete and Jodi Tucci (eh-VAR-ist-o) (TOOCH-ee) US, b. 1955, b. 1956

Fakeye, Lamidi O. (fay-KAY-yay, la-MEE-dee) Nigeria, b. 1927
Fischer, Ernst Georg Germany, 1815–1874
Francis, Sam US, b. 1923
Frasconi, Antonio Argentina, b. 1919
Frazer, Jim US, b. 1949
Fuller, Meta Warrick US, 1877–1968

Gehry, Frank (GEH-ree) US, b. 1929
Gherin, Jules (geh-rahn, zhool) 1800s-1900s
Giacometti, Alberto (jah-koe-MET-tee) Switzerland, 1901–1966
Gilbert, Cass US, 1911-1913
Glackens, William US, 1870-1938
Goncharova, Natalia (gehn-cheh-ROVE-eh, nah-TAL-ya) Russia, 1881-1962
Gordon, David S. US, b. 1955
Greenough, Horatio US, 1805-1852
Grooms, Red US, b. 1937

Hamilton, Ann US, b. 1956
Hanson, Ann US, b. 1959
Hanson, Duane US, b. 1925
Haozous, Robert (HAU-zoos) Apache/Navajo, b. 1943
Hartigan, Grace US, b. 1922
Hartley, Marsden US, 1877-1943
Hausa Nigeria, Giwa
Heade, Martin Johnson US, 1814 or 1819-1904
Henderson, Bill Canada, b. 1950
Henri, Robert (HEN-rye) US, 1865-1929
Herd, Stan US, b. 1950
Herrera, Joe US-Cochiti Pueblo, 21st century
Heward, Prudence Canada, 1896-1947
Hicks, Sheila US, b. 1934
Hine, Lewis US, 1874-1940
Hiroshige, Utagawa (hee-ro-shee-gay, oo-tah-gah-wah) Japan, 1797-1858
Hockney, David England, b. 1937
Hohokam (ho-HO-kahm) Southwestern US

Hokusai, Sakino [also known as Katsushika Hokusai] (ho-koo-sy, sah-keeno) Japan, 1760-1849
Holzer, Jenny (HOLT-ser) US, b. 1950
Hornell, Sven (hor-NELL) Sweden, 1919-1992
Huebner, George (HUBE-ner) US, 1757-1828
Hull, Lynn US, 21st century

Innerst, Mark (INN-erst) US, b. 1957
Inuit (INN-yoo-it) N. America, esp. Arctic Canada and Greenland
Iroquois (EER-oh-coy) Northeastern US

Jacobson, Margareta Sweden, 21st century
Jean-Gilles, Joseph (zhon-zheel, zhozef) Haiti, b. 1943
Jefferson, Thomas US, 1743-1826
Jiménez, Luis US, b. 1940
Johnson, Philip US, b. 1906
Johnson, William H. US, 1901-1970
Jones, Cleve US, b. 1964
Jones, Lois Mailou (jones, LOW-is MI-loo) US, b. 1905

Karan, Khem (KAR-on, kame) India, 1500s-1600s
Kirchner, Ernst Ludwig (KIRK-ner, ernst LOOT-vik) Germany, 1880-1938
Kiyotada, Torii (kee-oh-tah-dah, toh-ree) Japan, active 1720-1750
Klee, Paul (clay) Switzerland, 1879-1940
Kline, Franz US, 1910-1962
Kogge, Robert US, b. 1953
Krimmel, John Lewis US, 1789-1821
Kuhn, Justus Engelhardt (coon, YOU-stus) Germany, active 1708, d. 1717

Lane, Fitz Hugh US, 1804-1865
Lamb, A.A. US, active 1864 and after
Lawson, Ernest US, 1873-1939
Le Moyne, Jacques (luh moin, zhak) France, active 1564-1588
Lee, Russell US, 20th century
Lehman, Amanda (LAY-man) US, 21st century
Leicester, Andrew (LES-ter) Britain, b. 1948
Lenape (len-AH-pay) N. Amer. orig. from Delaware R. Valley, US
Leonardo da Vinci (lay-oh-nar-doe da VIN-chee) Italy, 1452-1519

Lin, Maya US, b. 1959
Lou, Liza (loo, LIE-za) US, 21st century
Luks, George (LOUKS) US, 1867–1933
Luna, James US, b. 1950

Mackain, Bonnie US, 21st century
Magafan, Ethel (MAG-a-fahn) US, b. 1916
Magritte, Rene (mah-greet, ren-ay) Belgium, 1898–1967
Manutuke New Zealand, Gisborne
Maori (mou-ree) New Zealand
Malevich, Kazimar (ma-LAY-vich) Russia, 1878–1935
Manley, Edna Jamaica, b. 1900
Martinez, Maria Montoya US, 1887–1980
Masanobu, Okumura (mah-sahn-o-boo, oh-koo-moor-a) 1686–1764
Matchitt, Paratene New Zealand, 21st century
Mayan (my-en) Mexico
Meyer, Blackwell 19th century
Mies van der Rohe, Ludwig (mees van der roe, loot-vik) Germany, 1886-1969
Mimbres (mim-brayz) Southwestern US
Minshall, Peter Trinidad, 21st century
Mitchell, Joan US, 1926–1992
Mixtec (MISH-tek) Mexico
Mogollan (MOH-gull-on) Southwestern US
Mohawk (MOE-hock) Northeast US, Southern Canada
Moore, Henry England, 1898–1986
Moses, Anna Mary Robertson (a.k.a. Grandma Moses) US, 1860–1961
Motley, Archibald Jr. US, b. 1981
Mughal School (MOH-gull) India, c. 1690–1710
Mukhina, Vera (moo-KEE-nah, vair-ah) USSR/Russia
Munch, Edvard (moongk, ED-vart) Norway, 1863–1944

Nagano, Paul T. US, 21st century
Nakashima, Tom (nah-kah-shee-mah) US, b. 1944
Navajo (NAV-ah-ho) Southwestern US
Njau, Elimo (nn-jaow, eh-lee-mo) East Africa
Noguchi, Isamu (noh-goo-chee, ees-sah-moo) Japan/US, 1904-1988
Normil, Andre (nor-mill) Haiti, b. 1934

O'Keeffe, Georgia US, 1887–1986
Otter, Thomas P. US, 1832–1890

Paik, Nam June (pike) Korea, b. 1932
Peale, Charles Willson US, 1741–1827
Pergola, Linnea (per-GOLE-ah, linn-AY-ah) US, b. 1953
Petrosky, Jeanne (peh-TROE-skee, jeen) US, b. 1957
Picasso, Pablo (pee-KAHS-oh, PAH-blo) Spain, 1881–1973
Pierce, Elijah US, 1892–1984
Prendergast, Maurice (PREN-der-gast) US, 1859–1924

Quick-to-See Smith, Jaune (kwik-too-see smith, zjhohn) US, b. 1940
Qin dynasty (chin) China

Rasjasthan, Jaipure, India
Rauschenberg, Robert (RAU-shen-berg) US, b. 1925
Reinders, Jim US, 21st century
Revelle, Barbara Jo (reh-VELL) US, b. 1946
Revere, Paul US, 1735–1818
Riis, Jacob (rees) b. Denmark, then US 1849-1914
Rivera, Diego (re-VAY-rah) Mexico, 1886-1957
Rodchenko, Aleksandr (ROTE-chen-ko) Russia, 1891–1956
Rodia, Simon (roh-dee-ah) Italy, 1875–1965
Rodin, Auguste (roh-dan, oh-goost) France, 1840–1917
Romero, Frank (ro-MAY-ro) US, b. 1941
Rosenberg, Nelson US, b. 1941
Rosenquist, James (ro-zen-kwist) US, b. 1933

Saint-Gaudens, Augustus (saynt-GOD-enz) US, 1848–1907
Schapiro, Miriam (shuh-PEER-o, MEER-ee-um) US/Canada, b. 1923
Schofield, David US, b. 1958
Segal, George (SEE-gel) US, b. 1924
Shinn, Everett US, 1876–1953
Skoglund, Sandy (Skoh-glend) US, b. 1946
Sloan, John US, 1871–1951
Smith, Kevin Warren Cherokee, b. 1958
Spencer, Niles US, 1893–1952
Steinberg, Saul Rumania/US, b. 1914
Steir, Pat (steer) US, b. 1938
Suikei, Sesson (soo-ee-kay, sess-ahn) Japan, 1504–1589
Sullivan, Louis US, 1856–1924
Swentzell, Roxanne US, b. 1962

Tansey, Mark (TAN-zee) US, b. 1949
Tennis, Kara Johns US, b. 1954
Tiffany, Louis Comfort US, 1848–1933
Thomas, Alma Woodsey US, 1891–1978
Thiebaud, Wayne (TEE-bo) US, b.1920
Tianren, Wang, Ge Demao China, 21st century
Twachtman, John Henry (TWOKT-men) US, 1853–1902

Ukeles, Miere Laderman (yoo-kell-ees, meer) US, b. 1939
Utzon, Joern (ootz-ahn, yorn) Netherlands, b. 1918

van Gogh, Vincent (vahn-GO, VIN-sent) Netherlands, 1853–1890
Van Der Zee, James US, 1886–1983
Vennerberg, Gunnar Gunnarson Sweden, active late 19th-early 20th century
Viola, Bill (vie-OH-la) US, b. 1951

Walters, Joe US, b. 1952
Waner, Elisabeth US, active 19th century
Wegman, William US, b. 1943
Wei Dynasty (way) China
West, Benjamin US, 1738-1820
White, John England, active 1585–1593
Wodiczko, Krzysztof (vo-DEECH-koe, SHIS-tof) Poland, b. 1943
Wood, Grant US, 1892–1942

Yellow Nose Cheyenne-Arapaho Reservation, late 19th century

Zalce, Alfredo (SAL-say, al-FRAY-tho) Mexico, b.1908
Zorn, Anders Sweden, 1860–1920

World Map

The best way to see what the world looks like is to look at a globe. The problem of showing the round earth on a flat surface has challenged mapmakers for centuries. This map is called a Robinson projection. It is designed to show the earth in one piece, while maintaining the shape of the land and size relationships as much as possible. However, any world map has distortions.

This map is also called a *political* map. It shows the names and boundaries of countries as they existed at the time the map was made. Political maps change as new countries develop.

Key to Abbreviations

ALB.	Albania
AUS.	Austria
B.-H.	Bosnia-Hercegovina
BELG.	Belgium
CRO.	Croatia
CZ. REP.	Czech Republic
EQ. GUINEA	Equatorial Guinea
HUNG.	Hungary
LEB.	Lebanon
LITH.	Lithuania
LUX.	Luxembourg
MAC.	Macedonia
NETH.	Netherlands
RUS.	Russia
SLOV.	Slovenia
SLCK.	Slovakia
SWITZ.	Switzerland
YUGO.	Yugoslavia

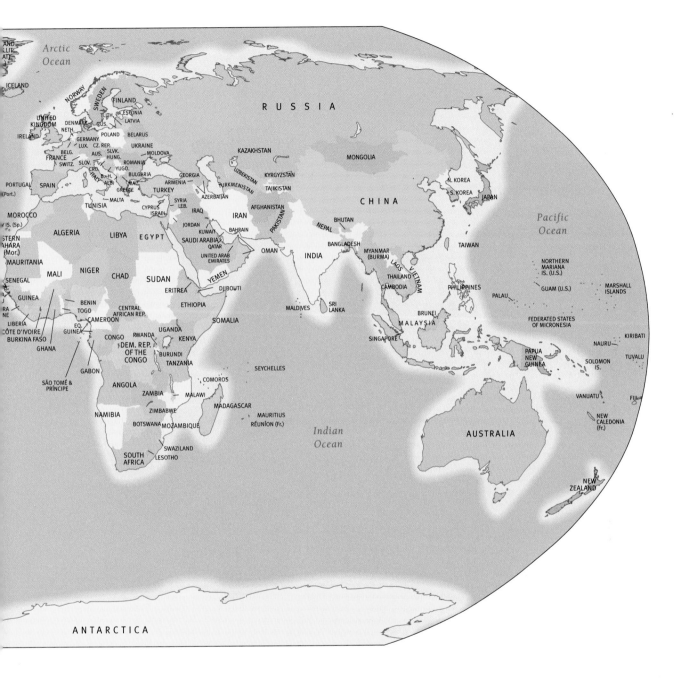

Arctic
Ocean

ICELAND

NORWAY
SWEDEN
FINLAND

UNITED
KINGDOM
DENMARK
NETH.
IRELAND
BELG.
LUX.
FRANCE
SWITZ.
GERMANY
POLAND
CZ. REP.
AUS. SLVK.
HUNG.
SLOV.
CRO.
B.-H.
ITALY
ALB.
MALTA
TUNISIA
PORTUGAL
(Port.)
SPAIN

ROMANIA
YUGO.
MAC.
GREECE
BULGARIA

ESTONIA
LITH.
BELARUS
RUS.
LATVIA

MOLDOVA
UKRAINE

GEORGIA
ARMENIA
TURKEY
AZERBAIJAN
CYPRUS
SYRIA
LEB.
ISRAEL
IRAQ

KAZAKHSTAN

UZBEKISTAN
TURKMENISTAN
TAJIKISTAN

KYRGYZSTAN

MONGOLIA

R U S S I A

N. KOREA
S. KOREA
JAPAN

Pacific
Ocean

CHINA

NORTHERN
MARIANA
IS. (U.S.)

MARSHALL
ISLANDS

GUAM (U.S.)

PALAU

FEDERATED STATES
OF MICRONESIA

MOROCCO
WESTERN
SAHARA
(Mor.)
IS. (Sp.)

ALGERIA
LIBYA
EGYPT

JORDAN
KUWAIT
BAHRAIN
SAUDI ARABIA
QATAR
UNITED ARAB
EMIRATES

AFGHANISTAN
PAKISTAN

IRAN

OMAN

NEPAL
BHUTAN

INDIA
BANGLADESH

MYANMAR
(BURMA)
LAOS
THAILAND
CAMBODIA
VIETNAM

TAIWAN

PHILIPPINES

MAURITANIA
MALI
NIGER
CHAD
SUDAN
SENEGAL
GUINEA

BENIN
TOGO
EQ.
GUINEA
CAMEROON
LIBERIA
CÔTE D'IVOIRE
BURKINA FASO
GHANA
GABON

CENTRAL
AFRICAN REP.

YEMEN
ERITREA
DJIBOUTI

ETHIOPIA

SOMALIA

MALDIVES
SRI
LANKA

BRUNEI
MALAYSIA

SINGAPORE

NAURU
KIRIBATI

TUVALU

SÃO TOMÉ &
PRÍNCIPE

CONGO
DEM. REP.
OF THE
CONGO

RWANDA
BURUNDI

UGANDA
KENYA

TANZANIA

SEYCHELLES

PAPUA
NEW
GUINEA

SOLOMON
IS.

ANGOLA
ZAMBIA
MALAWI

NAMIBIA
ZIMBABWE
BOTSWANA
MOZAMBIQUE

MADAGASCAR
COMOROS

MAURITIUS
RÉUNION (Fr.)

Indian
Ocean

AUSTRALIA

VANUATU
FIJI

NEW
CALEDONIA
(Fr.)

SOUTH
AFRICA
SWAZILAND
LESOTHO

NEW
ZEALAND

ANTARCTICA

Color Wheel

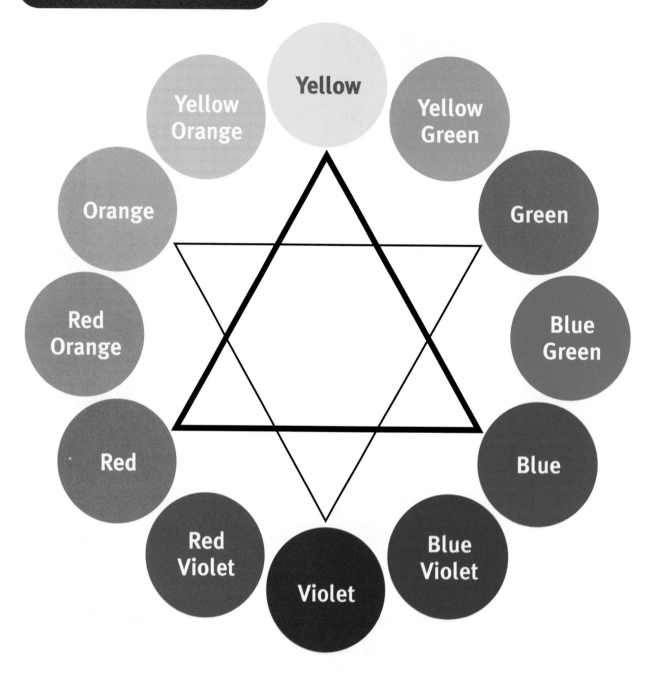

For easy study, the colors of the spectrum are usually arranged in a circle called a color wheel. Red, yellow, and blue are the three primary colors or hues. All other hues are made by mixing different amounts of these three colors.

If you mix any two primary colors, you will produce one of the three secondary colors. From experience, you probably know that red and blue make violet, red and yellow make orange, and blue and yellow make green. These are the three secondary colors.

The color wheel also shows six intermediate colors. You can create these by mixing a primary color with a neighboring secondary color. For example, yellow (a primary color) mixed with orange (a secondary color) creates yellow-orange (an intermediate color). Mixing the primary and secondary colors creates the six intermediate colors shown. Mixing different amounts of these colors produces an unlimited number of hues.

Bibliography

Aesthetics

Grimshaw, Caroline. *Connections: Art.* Chicago, IL: World Book, 1996.

Magee, Brian. *The Story of Philosophy.* NY: DK Publishing, 1998.

Varnedoe, Kirk. *A Fine Disregard: What Makes Modern Art Modern.* NY: Harry N. Abrams, Inc., 1994.

Weate, Jeremy. *A Young Person's Guide to Philosophy.* NY: DK Publishing, 1998.

Art Criticism

Antoine, Veronique. *Artists Face to Face.* Hauppauge, NY: Barron's, 1996.

Cumming, Robert. *Annotated Art.* NY: DK Publishing, 1998.

Franc, Helen M. *An Invitation to See: 150 Works from the Museum of Modern Art.* NY: Harry N. Abrams, Inc., 1996.

Greenberg, Jan and Sandra Jordan. *The American Eye.* NY: Delacorte, 1995.

--------------. *The Painter's Eye.* NY: Delacorte, 1991.

--------------. *The Sculptor's Eye.* NY: Delacorte, 1993.

Richardson, Joy. *Looking at Pictures: An Introduction to Art for Young People.* NY: Harry N. Abrams, Inc., 1997.

Rosenfeld, Lucy Davidson. *Reading Pictures: Self-Teaching Activities in Art.* Portland, ME: J. Weston Walch, 1991.

Roukes, Nicholas. *Humor in Art: A Celebration of Visual Wit.* Worcester, MA: Davis Publications, 1997.

Welton, Jude. *Looking at Paintings.* NY: DK Publishing, 1994.

Yenawine, Philip. *How to Look at Modern Art.* NY: Harry N. Abrams, Inc., 1991.

Art History
General

Barron's Art Handbook Series. *How to Recognize Styles.* Hauppauge, NY: Barron's, 1997.

Belloli, Andrea. *Exploring World Art.* Los Angeles, CA: The J. Paul Getty Museum, 1999.

D'Alelio, Jane. *I Know That Building.* Washington, DC: The Preservation Press, 1989.

Gebhardt, Volker. *The History of Art.* Hauppauge, NY: Barron's, 1998.

Hauffe, Thomas. *Design.* Hauppauge, NY: Barron's, 1996.

Janson, H.W. and Anthony F. Janson. *History of Art for Young People.* NY: Harry N. Abrams, Inc., 1997.

Remer, Abby. *Pioneering Spirits: The Life and Times of Remarkable Women Artists in Western History.* Worcester, MA: Davis Publications, 1997.

Stevenson, Neil. *Annotated Guides: Architecture.* NY: DK Publishing, 1997.

Thiele, Carmela. *Sculpture.* Hauppauge, NY: Barron's, 1996.

Wilkinson, Philip and Paolo Donati. *Amazing Buildings.* NY: DK Publishing, 1993.

Ancient World

Corbishley, Mike. *What Do We Know About Prehistoric People.* NY: Peter Bedrick Books, 1994.

Cork, Barbara and Struan Reid. *The Usborne Young Scientist: Archaeology.* London: Usborne Press, 1991.

Crosher, Judith. *Ancient Egypt.* NY: Viking, 1993.

Fleming, Stuart. *The Egyptians.* NY: New Discovery, 1992.

Giblin, James Cross. *The Riddle of the Rosetta Stone.* NY: Thomas Y. Crowell, 1990.

Haslam, Andrew, and Alexandra Parsons. *Make It Work: Ancient Egypt.* NY: Thomsom Learning, 1995.

Millard, Anne. *Pyramids.* NY: Kingfisher, 1996.

Morley, Jacqueline, Mark Bergin, and John Hames. *An Egyptian Pyramid.* NY: Peter Bedrick Books, 1991.

Powell, Jilliam. *Ancient Art.* NY: Thomsom Learning, 1994.

Classical World

Avi-Yonah, Michael. *Piece by Piece! Mosaics of the Ancient World.* Minneapolis, MN: Runestone Press, 1993.

Bardi, Piero. *The Atlas of the Classical World.* NY: Peter Bedrick Books, 1997.

Bruce-Mitford, Miranda. *Illustrated Book of Signs & Symbols.* NY: DK Publishing, 1996.

Chelepi, Chris. *Growing Up in Ancient Greece.* NY: Troll Associates, 1994.

Cohen, Daniel. *Ancient Greece.* NY: Doubleday, 1990.

Corbishley, Mike. *Ancient Rome.* NY: Facts on File, 1989.

Corbishley, Mike. *Growing Up in Ancient Rome.* NY: Troll Associates, 1993.

Hicks, Peter. *The Romans.* NY: Thomson Learning. 1993.

Loverance, Rowena and Wood. *Ancient Greece.* NY: Viking, 1993.

MacDonald, Fiona. *A Greek Temple.* NY: Peter Bedrick Books, 1992.

McCaughrean, G. *Greek Myths.* NY: Margaret McElderry Books, 1992.

Roberts, Morgan J. *Classical Deities and Heroes.* NY: Friedman Group, 1994.

Wilkinson, Philip. *Illustrated Dictionary of Mythology.* NY: DK Publishing, 1998.

Williams, Susan. *The Greeks.* NY: Thomson Learning, 1993.

The Middle Ages

Cairns, Trevor. *The Middle Ages.* NY: Cambridge University Press, 1989.

Caselli, Giovanni. *The Middle Ages.* NY: Peter Bedrick Books, 1993.

Chrisp, Peter. *Look Into the Past: The Normans.* NY: Thomson Learning. 1995.

Corrain, Lucia. *Giotto and Medieval Art.* NY: Peter Bedrick Books, 1995.

Howarth, Sarah. *What Do We Know About the Middle Ages.* NY: Peter Bedrick Books, 1995.

MacDonald, Fiona. *A Medieval Cathedral.* NY: Peter Bedrick Books, 1994.

Mason, Antony. *If You Were There in Medieval Times.* NY: Simon & Schuster, 1996.

Robertson, Bruce. *Marguerite Makes a Book.* Los Angeles, CA: The J. Paul Getty Museum, 1999.

Renaissance

Corrain, Lucia. *Masters of Art: The Art of the Renaissance.* NY: Peter Bedrick Books, 1997.

Di Cagno, Gabriella et al. *Michelangelo.* NY: Peter Bedrick Books, 1996.

Dufour, Alessia Devitini. *Bosch.* ArtBook Series. NY: DK Publishing, 1999.

Fritz, Jean, Katherine Paterson, et. al. *The World in 1492.* NY: Henry Holt & Co., 1992.

Giorgi, Rosa. *Caravaggio.* ArtBook Series. NY: DK Publishing, 1999.

Harris, Nathaniel. *Renaissance Art.* NY: Thomson Learning, 1994.

Herbert, Janis. *Leonardo da Vinci for Kids.* Chicago: Chicago Review Press, 1998.

Howarth, Sarah. *Renaissance People.* Brookfield, CT: Millbrook Press, 1992.

--------------. *Renaissance Places.* Brookfield, CT: Millbrook Press, 1992.

Leonardo da Vinci. ArtBook Series. NY: DK Publishing, 1999.

McLanathan, Richard. *First Impressions: Leonardo da Vinci.* NY: Harry N. Abrams, Inc., 1990.

--------------. *First Impressions: Michelangelo.* NY: Harry N. Abrams, Inc., 1993.

Medo, Claudio. *Three Masters of the Renaissance: Leonardo, Michelangelo, Raphael.* Hauppauge, NY: Barron's, 1999.

Milande, Veronique. *Michelangelo and His Times.* NY: Henry Holt & Co., 1995.

Muhlberger, Richard. *What Makes a Leonardo a Leonardo?* NY: Viking, 1994.

--------------. *What Makes a Raphael a Raphael?* NY: Viking, 1993.

Murray, Peter and Linda. *The Art of the Renaissance.* NY: Thames and Hudson, 1985.

Piero della Francesca. ArtBook Series. NY: DK Publishing, 1999.

Richmond, Robin. *Introducing Michelangelo.* Boston, MA: Little, Brown, 1992.

Romei, Francesca. *Leonardo da Vinci.* NY: Peter Bedrick Books, 1994.

Spence, David. *Michelangelo and the Renaissance.* Hauppauge, NY: Barron's, 1998.

Stanley, Diane. *Leonardo da Vinci.* NY: William Morrow, 1996.

Wood, Tim. *The Renaissance.* NY: Viking, 1993.

Wright, Susan. *The Renaissance.* NY: Tiger Books International, 1997.

Zuffi, Stefano. *Dürer.* ArtBook Series. NY: DK Publishing, 1999.

Zuffi, Stefano and Sylvia Tombesi-Walton. *Titian.* ArtBook Series. NY: DK Publishing, 1999.

Baroque and Rococo

Barron's Art Handbooks. *Baroque Painting.* Hauppague, NY: Barron's, 1998.

Bonafoux, Pascal. *A Weekend with Rembrandt.* NY: Rizzoli, 1991.

Jacobsen, Karen. *The Netherlands.* Chicago, IL: Children's Press, 1992.

Muhlberger, Richard. *What Makes a Goya a Goya?* NY: Viking, 1994.

--------------. *What Makes a Rembrandt a Rembrandt?* NY: Viking, 1993.

Pescio, Claudio. *Rembrandt and Seventeenth-Century Holland.* NY: Peter Bedrick Books, 1996.

Rodari, Florian. *A Weekend with Velázquez.* NY: Rizzoli, 1993.

Schwartz, Gary. *First Impressions: Rembrandt.* NY: Harry N. Abrams, Inc., 1992.

Spence, David. *Rembrandt and Dutch Portraiture.* Hauppauge, NY: Barron's, 1998.

Velázquez. ArtBook Series. NY: DK Publishing, 1999.

Vermeer. ArtBook Series. NY: DK Publishing, 1999.

Wright, Patricia. *Goya.* NY: DK Publishing, 1993.

Zuffi, Stefano. *Rembrandt.* ArtBook Series. NY: DK Publishing, 1999.

Neoclassicism, Romanticism, Realism

Friedrich. ArtBook Series. NY: DK Publishing, 1999.

Goya. Eyewitness Books. NY: DK Publishing, 1999.

Rapelli, Paola. *Goya.* ArtBook Series. NY: DK Publishing, 1999.

Impressionism & Post-Impressionism

Barron's Art Handbooks. *Impressionism.* Hauppauge, NY: Barron's, 1997.

Bernard, Bruce. *Van Gogh.* Eyewitness Books. NY: DK Publishing, 1999.

Borghesi, Silvia. *Cézanne.* ArtBook Series. NY: DK Publishing, 1999.

Crepaldi, Gabriele. *Gauguin.* ArtBook Series. NY: DK Publishing, 1999.

--------------. *Matisse.* ArtBook Series. NY: DK Publishing, 1999.

Kandinsky. ArtBook Series. NY: DK Publishing, 1999.

Monet. Eyewitness Books. NY: DK Publishing, 1999.

Muhlberger, Richard. *What Makes a Cassatt a Cassatt?* NY: Viking, 1994.

--------------. *What Makes a Degas a Degas?* NY: Viking, 1993.

--------------. *What Makes a Monet a Monet?* NY: Viking, 1993.

--------------. *What Makes a van Gogh a van Gogh?* NY: Viking, 1993.

Pescio, Claudio. *Masters of Art: Van Gogh.* NY: Peter Bedrick Books, 1996.

Rapelli, Paola. *Monet.* ArtBook Series. NY: DK Publishing, 1999.

Sagner-Duchting, Karin. *Monet at Giverny.* NY: Neueis Publishing, 1994.

Skira-Venturi, Rosabianca. *A Weekend with Degas.* NY: Rizzoli, 1991.

--------------. *A Weekend with van Gogh.* NY: Rizzoli, 1994.

Spence, David. *Cézanne.* Hauppague, NY: Barron's, 1998.

--------------. *Degas.* Hauppague, NY: Barron's, 1998.

--------------. *Gauguin.* Hauppague, NY: Barron's, 1998.

--------------. *Manet: A New Realism.* Hauppague, NY: Barron's, 1998.

--------------. *Monet and Impressionism.* Hauppague, NY: Barron's, 1998.

--------------. *Renoir.* Hauppague, NY: Barron's, 1998.

--------------. *Van Gogh: Art and Emotions.* Hauppague, NY: Barron's, 1998.

Torterolo, Anna. *Van Gogh.* ArtBook Series. NY: Dk Publishing, 1999.

Turner, Robyn Montana. *Mary Cassatt.* Boston, MA: Little, Brown, 1992.

Waldron, Ann. *Claude Monet.* NY: Harry N. Abrams, Inc., 1991.

Welton, Jude. *Impressionism.* NY: DK Publishing, 1993.

Wright, Patricia. *Manet.* Eyewitness Books. NY: DK Publishing, 1999.

20th Century

Antoine, Veronique. *Picasso: A Day in His Studio.* NY: Chelsea House, 1993.

Beardsley, John. *First Impressions: Pablo Picasso.* NY: Harry N. Abrams, Inc., 1991.

Cain, Michael. *Louise Nevelson.* NY: Chelsea House, 1990.

Children's History of the 20th Century. NY: DK Publishing, 1999.

Faerna, Jose Maria, ed. *Great Modern Masters: Matisse.* NY: Harry N. Abrams, Inc., 1994.

Faerna, Jose Maria, ed. *Great Modern Masters: Picasso.* NY: Harry N. Abrams, Inc., 1994.

Gherman, Beverly. *Georgia O'Keeffe: The Wideness and Wonder of Her World.* NY: Simon & Schuster, 1994.

Greenberg, Jan and Sandra Jordan. *Chuck Close Up Close.* NY: DK Publishing, 1998.

Heslewood, Juliet. *Introducing Picasso.* Boston, MA: Little, Brown, 1993.

Paxman, Jeremy. *20th Century Day by Day.* NY: DK Publishing, 1991.

Ridley, Pauline. *Modern Art.* NY: Thomson Learning, 1995.

Rodari, Florian. *A Weekend with Matisse.* NY: Rizolli, 1992.

--------------. *A Weekend with Picasso.* NY: Rizolli, 1991.

Spence, David. *Picasso: Breaking the Rules of Art.* Hauppauge, NY: Barron's, 1998.

Tambini, Michael. *The Look of the Century.* NY: DK Publishing, 1996.

Turner, Robyn Montana. *Georgia O'Keeffe.* Boston, MA: Little, Brown, 1991.

Woolf, Felicity. *Picture This Century: An Introduction to Twentieth-Century Art.* NY: Doubleday, 1993.

United States

Howard, Nancy Shroyer. *Jacob Lawrence: American Scenes, American Struggles.* Worcester, MA: Davis Publications, 1996.

--------------. *William Sidney Mount: Painter of Rural America.* Worcester, MA: Davis Publications, 1994.

Panese, Edith. *American Highlights: United States History in Notable Works of Art.* NY: Harry N. Abrams, Inc., 1993.

Sullivan, Charles, ed. *African-American Literature and Art for Young People.* NY: Harry N. Abrams, Inc., 1991.

--------------. *Here Is My Kingdom: Hispanic-American Literature and Art for Young People.* NY: Harry N. Abrams, Inc., 1994.

--------------. *Imaginary Gardens: American Poetry and Art for Young People.* NY: Harry N. Abrams, Inc., 1989.

Native American

Burby, Liza N. *The Pueblo Indians.* NY: Chelsea House, 1994.

D'Alleva, Anne. *Native American Arts and Culture.* Worcester, MA: Davis Publications, 1993.

Dewey, Jennifer Owings. *Stories on Stone.* Boston, MA: Little, Brown, 1996.

Garborino, Merwyn S. *The Seminole.* NY: Chelsea House, 1989.

Gibson, Robert O. *The Chumash.* NY: Chelsea House, 1991.

Graymont, Barbara, *The Iroquois.* NY: Chelsea House, 1988.

Griffin-Pierce, Trudy. *The Encyclopedia of Native America.* NY: Viking, 1995.

Hakim, Joy. *The First Americans.* NY: Oxford University Press, 1993.

Howard, Nancy Shroyer. *Helen Cordero and the Storytellers of Cochiti Pueblo.* Worcester, MA: Davis Publications, 1995.

Jensen, Vicki. *Carving a Totem Pole.* NY: Henry Holt & Co., 1996.

Littlechild, George. *This Land Is My Land.* Emeryville, CA: Children's Book Press, 1993.

Moore, Reavis. *Native Artists of North America.* Santa Fe, NM: John Muir Publications, 1993.

Perdue, Theda. *The Cherokee.* NY: Chelsea House, 1989.

Remer, Abby. *Discovering Native American Art.* Worcester, MA: Davis Publications, 1996.

Sneve, Virginia Driving Hawk. *The Cherokees.* NY: Holiday House, 1996.

Art of Global Cultures
General

Bowker, John. *World Religions.* NY: DK Publishing, 1997.

Eyewitness World Atlas. DK Publishing (CD ROM)

Wilkinson, Philip. *Illustrated Dictionary of Religions.* NY: DK Publishing, 1999.

World Reference Atlas. NY: DK Publishing, 1998.

Africa

Ayo, Yvonne. *Africa.* NY: Alfred A. Knopf, 1995.

Bohannan, Paul and Philip Curtin. *Africa and Africans.* Prospect Heights, IL: Waveland Press, 1995.

Chanda, Jacqueline. *African Arts and Culture.* Worcester, MA: Davis Publications, 1993.

--------------. *Discovering African Art.* Worcester, MA: Davis Publications, 1996.

Gelber, Carol. *Masks Tell Stories.* Brookfield, CT: Millbrook Press, 1992

La Duke, Betty. *Africa: Women's Art. Women's Lives.* Trenton, NJ: Africa World Press, 1997.

--------------. *Africa Through the Eyes of Women Artists.* Trenton, NJ: Africa World Press, 1996.

McKissack, Patricia and Fredrick McKissack. *The Royal Kingdoms of Ghana, Mali, and Songhay.* NY: Henry Holt & Co., 1994.

Mexico, Mesoamerica, Latin America

Baquedano, Elizabeth, *Eyewitness Books: Aztec, Inca, and Maya.* NY: Alfred A. Knopf, 1993.

Berdan, Frances F. *The Aztecs.* NY: Chelsea House, 1989.

Braun, Barbara. *A Weekend with Diego Rivera.* NY: Rizzoli, 1994.

Cockcroft, James. *Diego Rivera.* NY: Chelsea House, 1991.

Goldstein, Ernest. *The Journey of Diego Rivera.* Minneapolis, MN: Lerner, 1996.

Greene, Jacqueline D. *The Maya.* NY: Franklin Watts, 1992.

Neimark, Anne E. *Diego Rivera: Artist of the People.* NY: Harper Collins, 1992.

Platt, Richard. *Aztecs: The Fall of the Aztec Capital.* NY: DK Publishing, 1999.

Sherrow, Victoria. *The Maya Indians.* NY: Chelsea House, 1994.

Turner, Robyn Montana. *Frida Kahlo.* Boston, MA: Little, Brown, 1993.

Winter, Jonah. *Diego.* NY: Alfred A. Knopf, 1991.

Asia

Doherty, Charles. *International Encyclopedia of Art: Far Eastern Art.* NY: Facts on File, 1997.

Doran, Clare. *The Japanese.* NY: Thomson Learning, 1995.

Ganeri, Anita. *What Do We Know About Buddhism.* NY: Peter Bedrick Books, 1997.

--------------. *What Do We Know About Hinduism.* NY: Peter Bedrick Books, 1996.

Lazo, Caroline. *The Terra Cotta Army of Emperor Qin.* NY: Macmillan, 1993.

MacDonald, Fiona, David Antram and John James. *A Samurai Castle.* NY: Peter Bedrick Books, 1996.

Major, John S. *The Silk Route.* NY: Harper Collins, 1995.

Martell, Mary Hazel. *The Ancient Chinese.* NY: Simon & Schuster, 1993.

Pacific

D'Alleva, Anne. *Arts of the Pacific Islands.* NY: Harry N. Abrams, 1998.

Haruch, Tony. *Discovering Oceanic Art.* Worcester, MA: Davis Publications, 1996.

Niech, Rodger and Mick Pendergast. *Traditional Tapa Textiles of the Pacific.* NY: Thames and Hudson, 1998.

Thomas, Nicholas. *Oceanic Art.* NY: Thames and Hudson, 1995.

Studio

Drawing Basic Subjects. Hauppauge, NY: Barron's, 1995.

Ganderton, Lucinda. *Stitch Sampler.* NY: DK Publishing, 1999.

Grummer, Arnold. *Complete Guide to Easy Papermaking.* Iola, WI: Krause Publications, 1999.

Harris, David. *The Art of Calligraphy.* NY: DK Publishing, 1995.

Horton, James. *An Introduction to Drawing.* NY: DK Publishing, 1994.

Learning to Paint: Acrylics. Hauppauge, NY: Barron's, 1998.

Learning to Paint: Drawing. Hauppauge, NY: Barron's, 1998.

Learning to Paint: Mixing Watercolors. Hauppauge, NY: Barron's, 1998.

Learning to Paint in Oil. Hauppauge, NY: Barron's, 1997.

Learning to Paint in Pastel. Hauppauge, NY: Barron's, 1997.

Learning to Paint in Watercolor. Hauppauge, NY: Barron's, 1997.

Lloyd, Elizabeth. *Watercolor Still Life.* NY: DK Publishing, 1994.

Slafer, Anna and Kevin Cahill. *Why Design?* Chicago, IL: Chicago Review Press, 1995.

Smith, Ray. *An Introduction to Acrylics.* NY: DK Publishing, 1993.

--------------. *An Introduction to Oil Painting.* NY: DK Publishing, 1993.

--------------. *An Introduction to Watercolor.* NY: DK Publishing, 1993.

--------------. *Drawing Figures.* Hauppauge, NY: Barron's, 1994.

--------------. *Oil Painting Portraits.* NY: DK Publishing, 1994.

--------------. *Watercolor Color.* NY: DK Publishing, 1993.

Wright, Michael. *An Introduction to Pastels.* NY: DK Publishing, 1993.

Wright, Michael and Ray Smith. *An Introduction to Mixed Media.* NY: DK Publishing, 1995.

--------------. *An Introduction to Perspective.* NY: DK Publishing, 1995.

Perspective Pack. NY: DK Publishing, 1998.

Glossary

abstract Art that is based on a subject you can recognize, but the artist simplifies, leaves out, or rearranges some elements so that you may not recognize them. (*arte abstracto*)

activism The practice of working to change attitudes or beliefs related to politics or other issues within a community. (*activismo*)

aesthetician (*es-tha-TISH-un*) A person who wonders about art or beauty and asks questions about why art was made and how it fits into society. (*estético*)

analogous colors (*an-AL-oh-gus*) Colors that are closely related because they have one hue in common. For example, blue, blue-violet, and violet all contain the color blue. Analogous colors appear next to one another on the color wheel. (*colores análogos*)

appliqué (*ah-plee-KAY*) A process of stitching and/or gluing cloth to a background, similar to collage. (*aplicación*)

armature (*AR-mah-chur*) A system of support, similar to a skeleton, used to make a sculpture. (*armadura*)

art critic A person who expresses a reasoned opinion on any matter concerning art. (*crítico de arte*)

art form A category or kind of art such as painting, sculpture, or photography. (*forma artística*)

art historian A person who studies art—its history and contributions to cultures and societies. (*historiador de arte*)

artist A person who makes art. (*artista*)

art media The materials used by the artist to produce a work of art. (*medios artísticos*)

Art Nouveau (*art noo-VOH*) 1900–1915. A French phrase that means "New Art." A design style that explored the flowing lines, curves, and shapes of nature. (*art nouveau*)

Ash Can School 1908–1914. A group of American artists who painted pictures of real scenes of city life. The group's original name was "The Eight." (*escuela "Ash Can"*)

assemblage (*ah-SEM-blij*) A sculpture made by combining discarded objects such as boxes, pieces of wood, parts of old toys, and so on. (*ensambladura*)

asymmetrical (*ay-sim-MET-tri-kal*) A type of visual balance in which the two sides of the composition are different yet balanced; visually equal without being identical. Also called informal balance. (*asimétrico*)

avant-garde (*ah-vant-GARD*) An art term that describes art that is original and different from traditional styles of art. Avant-garde artists often experiment with new materials and ways of expressing ideas. (*vanguardismo*)

balance A principle of design that describes how parts of an artwork are arranged to create a sense of equal weight or interest. An artwork that is balanced seems to have equal visual weight or interest in all areas. Types of balance are symmetrical, asymmetrical, and radial. (*equilibrio*)

bisqueware (*BISK-wair*) Ceramic that has been fired once but not glazed. (*bizcocho de porcelana*)

cause A belief or issue that moves people to action. (*causa*)

celebration An observation of an event or local tradition with other members of a community. (**celebración**)

ceramics (*sir-AM-miks*) The art of making objects from clay, glass, or other minerals by baking or firing them at high temperatures in an oven known as a kiln. Ceramics are also the products made in this way. (*cerámica*)

Christian art A type of art that began in Africa in the fifteenth century and continues today. The primary aim of mission art is to teach people in African communities about Christian religions. (*arte cristiana*)

cinematography The art of making "moving" or motion pictures. (*cinematografía*)

cityscape An artwork that shows a view of a city (buildings, streets, shops) as subject matter. (*paisaje urbano*)

codex A type of book whose pages are hinged together at both sides, similar to an accordion. (*códice*)

collaborate To work together with others. (*colaborar*)

collage (*coh-LAHZ*) A work of art created by gluing bits of paper, fabric, scraps, photographs, or other materials to a flat surface. (*collage*)

color Another word for hue, which is the common name of a color in or related to the spectrum, such as yellow, yellow-orange, blue-violet, green. See hue. (*color*)

color scheme A plan for selecting or organizing colors. Common color schemes include: warm, cool, neutral, monochromatic, analogous, complementary, split-complementary and triad. (*combinación de colores*)

commemorate (*co-MEM-or-ate*) To honor or remember a person or event. (*conmemorar*)

communication The exchange of information, thoughts, feelings, ideas, opinions, and so on, either in spoken, written, or visual form. (*comunicación*)

communism A form of government in Russia whose main idea was to create communities in which people worked together. (*comunismo*)

complementary (*com-ple-MEN-tah-ree*) Colors that are directly opposite each other on the color wheel, such as red and green, blue and orange, and violet and yellow. When complements are mixed together, they make a neutral brown or gray. When they are used next to each other in a work of art, they create strong contrasts. (*complementarios*)

computer art Art whose main medium is the computer. (*arte generado por computadora*)

contour drawing A drawing that shows only the edges (contours) of objects. (*dibujo de contorno*)

cool colors Colors often connected with cool places, things, or feelings. The family of colors ranging from the greens through the blues and violets. (*colores frescos*)

crafts Works of art, either decorative or useful, that are skillfully made by hand. (*artesanías*)

Cubism 1907–1914. An art history term for a style developed by the artists Pablo Picasso and Georges Braque. In Cubism, the subject matter is broken up into geometric shapes and forms. The forms are put back together into an abstract composition. Often, three-dimensional objects seem to be shown from many different points of view at the same time. (*cubismo*)

Dada 1915–1923. An art movement that was known for rejecting traditional art styles and materials. These artists created artworks based on chance, and often used found objects to create new art forms. Many artists involved in the Dada movement became leaders of Surrealism and other new styles of art. (*dadaísmo*)

dailies The film shot each day during a film shoot. (*toma del día*)

designers Artists who plan the organization and composition of an artwork, object, place, building, and so on. Designers plan clothing (fashion design), outdoor spaces (landscape design), indoor spaces (furniture and interior design), signs and ads (graphic design), and so on. (*diseñadores*)

document (*DOK-you-ment*) To make or keep a record of. (*documentar*)

dry media Art materials such as pencils, chalk (pastels), and crayons that are not wet and do not require the use of a liquid. (*medios secos*)

Earth Art An art movement in which land and earth are important as ideas or used as a media for expression. (*arte Tierra*)

earthworks Any work of art in which land and earth are important media. See earth art. (*earthworks*)

elements of design The visual "tools" artists use to create art. The elements include color, value, line, shape, form, texture, and space. (*elementos de diseño*)

emphasis Areas in a work of art that catch and hold the viewer's attention. These areas usually have contrasting sizes, shapes, colors, or other distinctive features. (*acentuación*)

form An element of design. Any three-dimensional object such as a cube, sphere, pyramid, cylinder. A form can be measured from top to bottom (height), side to side (width), and front to back (depth). Form is also a general term that means the structure or design of a work. (*forma*)

found objects Materials that artists find and use for artwork, such as scraps of wood, metal, or ready-made objects. (*objetos encontrados*)

frame A single image from a video or sound installation. (*cuadro*)

fresco (*FRES-coh*) A technique of painting in which pigments are applied to a thin layer of wet plaster so that they will be absorbed. The painting becomes part of the wall. (*fresco*)

geometric A shape or form that has smooth, even edges. Geometric shapes include circles, squares, rectangles, triangles, and ellipses. Geometric forms include cones, cubes, cylinders, slabs, pyramids, and spheres. (*geométricas*)

gesture drawing A quick drawing that captures the gestures or movements of the body. (*dibujo gestual*)

global community The interaction and sharing of ideas and knowledge of people and populations worldwide. (*comunidad global*)

global style A style of art that cannot be linked to just one culture or tradition of art. Global style comes about from exchanges of ideas among artists of many nations and cultures around the world. (*estilo global*)

graphic design A general term for artwork in which letter forms (writing, typography) are an important part of the artwork. (*diseño gráfico*)

graphic designer An artist who designs such things as packages, wrapping papers, books, posters, and greeting cards. (*diseñador gráfico*)

Harlem Renaissance (*HAR-lem ren-eh-SAHNSS*) 1920–1940. A name of a period and a group of artists who lived and worked in Harlem, New York City. They used a variety of art forms to express their lives as African Americans. (*Renacimiento de Harlem*)

horizon line The flat line where water or land seems to end and the sky begins. It is usually on the eye level of the observer. If the horizon cannot be seen, its location must be imagined. (*línea de horizonte*)

hue Another word for color. See color. (*tonalidad*)

immigrants People who move from one country to another. (*inmigrantes*)

implied line The way objects are set up so as to produce the effect of seeing lines in a work, but where lines are not actually present. (*línea implícita*)

implied texture The way a surface appears to look, such as rough or smooth. (*textura implícita*)

Impressionists 1875–1900. A group of artists who worked outside and painted directly from nature. Impressionist artists used rapid brushstrokes to capture an impression of light and color. (*impresionistas*)

installations Temporary arrangements of art objects in galleries, museums, or outdoors. (*instalaciones*)

intaglio print (*in-TAH-lee-oh*) A print in which the artist scratches lines into a smooth metal plate, inks the plate, and then pulls the print using a printing press to apply even pressure between the plate and the paper. (*impresión en huecograbado*)

intermediate color or hue A color made by mixing a secondary color with a primary color. Blue-green, yellow-green, yellow-orange, red-orange, red-violet, and blue-violet are intermediate colors. (*color intermedio*)

kinetic art (*kih-NET-ick*) A general term for all artistic constructions that include moving elements, whether actuated by motor, by hand crank, or by natural forces as in mobiles. (*arte cinético*)

kinetic sculpture A sculpture that moves or has moving parts. The motion may be caused by many different forces, including air, gravity, and electricity. (*escultura cinética*)

kivas The rounded ceremonial rooms in an Anasazi pueblo. (*escultura cinética*)

limner (*LIM-ner*) An early American self-taught artist who painted signs, houses, and portraits. (*limner*)

line A mark with length and direction, created by a point that moves across a surface. A line can vary in length, width, direction, curvature, and color. Line can be two-dimensional (a pencil line on paper), three-dimensional (wire), or implied. (*línea*)

linear perspective (*lin-EE-er per-SPEK-tiv*) A technique used to show three-dimensional space on a two-dimensional surface. (*perspectiva lineal*)

linoleum cut A relief print that is made from a linoleum block. The linoleum is cut away. The uncut relief areas are covered with ink, paper is placed on top, and the print is made by rubbing the back of the paper. (*impresión en linóleo*)

lithographic print (*lith-oh-GRAF-ik*) A print made when an artist draws an image on a flat slab of stone (or a special metal plate) with a greasy crayon or paint. A special acid removes the part of the stone not covered with crayon. The crayoned part is then inked, and the print is made using a printing press. (*litografía*)

maquette (*mah-KET*) A small-scale model of a larger sculpture. (*maqueta*)

memorial Artworks or other objects that help people remember things, such as important events or people. (*obra conmemorativa*)

miniature A very small, detailed painting. (*miniatura*)

mixed media Any artwork that is made with more than one medium, such as ink and watercolor, painting and collage, and so on. (*medios mixtos*)

mobile (*MOH-beel*) A hanging balanced sculpture with parts that can be moved, especially by the flow of air. Invented by Alexander Calder in 1932. (*móvil*)

Modern architecture 1900–1970. A style of architecture that used steel, concrete, and glass to create tall buildings. Modern architecture was characterized by simple lines and a lack of decoration. (*estilo arquitectónico moderno*)

monochromatic (*mah-no-crow-MAT-ik*) Made of only a single color or hue and its tints and shades. (*monocromático*)

monoprint A printing process in which one image is transferred from a painted or inked surface onto a sheet of paper. Monoprinting usually involves creating one unique print instead of many. (*monoimpresión*)

montage (*mon-TAHJ*) An artwork created by combining photographic images onto a flat surface. (*montaje*)

monument An artwork created for a public place that preserves the memory of a person, event, or action. (*monumento*)

mosaic (mo-ZAY-ik) Artwork made by fitting together tiny pieces of colored glass or tiles, stones, paper, or other materials. These small materials are called tesserae. (*mosaico*)

motif (moh-TEEF) A single or repeated design or part of a design or decoration. (*motivo*)

movement A way of combining visual elements to produce a sense of action. This combination of elements helps the viewer's eye to sweep over the work in a definite manner. (*movimiento*)

multimedia Artworks that use the tools and techniques of more than one medium. (*multimedia*)

mural movement A movement begun by American artists in the 1970s that focused on adding beauty to city neighborhoods through the creation of large, public paintings, often on the walls of public buildings. (*movimiento muralista*)

negative shape/space The empty space surrounding shapes or solid forms in a work of art. (*forma o espacio negativo*)

Neoclassical 1776–1860. A style of art inspired by ancient Greek and Roman art. (*estilo neoclásico*)

neutral colors A color not associated with a hue, such as black, white, gray, or brown. (*colores neutros*)

nonobjective art A style of art that does not have a recognizable subject matter; the subject is the composition of the artwork. Nonobjective is often used as a general term for art that contains no recognizable subjects. Also known as nonrepresentational art. (*arte no figurativo*)

organic A shape or form that is irregular in outline, such as things in nature. (*orgánicas*)

pan The movement of the camera during filming. (*panorámica*)

pattern A choice of lines, colors, or shapes, repeated over and over in a planned way. A pattern is also a model or guide for making something. (*patrón*)

Performance Art A form of visual art closely related to theater that combines any of the creative forms of expression, such as poetry, theater, music, architecture, painting, film, slides, and so on. (*arte de la representación*)

pigments Coloring materials made from earth, crushed minerals, plants, or chemicals. Pigments are mixed with a liquid or binder (such as glue, egg, wax, or oil) to make paint, ink, dyes, or crayons. (*pigmentos*)

planned pattern Patterns thought out and created in a systematic and organized way. Whether manufactured or natural, they are precise, measurable, and consistent. (*patrón planificado*)

pointillism 1880–1900. A style of painting in which small dots of color are placed side by side. When viewed from a distance, the eye tends to see the colors as mixed. (*puntillismo*)

Pop Art 1940 to the present. A style of art whose subject matter comes from popular culture (mass media, advertising, comic strips, and so on). (*arte pop*)

portrait An artwork that shows a specific person or group of people. (*retrato*)

portraiture The art of creating portraits. (*retratismo*)

positive space/shape The objects in a work of art, not the background or the space around them. (*espacio o forma positiva*)

Post-Modern architecture 1970–present. A style of architecture that combined some styles from the past with more decoration, line, and color. (*arquitectura postmoderna*)

pre-Columbian An art history term used to describe the art and civilizations in North and South America before the time of the Spanish conquests. (*precolombino*)

primary color or hue One of three basic colors (red, yellow, and blue) that cannot be made by mixing colors. Primary colors are used for mixing other colors. (*color primario*)

principles of design Guidelines that help artists to create designs and control how viewers are likely to react to images. Balance, contrast, proportion, pattern, rhythm, emphasis, unity, and variety are examples of principles of design. (*principios de diseño artístico*)

Productivists A group of Russian avant-garde artists who believed that art is useful to society. They felt that combining art, craftsmanship, and industry could help build a better world. (*productivistas*)

proportion The relation of one object to another in size, amount, number, or degree. (*proporción*)

proportions The relation between one part of the body and another in terms of size, quantity, and degree. (*proporciones*)

pueblo A Native-American village of the southwestern United States. (*pueblo*)

pulp Mashed up material, usually wood or plant fibers, used to make paper. (*pulpa*)

radial A kind of balance in which lines or shapes spread out from a center point. (*radial*)

random pattern Patterns caused by accidental arrangement or produced without consistent design. Random patterns are usually asymmetrical, non-uniform, and irregular. (*patrón aleatorio*)

Realistic style 1850–1900. A style of art that shows people, scenes, and events as the eye sees them. It was developed in the mid-nineteenth century by artists who did not follow the style of Neoclassicism and the drama of Romanticism. See Neoclassical, Romantic style. (*estilo realista*)

redware A general term for pottery made from clay that has a red color due to high levels of iron. Also a specific term for the unfired pottery of Pennsylvania that has the red color of the natural clay in this region. (*barro cocido*)

Regionalist An artist whose artworks focus on a specific region or section of the country. (*regionalista*)

relief print A print created using a printing process in which ink is placed on the raised portions of the block or plate. (*impresión en relieve*)

relief sculpture A sculpture with parts that are raised from a background. (*escultura en relieve*)

rhythm A type of visual or actual movement in an artwork. Rhythm is a principle of design. It is created by repeating visual elements. Rhythms are often described as regular, alternating, flowing, progressive, or jazzy. (*ritmo*)

Romantic style 1815–1975. A style of art in which foreign places, myths, and legends and imaginary events were popular subjects. (*estilo romántico*)

scientific record Accurate and highly detailed artworks or written works, used to help document or classify species. (*récord científico*)

sculpture An artwork that has three dimensions: height, width, and depth or thickness. (*escultura*)

secondary color or hue A color made by mixing equal amounts of two primary colors. Green, orange, and violet are the secondary colors. Green is made by mixing blue and yellow. Orange is made by mixing red and yellow. Violet is made by mixing red and blue. (*color secundario*)

serigraph (SEHR-i-graf) A print, also known as a silkscreen print, made by squeezing ink through a stencil and silk-covered frame to paper below. (*serigrafía*)

sgrafitto (sgra-FEET-toh) A pottery technique in which designs are scratched onto a clay object through a thin layer of colored slip before the pottery is glazed and fired. (*esgrafiado*)

shade Any dark value of a color, usually made by adding black. (*sombra*)

shading A gradual change in value from dark to light. *(sombreado)*

shape A flat figure created when actual or implied lines meet to surround a space. A change in color or shading can define a shape. Shapes can be divided into several types: geometric (square, triangle, circle) and organic (irregular in outline). *(figura)*

skyscrapers High-rise buildings. *(rascacielos)*

slurry A watery mixture used to make paper. *(lechada)*

space The empty or open area between, around, above, below, or within objects. Space is an element of art. Shapes and forms are made by the space around and within them. Space is often called three-dimensional or two-dimensional. Positive space is filled by a shape or form. Negative space surrounds a shape or form. *(espacio)*

split complement A color scheme based on one hue and the hues on each side of its complement on the color wheel. Orange, blue-violet, and blue-green are split complementary colors. *(complemento fraccionario)*

still life Art based on an arrangement of objects that are not alive and cannot move, such as fruit, flowers, or bottles. The items are often symbols for abstract ideas. A book, for example, may be a symbol for knowledge. A still life is usually shown in an indoor setting. *(naturaleza muerta)*

storyboard A set of words and sketches that are made to plan a motion picture or television program. Each sketch shows a scene in the story. *(guión sinóptico)*

style The result of an artist's means of expression—the use of materials, design qualities, methods of work, and choice of subject matter. In most cases, these choices show the unique qualities of an individual, culture, or time period. The style of an artwork helps you to know how it is different from other artworks. *(estilo)*

stylize To simplify shapes or forms found in nature. *(estilizar)*

subject A topic or idea shown in an artwork, especially anything recognizable such as a landscape or animals. *(tema)*

subtractive process Sculptural process in which material (clay, for example) is carved or cut away to create form. In an additive process, material is added to create form. *(proceso de substracción)*

Surrealism A style of art in which dreams, fantasy, and the human mind are the source of ideas for artists. Unrelated objects and situations are often set in unnatural surroundings. Artists who work in this style are known as Surrealists. *(surrealismo)*

symmetrical *(sim-MET-ri-kal)* A type of balance in which both sides of a center line are exactly or nearly the same, like a mirror image. For example, the wings of a butterfly are symmetrical. Also known as formal balance. *(simétrico)*

technology The art of creating things to make human life easier. *(tecnología)*

texture The way a surface feels (actual texture) or how it may look (implied texture). Texture can be sensed by touch and sight. Textures are described by words such as rough, silky, pebbly. *(textura)*

theme The artist's interpretation of a subject or topic of a work of art. For example, a landscape can have a theme of the desire to save nature, or to destroy nature. A theme such as love, power, or respect can be shown through a variety of subjects. *(idea central)*

thumbnail sketches Small, quick sketches that record ideas and information for a final work of art. *(esquemas)*

tint A light value of a pure color, usually made by adding white. For example, pink is a tint of red. *(matiz claro)*

tohunga *(toh-HUN-gah)* A Maori term that means "craftsman-priest." A great master carver of the Maori of New Zealand.

trade art Art that is created primarily for sale to tourists or for export to foreign markets. *(intercambio de arte)*

traditional art Artwork created in almost the same way year after year because it is part of a culture, custom, or belief. *(arte tradicional)*

traditions Customs, actions, thoughts, or beliefs that are passed on or handed down from generation to generation, either by word of mouth or by example. *(tradiciones)*

triad *(TRY-ad)* Three colors spaced equally apart on the color wheel, such as orange, green, and violet. *(tríada)*

two-point perspective A method of creating the illusion of deep space on a flat surface. In two-point perspective there are two vanishing points on the horizon line. *(perspectiva de dos puntos)*

ukiyo-e *(oo-key-OH-eh)* Japanese pictures of the ""floating world" district of Edo. These were first made in paint, but were more commonly produced in editions of woodcuts of many colors. They are the unique creation of the Edo period (1603–1868). *(ukiyo-e)*

unity A feeling that all parts of a design are working together as a team. *(unidad)*

value An element of art that means the darkness or lightness of a surface. Value depends on how much light a surface reflects. Tints are light values of pure colors. Shades are dark values of pure colors. Value can also be an important element in works of art in which there is little or no color (drawings, prints, photographs, most sculpture and architecture). *(valor)*

variety The use of different lines, shapes, textures, colors, and other elements of design to create interest in a work of art. *(variedad)*

video art Art created by or using video technology. *(arte generado por video)*

warm colors Colors that are often associated with fire and the sun and remind people of warm places, things, and feelings. Warm colors range from the reds through the oranges and yellows. *(colores cálidos)*

wet media Drawing and painting materials which have a fluid or liquid ingredient. *(medios húmedos)*

whole-to-part drawing A drawing in which the largest shapes are drawn first, and then details are gradually filled in. *(dibujo del todo a las partes)*

Spanish Glossary

acentuación Parte de una obra artística que captura y retiene la atención del espectador. Por lo general, esta área exhibe contrastes en tamaño, forma, color u otros rasgos distintivos. (*emphasis*)

activismo La práctica de tratar de cambiar las actitudes, creencias políticas u otros asuntos en una comunidad. (*activism*)

aplicación Proceso parecido al collage en el cual trozos de tela se cosen y/o se pegan a un fondo. (*appliqué*)

armadura Un conjunto de piezas, similar a un esqueleto, que sirve de soporte para hacer una escultura. (*armature*)

arquitectura postmoderna 1970–actualidad. Un estilo arquitectónico que toma como base algunos estilos del pasado y los combina con más decoración, líneas y colores. (*Post-Modern architecture*)

arte abstracto Arte que se basa en un tema reconocible pero en el que el artista ha simplificado, excluido o reordenado algunos elementos de modo que no podamos reconocerlos. (*abstract*)

arte cinético Término general que se usa para describir cualquier construcción artística que incluya elementos móviles, ya sea mediante un motor, una manivela o fuerzas naturales, como en el caso de los móviles. (*kinetic art*)

arte cristiana Estilo artístico que se originó en África en el siglo XV y que continúa existiendo en la actualidad. El objetivo principal de este estilo artístico es enseñar las religiones cristianas a los pueblos africanos. (*Christian art*)

arte de la representación Una forma de arte visual estrechamente relacionada con el teatro que integra cualquiera de las formas creativas de expresión, como la poesía, el teatro, la música, la arquitectura, la pintura, el cine, la fotografía, etc. (*Performance art*)

arte generado por computadora Arte creado principalmente con una computadora. (computer art)

arte generado por video Arte que se crea usando la tecnología de video. (*video art*)

arte no figurativo 1917–1932. Estilo de arte que no posee un tema reconocible; el tema es la composición de la obra artística. A menudo, se usa como un término general para el arte que contiene temas irreconocibles. También se le conoce como arte abstracto. (*nonobjective art*)

arte pop De 1940 hasta el presente. Tendencia artística cuyos temas provienen de la cultura popular (medios de comunicación, publicidad y tiras cómicas, entre otros). (*Pop Art*)

artesanías Obras de arte, con valor tanto decorativo como útil, que han sido hábilmente hechas a mano. (*crafts*)

arte Tierra Movimiento artístico en el cual el suelo y la Tierra son ideas importantes o se emplean como medios de expresión. (*Earth Art*)

arte tradicional Arte que se crea casi de manera idéntica año tras año, debido a que es parte de una cultura, costumbre o creencia. (*traditional art*)

artista Persona que hace arte. (*artist*)

art nouveau 1900–1915. Un término que en francés significa "arte nuevo". Un estilo de diseño que exploraba las líneas, curvas y formas de la naturaleza. (*Art Nouveau*)

asimétrico Tipo de equilibrio visual en el cual los dos lados de una composición son diferentes pero están equilibrados; son iguales visualmente pero no idénticos. También se denomina equilibrio irregular. (*asymmetrical*)

barro cocido Término que se usa para denominar la cerámica hecha con arcilla que tiene un color rojizo debido a su alto contenido de hierro. Su equivalente en inglés, redware, también se emplea para referirse a la cerámica sin hornear de Pennsylvania, que es del color rojizo natural de la arcilla que se encuentra en esa región. (*redware*)

bizcocho de porcelana Cerámica que ha sido horneada una vez pero no esmaltada. (*bisqueware*)

causa Una creencia o asunto que lleva a las personas a tomar algún tipo de medida. (*cause*)

celebración La observación de un suceso o tradición local con otros miembros de la comunidad. (*celebration*)

cerámica Arte de fabricar objetos de barro, vidrio u otros minerales cociéndolos o quemándolos a altas temperaturas en un horno de secar. La palabra también se refiere a los productos que se forman de esta manera. (*ceramics*)

cinematografía El arte de la reproducción fotográfica de imágenes en movimiento. (*cinematography*)

códice Un tipo de libro cuyas páginas están unidas en los dos lados, como un acordeón. (*codex*)

colaborar Trabajar junto con otros. (*collaborate*)

collage Una obra de arte que se crea pegando trocitos de papel, tela, recortes, fotografías u otros materiales sobre una superficie plana. (*collage*)

color intermedio Color que se produce al mezclar un color secundario con un color primario. El azul-verde, el verde-amarillo, el amarillo-anaranjado, el rojo-anaranjado, el rojo-violeta y el azul-violeta son colores intermedios. (*intermediate color*)

color Otro término para denominar el matiz, que es el nombre común de un color que está en el espectro o que está relacionado con él, por ejemplo, amarillo, amarillo anaranjado, azul violeta y verde. (*color*)

color primario Uno de los tres colores básicos (amarillo, rojo y azul) que no se puede producir mezclando colores. Los colores primarios se usan para formar otros colores. (*primary color*)

color secundario Color que se produce al mezclar dos colores primarios en cantidades iguales. El verde, el anaranjado y el violeta son colores secundarios. El verde es la combinación de azul con amarillo. El anaranjado se obtiene al mezclar el rojo y el amarillo. El color violeta se produce al mezclar el rojo con el azul. (*secondary color*)

colores análogos Colores estrechamente relacionados debido a un matiz que comparten en común. Por ejemplo, el azul, el azul-violeta y el violeta contienen el color azul. En la rueda de colores, los colores análogos se encuentran uno al lado del otro. (*analogous color*)

colores cálidos Reciben este nombre porque a menudo se les asocia con el fuego y el Sol. Asimismo, nos recuerdan lugares, cosas y sensaciones cálidas. Los colores cálidos van desde distintas tonalidades de rojo hasta el anaranjado y amarillo. (*warm colors*)

colores frescos Colores que se relacionan, a menudo, con lugares, cosas o sentimientos que proyectan frescura. Familia de colores que va del verde al azul y violeta. (*cool colors*)

colores neutros Aquellos colores que no se asocian con una tonalidad, como el negro, el blanco, el gris o el café. (*neutral colors*)

combinación de colores Plan para seleccionar u organizar los colores. Entre las combinaciones de colores comunes se encuentran las siguientes: cálido, fresco, neutro, monocromático, análogo, complementario, complementario fraccionado y tríada. (*color scheme*)

complementarios Colores directamente opuestos entre sí en la rueda de colores. Por ejemplo, el rojo y el verde, el azul y el anaranjado, el violeta y el amarillo. Cuando los colores complementarios se mezclan, el resultado es un color marrón o gris neutro. Cuando se usan uno al lado del otro en una obra artística, producen contrastes intensos. (*complementary*)

complemento fraccionario Combinación de colores que se basa en un matiz y en los matices de cada lado de su complemento en la rueda de colores. El anaranjado, el azul-violeta y el azul-verde son colores complementarios fraccionados. (*split complement*)

comunicación El intercambio de información, pensamientos, sentimientos, ideas, opiniones, etc., de forma oral, escrita o visual. (*communication*)

comunidad global La interacción e intercambio de ideas y conocimientos entre los pueblos y comunidades de todo el mundo. (*global community*)

comunismo Una forma de gobierno que se aplicó en Rusia, la cual se basaba en la idea de crear pequeñas comunidades donde las personas compartieran el trabajo. (*communism*)

conmemorar Honrar o recordar a una persona o acontecimiento. (*commemorate*)

crítico de arte Persona que expresa una opinión razonada acerca de cualquier asunto relacionado con el arte. (*art critic*)

cuadro Una sola imagen de un video o instalación de sonido. (*frame*)

cubismo 1907–1914. Término de arte que denota un estilo desarrollado por Pablo Picasso y Georges Braque. En el cubismo, el tema se descompone en formas y figuras geométricas. Éstas se analizan y luego se vuelven a juntar en una composición abstracta. A menudo, da la impresión de que los objetos tridimensionales se están mostrando desde muchos puntos de vista diferentes al mismo tiempo. (*Cubism*)

dadaísmo 1915–1923. Un movimiento artístico que rechazaba los materiales y estilos artísticos tradicionales. Los integrantes de este movimiento creaban obras de arte en base al azar, y a menudo usaban objetos encontrados para crear nuevas formas artísticas.

Muchos de los artistas que participaron en este movimiento se convirtieron en líderes del surrealismo y de otros estilos artísticos nuevos. (*Dada*)

dibujo de contorno Un dibujo que muestra sólo los bordes (el contorno) de los objetos. (*contour drawing*)

dibujo del todo a las partes Un dibujo en el cual primero se hacen los objetos más grandes y después se van agregando gradualmente los detalles. (*whole-to-part drawing*)

dibujo gestual Un dibujo que se realiza rápidamente para captar los gestos o movimientos del cuerpo. (*gesture drawing*)

diseñador gráfico Un artista que diseña objetos tales como paquetes, papel de envolver, libros, carteles y tarjetas de felicitaciones. (*graphic designer*)

diseñadores Artistas que se encargan de planear la organización y composición de una obra de arte, objeto, lugar, edificio, etc. Hay diseñadores de prendas de vestir (diseñadores de modas), de espacios al aire libre (diseñadores de exteriores), de espacios dentro de los edificios (diseñadores de muebles y de interiores), diseñadores de carteles y anuncios (diseñadores gráficos), etc. (*designers*)

diseño gráfico Un término general que designa aquellas obras de arte en las cuales la forma de las letras (escritura, tipografía) cumple un papel importante. (*graphic design*)

documentar Llevar un registro de algo. (*document*)

earthworks Cualquier obra de arte en la que el suelo y la Tierra son medios importantes. *Ver* arte Tierra.

elementos de diseño Las "herramientas" visuales que los artistas usan para crear arte. Entre los elementos se incluyen el color, el valor, la línea, la figura, la forma, la textura, y el espacio. (*elements of design*)

ensambladura Una escultura hecha con objetos que se han desechado, como cajas, trozos de madera, partes de juguetes viejos, etc. (*assemblage*)

equilibrio Principio de diseño que describe la manera en que se encuentran ordenadas las partes de una obra artística con el fin de crear la sensación de igual peso o interés. Una obra artística equilibrada ofrece un peso visual o un interés igual en todas sus áreas. Los tipos de equilibrio son simétrico, asimétrico y radial. (*balance*)

escuela "Ash Can" 1908–1914. Un grupo de artistas estadounidenses que pintaban escenas de la vida real en la ciudad. Originalmente este grupo se dio a conocer con el nombre de "el grupo de los ocho". (*Ash Can School*)

escultura cinética Una escultura que se mueve o que tiene partes móviles. El movimiento puede ser el resultado de distintas fuerzas, como el aire, la gravedad y la electricidad. (*kinetic sculpture*)

escultura en relieve Una escultura en la cual algunas partes sobresalen del fondo. (*relief sculpture*)

escultura Una obra de arte que tiene tres dimensiones: altura, anchura y profundidad. (*sculpture*)

esgrafiado Una técnica que se emplea en cerámica mediante la cual se graba un diseño en un objeto de arcilla a través de una cinta delgada de color, mientras que el objeto todavía está húmedo, antes de esmaltarlo y hornearlo. (*sgrafitto*)

espacio La extensión vacía o abierta que se encuentra entre objetos, alrededor de ellos, encima de ellos, debajo de ellos o dentro de los mismos. El espacio es un elemento artístico. Las figuras y las formas se producen debido al espacio que existe a su derredor y dentro de ellas. A menudo nos referimos al espacio como tridimensional o bidimensional. Una figura o una forma llenan el espacio positivo mientras que el espacio negativo rodea una figura o una forma. (*space*)

espacio o forma positiva Los objetos de una obra artística que no constituyen ni el fondo ni el espacio que se halla a su alrededor. (*positive space/shape*)

esquemas Bosquejos pequeños y rápidos que se realizan para anotar ideas e información con el fin de usarlos en la obra de arte final. (*thumbnail sketches*)

estético Persona que se dedica al estudio del arte o la belleza. Persona que cuestiona cómo se produce el arte y el papel que juega en la sociedad. (*aesthetician*)

estilizar Simplificar las formas de la naturaleza. (*stylize*)

estilo arquitectónico moderno 1900–1970. Un estilo arquitectónico que emplea acero, hormigón y vidrio para la construcción de edificios altos. Las líneas simples y la falta de decoración son características del estilo arquitectónico moderno. (*Modern architecture*)

estilo global Un estilo artístico que no se puede relacionar con una sola cultura o tradición artística. El estilo global es el resultado del intercambio de ideas entre los artistas de distintas naciones y culturas del mundo. (*global style*)

estilo neoclásico 1776–1860. Un estilo artístico inspirado en los antiguos artes griego y romano. *(Neoclassical)*

estilo realista 1850–1900. Un estilo artístico que representa a las personas, los lugares y los sucesos tal como los percibe el ojo humano. Este estilo fue desarrollado a mediados del siglo XIX por artistas que no seguían el estilo del neoclasicismo y el dramatismo del romanticismo. *Ver* estilo neoclásico, estilo romántico. *(Realistic style)*

estilo Resultado de los medios de expresión de un artista: el uso de materiales, la calidad del diseño, los métodos de trabajo y la selección del tema. En la mayoría de los casos, estas selecciones muestran las cualidades singulares de un individuo, una cultura o un período de tiempo. El estilo de una obra artística nos ayuda a distinguirla de otras obras de arte. *(style)*

estilo romántico 1815–1975. Un estilo artístico en el cual los lugares lejanos, los mitos, las leyendas y los sucesos imaginarios son temas comunes. *(Romantic style)*

figura Forma plana que se crea cuando se juntan líneas implícitas o reales que cierran un espacio. Un cambio de color o una sombra pueden definir una figura. Las figuras se pueden dividir en varios tipos: geométricas (cuadrado, triángulo, círculo) y orgánicas (contornos irregulares). *(shape)*

forma artística Técnica o método utilizado en la creación de una obra artística, como una pintura, una fotografía o un collage. *(art form)*

forma o espacio negativo El espacio vacío que rodea las formas o los cuerpos geométricos en una obra artística. *(negative shape/space)*

formas orgánicas Formas cuyos perfiles son irregulares, como por ejemplo, los objetos que se hallan en la naturaleza. *(organic shapes)*

fresco Técnica de pintura mural que consiste en aplicar pigmentos a una capa delgada de yeso húmedo. El yeso absorbe los pigmentos y la pintura se convierte en parte de la pared. *(fresco)*

geométricas Figuras o formas que parecen mecánicas. También se pueden usar fórmulas matemáticas para describir algo que es geométrico. *(geometric)*

guión sinóptico Conjunto de texto y bosquejos que se crean para planear una película o programa de televisión. Cada bosquejo muestra una escena del guión. *(storyboard)*

historiador de arte Persona que estudia el arte: su historia y aportaciones a las culturas y sociedades. *(art historian)*

idea central Tema o tópico de una obra artística. Por ejemplo, un paisaje puede tener como idea central el deseo de salvar la naturaleza o de destruirla. Una idea central como el amor, el poder o el respeto se pueden mostrar a través de una variedad de temas. Por lo general, la frase "idea central y variaciones" se usa para expresar varias maneras de mostrar una idea. *(theme)*

impresión en huecograbado Un tipo de impresión que se logra cuando el artista graba líneas sobre una placa lisa de metal, recubre la placa de tinta y después crea la lámina con una imprenta que ejerce presión de manera uniforme entre la placa y el papel. *(intaglio print)*

impresión en linóleo Un tipo de impresión en relieve que se hace con un clisé o bloque de linóleo. Primero se recorta el linóleo y se recubren de tinta las partes no recortadas. Después se coloca una hoja de papel encima del linóleo y la estampa se imprime frotando el reverso de la hoja de papel. *(linoleum cut)*

impresión en relieve Impresión que se crea al usar un proceso de imprimir en el cual se coloca tinta en las partes elevadas del clisé topográfico. *(relief print)*

impresionistas 1875–1900. Grupo de artistas que trabajaban al aire libre y pintaban directamente observando la naturaleza. Los pintores impresionistas usaban rápidas pinceladas para reproducir el efecto de la luz y el color. *(impressionists)*

inmigrantes Personas que se mudan de un país a otro. *(immigrants)*

instalaciones Arreglos temporales de objetos de arte en galerías, museos o al aire libre. *(installations)*

intercambio de arte Arte que ha sido creado principalmente para vender a los turistas o para exportar al extranjero. *(trade art)*

kivas Las cámaras ceremoniales circulares de los anasazi. *(kivas)*

lechada Una mezcla acuosa que se usa para hacer papel. *(slurry)*

limner Un artista estadounidense autodidacta de la época temprana del país, que pintaba carteles, casas y retratos. *(limner)*

línea de horizonte Línea de nivel donde parece que el agua o la tierra terminan y comienza el cielo. Por lo general, se encuentra al nivel de los ojos del espectador. Si el horizonte no se puede ver, entonces se debe imaginar su ubicación. *(horizon line)*

línea implícita Manera en que se arreglan los objetos con el fin de producir el efecto de que se vean líneas en una obra, aunque estas líneas en realidad no están presentes. *(implied line)*

línea Trazo que muestra longitud y dirección, creado por un punto que se mueve por una superficie. Una línea puede variar en longitud, ancho, dirección, curvatura y color. Puede ser bidimensional (una línea hecha con un lápiz sobre papel), tridimensional (alambre) o puede estar implícita. *(line)*

litografía Un tipo de impresión que se logra cuando un artista dibuja una imagen en una losa de piedra plana (o una lámina de metal especial) con un carboncillo aceitoso o con pintura. Con un ácido especial se quita la parte de la piedra que no está cubierta por la pintura o carboncillo. Después se recubren de tinta las partes pintadas con el carboncillo y se hace la estampa con una imprenta. *(lithographic print)*

maqueta Modelo, a escala reducida, de una escultura. *(maquette)*

matiz claro Valor leve de un color puro, que se produce generalmente al añadir blanco. Por ejemplo, el rosado es un matiz claro del rojo. *(tint)*

medios artísticos Material o medios técnicos para realizar una expresión artística. *(art media)*

medios húmedos Materiales de dibujo o materiales para pintar que tienen un ingrediente líquido. *(wet media)*

medios mixtos Toda obra de arte que está compuesta por más de un medio, como tinta y acuarelas, pintura y collage, etc. *(mixed media)*

medios secos Materiales de arte, como lápices, tiza (pasteles) y lápices de cera, que no son húmedos y que no requieren el uso de ningún líquido. *(dry media)*

miniatura Una pintura muy pequeña y con mucho detalle. *(miniature)*

monocromático Hecho de un solo color o matiz y sus tintes y tonos. *(monochromatic)*

monoimpresión Proceso de impresión en el cual se transfiere una imagen de una superficie pintada o recubierta de tinta a una hoja de papel. Por lo general, el resultado de este proceso es la creación de una sola y exclusiva estampa, en lugar de muchas a la vez. *(monoprint)*

montaje Obra de arte que resulta de la combinación de varias imágenes fotográficas sobre una superficie plana. *(montage)*

monumento Una obra de arte que ha sido creada para exhibir en un lugar público con el fin de recordar a una persona, un suceso o una acción. *(monument)*

mosaico Obra artística compuesta de pequeños trozos de vidrio o azulejos, piedras, papel u otros materiales, de diversos colores. Estos materiales reciben el nombre de teselas. *(mosaic)*

motivo Un diseño, o parte de un diseño o decoración, que se repite una o muchas veces. *(motif)*

móvil Escultura equilibrada en suspensión que tiene partes que pueden entrar en movimiento, especialmente por la acción del viento. Ideada por Alexander Calder en 1932. *(mobile)*

movimiento Manera de combinar elementos visuales con el fin de producir una sensación de acción. Gracias a esta combinación de elementos, los ojos del espectador recorren la obra de arte de una manera definida. *(movement)*

movimiento muralista Un movimiento que iniciaron los artistas estadounidenses en los años 70 con el propósito de embellecer los vecindarios urbanos mediante la creación de grandes pinturas, a menudo en las paredes de los edificios públicos. *(mural movement)*

multimedia Obras de arte que usan las herramientas y las técnicas de varios medios. *(multimedia)*

naturaleza muerta Arte que se basa en un arreglo de objetos inertes e inmóviles, como por ejemplo, frutos, flores o botellas. Estos objetos expresan, a menudo, ideas abstractas. Por ejemplo, un libro puede representar un símbolo para el conocimiento. Por lo general, una naturaleza muerta se muestra en un ambiente interior. *(still life)*

objetos encontrados Materiales que los artistas encuentran y usan en sus obras de arte, como recortes de madera, metal u otros objetos ya acabados. *(found objects)*

obra conmemorativa Obra de arte u otro objeto que ayuda a las personas a recordar algo, como un suceso o una persona importante. *(memorial)*

orgánicas Formas cuyos perfiles son irregulares, como por ejemplo, los objetos que se hallan en la naturaleza. *(organic)*

paisaje urbano Una obra de arte cuyo tema es una vista de una ciudad (edificios, calles, tiendas). *(cityscape)*

panorámica El movimiento de la cámara durante la filmación. *(pan)*

patrón aleatorio Patrones originados por arreglos accidentales o que se reproducen sin un diseño consistente. Por lo general, los patrones aleatorios son asimétricos, irregulares y no uniformes. *(random pattern)*

patrón planificado Patrón desarrollado y creado de manera sistemática y organizada. Ya sean manufacturados o naturales, estos patrones son precisos, mensurables y consistentes. *(planned pattern)*

patrón Selección de líneas, colores o formas, que se repiten constantemente de manera planificada. Un patrón es también un modelo o guía para realizar algo. *(pattern)*

perspectiva de dos puntos Un método para crear la ilusión de profundidad en una superficie plana. En la perspectiva de dos puntos hay dos puntos de fuga en la línea del horizonte. *(two-point perspective)*

perspectiva lineal Técnica que se utiliza para mostrar un espacio tridimensional sobre una superficie bidimensional. *(linear perspective)*

pigmentos Materiales para colorear que se hacen con tierra, minerales triturados, plantas o productos químicos. Los pigmentos se mezclan con un líquido o substancia aglutinante (como pegamento, huevo, cera o aceite) para hacer pintura, tinta, colorantes o lápices de cera. *(pigments)*

precolombino Un término que se usa en historia del arte para describir el arte y las civilizaciones de América del Norte y del Sur, anteriores a la época de la conquista española. *(pre-Columbian)*

principios de diseño artístico Directrices que ayudan a los artistas a componer diseños y a controlar la manera cómo los observadores puedan reaccionar con las imágenes. El equilibrio, el contraste, la proporción, el patrón, el ritmo, el énfasis, la unidad, y la variedad son principios de diseño. *(principles of design)*

proceso de substracción En escultura, proceso mediante el cual se talla o se recorta el material (arcilla, por ejemplo) para crear la forma. En un proceso de adición, por el contrario, se agrega material para crear la forma. *(subtractive process)*

productivistas Un grupo de artistas rusos vanguardistas que sostenían que el arte es útil para la sociedad. Creían que podíamos lograr un mundo mejor mediante la combinación del arte, las labores artesanales y la industria. *(Productivists)*

proporción Relación de un objeto con otro en cuanto a tamaño, cantidad, número o grado. *(proportion)*

proporciones La relación entre dos partes del cuerpo en cuanto a su tamaño, cantidad y grado. *(proportions)*

pueblo Una tribu de indígenas del sudoeste de los Estados Unidos. *(pueblo)*

pulpa Material triturado, por lo general fibra de madera o de plantas, que se usa para hacer papel. *(pulp)*

puntillismo 1880–1900. Un estilo de pintar en el que se colocan pequeños puntos de colores uno junto a otro. Cuando la obra se observa desde lejos, el ojo tiende a ver los colores mezclados. *(pointillism)*

radial Especie de equilibrio en el cual las líneas o las formas se extienden a partir de un punto central. *(radial)*

rascacielos Edificios muy altos. *(skyscrapers)*

récord científico Obras de arte u obras escritas que cuentan con un nivel muy alto de exactitud y de detalle, utilizadas para documentar o clasificar las especies. *(scientific record)*

regionalista Artista cuyo arte está orientado hacia una región o sección en particular del país. *(Regionalist)*

Renacimiento de Harlem 1920–1940. Nombre de un período y de un grupo de artistas que vivieron y trabajaron en Harlem, en la ciudad de Nueva York. Estos artistas expresaron de distintas formas su experiencia como afroamericanos. *(Harlem Renaissance)*

retratismo El arte de hacer retratos. *(portraiture)*

retrato Una obra de arte que muestra a una persona o un grupo de personas en particular. *(portrait)*

ritmo Tipo de movimiento visual o real en una obra artística. El ritmo es un principio de diseño. Se crea mediante la repetición de elementos visuales. A menudo, el ritmo se describe como regular, alternativo, fluido, progresivo o animado. *(rhythm)*

serigrafía Un tipo de impresión que se logra haciendo pasar la tinta a través de una pantalla de seda hasta el papel que se encuentra debajo, donde se imprime la estampa. *(serigraph)*

simétrico Tipo de equilibrio en el cual los dos lados de una línea central son exactamente o casi iguales, como un reflejo exacto. Por ejemplo, las alas de una mariposa son simétricas. A este tipo de equilibrio también se le denomina equilibrio formal. *(symmetrical)*

sombra Cualquier pigmento oscuro de un color que, por lo general, se crea al añadir negro. *(shade)*

sombreado Un cambio gradual en la intensidad, de más oscuro a más claro. *(shading)*

surrealismo Un estilo artístico en el cual los sueños, la imaginación y la mente humana son la fuente de inspiración artística. A menudo, objetos y situaciones que normalmente no están relacionados entre sí confluyen en un mismo ambiente no natural. Se conoce como surrealistas a los artistas de esta escuela. (*Surrealism*)

tecnología El arte de crear cosas para hacernos la vida más fácil. (*technology*)

tema Tópico o idea que se muestra en una obra artística, en particular cualquier cosa que sea reconocible, como un paisaje o los animales. (*subject*)

textura implícita Manera en que parece verse una superficie: áspera o lisa. (*implied texture*)

textura Manera en que se siente una superficie (textura real) o cómo se ve (textura implícita). Podemos sentir la textura gracias al tacto y a la vista. Palabras como áspera, sedosa, rugosa se usan para describir la textura. (*texture*)

tohunga Un término de la tribu maori que significa "sacerdote artesano". Un maestro escultor de la tribu maori de Nueva Zelanda. (*tohunga*)

toma del día La filmación que se realiza en un día durante el rodaje de una película. (*dailies*)

tonalidad Matiz de color. (*hue*)

tradiciones Costumbres, acciones, pensamientos o creencias que se transmiten de una generación a otra, ya sea de forma oral o mediante el ejemplo. (*traditions*)

tríada Tres colores igualmente espaciados entre sí en la rueda de colores, como por ejemplo, el anaranjado, el verde y el violeta. (*triad*)

ukiyo-e Dibujos japoneses que representan el "mundo flotante" del distrito de Edo. Al comienzo se hacían con pintura, pero son más comunes las xilografías de diversos colores. Son una creación exclusiva del período Edo (1603–1868). (*ukiyo-e*)

unidad Sensación de que todas las partes de una obra artística funcionan juntas como un conjunto. (*unity*)

valor Elemento artístico que denota el grado de oscuridad o claridad de una superficie. El valor depende de la cantidad de luz que puede reflejar una superficie. Los matices claros son valores leves de los colores puros. Las sombras son valores oscuros de los colores puros. El valor también tiene importancia como elemento en las obras artísticas que muestran una cantidad mínima o inexistente de color (dibujos, grabados, fotografías, la mayor parte de la escultura y la arquitectura). (*value*)

vanguardismo Un término que describe las manifestaciones artísticas originales y que se distinguen de los estilos artísticos tradicionales. Los artistas vanguardistas a menudo experimentan con nuevos materiales y nuevas formas de expresar sus ideas. (*avant-garde*)

variedad Uso de diferentes líneas, formas, texturas, colores y otros elementos del diseño con el fin de crear interés en la obra artística. (*variety*)

Index